Figures in Ariosto's Tapestry

Peter DeSa Wiggins

Figures
in Ariosto's
Tapestry

Character and Design
in the *Orlando Furioso*

The Johns Hopkins University Press

Baltimore and London

This book has been brought to publication with the generous assistance of the Andrew W. Mellon Foundation and the College of William and Mary.

The Johns Hopkins University Press
701 West 40th Street
Baltimore, Maryland 21211
The Johns Hopkins Press Ltd., London

The paper in this book is acid-free and meets the guidelines for permanence and durability of the Committee on Production Guidelines for Book Longevity of the Council on Library Resources.

Library of Congress Cataloging in Publication Data
Wiggins, Peter DeSa.
    Figures in Ariosto's tapestry.

    Bibliography: p.
    Includes index.
    1. Ariosto, Lodovico, 1474–1533. Orlando furioso.
2. Roland—Romances—History and criticism.   3. Ariosto,
Lodovico, 1474–1533—Characters.   I. Title.
PQ4569.W5 1985   851'.3   85-7576
ISBN 0-8018-2663-2 (alk. paper)

To Kathy, Emily, Elmira, and Ed
"tanta fede e tanto amor"

Contents

Acknowledgments

I would like to thank Eduardo Saccone for reading and criticizing the manuscript of this work and for his friendship and encouragement. He among modern critics and Galileo among the early ones were my guides through the Ariostan labyrinth. I would also like to thank James V. Mirollo for reading the first two chapters in their crudest form and for helping me to get started. To Thomas G. Bergin, for his encouragement of both my first work on Ariosto and now of my latest, I owe a lasting debt of gratitude. To Maurice Valency, who drew my attention to Ariosto when I was a graduate student, I must always be grateful.

The College of William and Mary provided the semester grant that enabled me to write the first draft and then provided a generous subsidy toward publication of the final version. A summer stipend from the National Endowment for the Humanities supported a major portion of the research. The first three chapters, in early form, were published as articles in *Italica* 57 (Winter 1980), *Forum Italicum* 16 (Spring–Fall 1982) and *MLN* 98 (1983); I thank the editors for their permission to reprint. Lastly, I wish to thank Ellen Noel, manuscript editor at the Johns Hopkins University Press, for her sharp eye and good judgment.

Figures in Ariosto's Tapestry

1
Introduction: Galileo's Telescope

That (said Don Quixote), is another error incident to many people, who do not believe that any such knights ever existed; and I have, on diverse and sundry occasions, endeavoured to dissipate that almost general mistake by the light of truth: sometimes, indeed, I have not succeeded in my attempts; however, I have frequently gained my point, by supporting it on the shoulders of demonstration; and truly the case is so clear, that I could almost affirm I have with my own eyes beheld Amadis de Gaul, who was a tall man, of a fair complexion, well furnished with a black beard, his aspect something between mild and severe, concise of speech, slow to anger, and soon appeased. In the same manner, methinks, I could delineate and paint all the knights-errant that ever were recorded in history; for, according to the ideas formed by reading these histories, and by comparing their exploits and dispositions, sound philosophy may discover their lineaments, statures, and complexions.

—Cervantes, *Don Quixote*, translated by Tobias Smollett

he idea that Ariosto might have invested his characters with his most serious meanings has been so unpopular in the past century of Ariosto criticism that anyone entering the lists in its behalf must feel an uncomfortable kinship with the ingenious gentleman of La Mancha. The dictum of Burckhardt, voiced in 1860 in part 4 of his great culture history of the Renaissance, has had a decisive influence on all subsequent Ariosto criticism: it is inappropriate, Burckhardt declared, it is anachronistic to judge the *Orlando Furioso* on its efficacy in the representation of character; the poem does not depend for its effect on its characters, and the critic who lays stress on them will only cause it to lose, rather than gain, in grandeur. Assent to this proposition has been universal, if not always expressed openly or with the same conviction. Critics of the *Furioso* have for the most part devoted themselves to questions of style,

1

structure, theme, and rhetorical strategy, and have not founded their arguments on analysis of character. The resulting discourse has often resembled discreet murmurings about a respected friend with an embarrassing flaw in his physiognomy.

Criticism has had about as much success in its attempt to explain why the *Furioso,* despite its horde of puppetlike characters, is a great narrative as we might expect if we tried to distract attention from our friend's proboscis by exclaiming over the serenity of his brow and his commanding gaze. On rare occasions, we find a critic who tacitly concedes that strong characterization is essential to first-rate narrative and who goes on to center his discussion of the *Furioso* on one or more of its characters. However, the Burckhardtian influence generally exercises itself on these occasions by fastening the critic's attention on a single episode of a character's career, as if it were daring enough to address the question of characterization at all without risking to open the Pandora's box of the requisite of consistency in characterization laid down for longer narratives ever since Aristotle's time.

One critic stands out in the history of Ariosto criticism for having praised the *Orlando Furioso* above all for its consistency in the representation of character. Galileo Galilei admired Ariosto for precisely that "extraordinary Degree of Judgment" and that "exact Knowledge of human Nature" the novelist Henry Fielding was later to commend in authors who exhibited in their works what he called "Conservation of Character" (*The History of Tom Jones,* bk. 8, ch. 1). Since the analysis of the *Furioso* ensuing in these pages takes its inspiration from Galileo, a close study of his methods as a reader must serve as introduction.

Writing from the Villa d'Arcetri in his seventy-sixth year—excusing himself to an aristocratic acquaintance for his inability, due to his blindness and the loss of a manuscript, to supply as thorough a comparison of Ariosto and Tasso as the one requested of him—Galileo sketches nevertheless a cursory outline of his views, and in conclusion he comments, "In Ariosto the observation of character is marvelous."[1] He has just been comparing Rinaldo and Armida in Tasso's *Gerusalemme Liberata* to Ruggiero, Bradamante, and Alcina in Ariosto's work. His comment echoes many others that he made years earlier in the *Considerazioni al Tasso* and the *Postille all'Ariosto* and sums up his admiration for Ariosto within one of the categories to which he returns over and over again. Readers of Galileo's criticism will always be impressed with his concern over characterization, which he carries to the point of apostrophizing certain characters with reproaches and exhortations when he finds them behaving in a way that offends his sense of reality. In "Galileo,

Man of Letters," Dante della Terza observes that "one of the most vivid traits of Galileo's criticism is his insistence on the sharpness of the psychological focus, indicative of a taste for rigorously delineated portraiture. . . . A whole category of the *Considerazioni* could be said to be dedicated to this psychological coherence in the design of characters."[2] In the *Postille,* as well as the *Considerazioni,* this concentration on characterization is so pervasive and so regularly coupled with a demand for verisimilitude that the reader must often wonder if Galileo did not implicitly regard literature as a protoscience of psychology. In any case, it has been demonstrated that one aspect of Galileo's distaste for the *Gerusalemme Liberata,* far from being based on a priori notions of what an epic or a romance should be, derives from direct observation of Tasso's poetic practice in endowing most of his characters with a peculiar perplexity and wavering hesitation followed by impulsive, uncontrolled action.[3] The acuteness of this observation is undeniable, whether or not Galileo expressed a liking for what he saw, and despite his effort to use all of his observations in the service of a proof that one poet was better than the other. The Tasso enthusiast is left with the stark truth that Galileo, with his focus on psychological portraiture, is perhaps the first critic on record to have observed certain essential features of Tasso's poetry, and he considered them abominable.

Now it would seem that the Ariosto enthusiast should have little difficulty, given Galileo's predilection for Ariosto, in tapping the *Considerazioni* and the *Postille* for a steady flow of first-rate and immediately intelligible observations about the characters of the *Orlando Furioso.* Unfortunately, this is not the case at all. Galileo seems to have been much more concerned to prove the inferiority of Tasso than to establish what he considered obvious—the excellence of the *Orlando Furioso.* The rhetoric of vilification abounds in his criticism, almost as if he enjoyed it for its own sake, while there is very little direct and substantial commentary on passages in Ariosto's work. Hence, one must take whatever there is and interpret it in light of its context, often comparing statements of a very general nature to be found in the *Considerazioni* with those notes, or *postille,* that Galileo jotted down in apparent haste next to specific lines and stanzas in his personal copy of the *Furioso.* In other words, one is left in the uncomfortable position of having to fill in the blanks between the general and the particular in order to get an approximation of Galileo's views of the *Orlando Furioso* and its characters. Naturally, conjecture must enter such a process, but the value of the conjecture can be judged, from one vantage point, by whatever consistency of outlook it reveals in the totality of Galileo's criticism, and from another more important vantage point, by the fruits it bears in an actual exegesis of Ariosto's text. Furthermore, because theorists in the field of narrative, with very few exceptions, have dodged the *Orlando Furioso* as nimbly as they could, a sensibility as extraordinary as Galileo's may provide a better than average occasion for attempting to place Ariosto's work closer to the position it deserves in the spectrum of narrative art from Homer to the present.[4]

After struggling through the pages of the *Postille* as they come at one in the standard edition of Galileo's works,[5] awhirl with corrections of printer's errors and with finicky adjustments to Ariosto's diction and rhetoric, one finds, on the next-to-last page, a pleasant refuge from one's mounting disappointment. Evidently, Galileo, as an afterthought, or else lacking space in the margins of his copy, added to the blank part of its last page four brief notes. One of them deals with an episode in which Orlando and Isabella, having caught sight of a mob dragging a man off to be quartered, learn upon closer inspection that he is none other than Isabella's beloved Zerbino, whereupon Orlando rescues him and the three ride away together. The note reads, quite simply:

> Mark the characterization wonderfully observed, always in all things, and in Orlando, who is always portrayed as distracted and taciturn to the point of madness: questioned by Isabella, he answers only, "I don't know," c. 23, st. 55; and further down, st. 67, "They arrived taciturn," etc. (p. 193).

If one has plowed through the *Considerazioni* and the *Postille* from beginning to end, this observation, terse as it is, comes as a startling and crystalline result, in the form of practical criticism, of much that has been interesting on a more abstract plane. It has the effect of rendering clear in one luminous moment the literary critical implications of such famous passages in the *Considerazioni* as the one in which Galileo compares the *Gerusalemme Liberata* to a work of marquetry and the *Orlando Furioso* to an oil painting (p. 63), or the one in which he takes exception to the use of allegory, comparing its effect on the flow of a narrative to the effect of anamorphic distortions of perspective on the appearance of a work of art (pp. 129–30). The actual verse fragments of the *Orlando Furioso* under observation in this note appear to be very close literary counterparts of those "shadings" [*sfumature*] that, in Galileo's opinion, lend force, depth, and wholeness to an oil painting, while the concept of character implicit in the note suggests that its author did not attach any conventional allegorical or typological meaning to Orlando. Instead, one of the most striking things about this note is that it resembles the sort of observation that a twentieth-century critic might make about a character in a realistic novel.

According to Galileo, Ariosto created in Orlando a character who "always" exhibits symptoms of madness. The smallest details of his behavior in every episode prior to his actual mad scene reveal in him a potential for becoming insane. They *shade into* the mad scene, causing it to appear to be the natural outcome of a predisposition, and consequently, they lend coherence and three-dimensionality to Orlando's character, as well as unity to at least the portion of the narrative that involves him. At the same time, his learning of Angelica's lost virginity, with all of the important issues that it brings to culmination, must be regarded, in consequence of these shadings, more as the immediate cause of his madness—perhaps, the inciting incident—than as the formal cause, which appears to remain embedded in his character, retrievable only through a close reading of all of the episodes in which he takes part. If we follow Galileo's perception this far, we find ourselves with a view of the *Orlando Furioso* that has character taking precedence over incident, and this in one of the most intricately plotted works in the history of Western literature. At least it becomes extremely difficult to consider plot and rhetoric as compensating for a deficiency of careful, subtle delineation in the realm of character. Instead, we are inclined to regard the intricate plotting as a web taking its origin from characters whose psyches have been developed to a complexity not customarily encountered in romance.

It is true that Ariosto's characters meet the eye with all of the metaphorical and symbolic trappings of medieval romance, and no doubt this facilitated the work of the allegorists who transmitted their version of the *Orlando Furioso* to Spenser. For the reader schooled on *The Faerie Queene,* it takes uncommon restraint not to attempt allegorical interpretations of episodes and characters in Ariosto's work. Even when the critic professes sophistication in this regard, we may still find him allegorizing under cover of a scholarly exegesis based on study of influence or cultural context. However, Galileo's perception of Orlando divests the baron of his symbolic paraphernalia just as the cast of mind giving rise to such perceptions tends to transform the knights and ladies and wizards and enchantresses of Ariosto's vision into people, into detailed, complex representations of reality as opposed to signs pointing to easily recognizable concepts or types in moral philosophy. The pursuit of Galileo's antiallegorical reading then becomes an exercise in measuring the *displacement* (to use Northrop Frye's term[6]) in the direction of the *real* (as the term *real* is understood in discussions of eighteenth- and nineteenth-century fiction) undergone by the characters of the *Orlando Furioso*. According to Galileo, their complexities and ambiguities as representations of real people would have to be accounted for before it would be possible to interpret them as figures in the pattern of a moral philosophical vision; psychology would have to precede philosophy.

On the one hand, Galileo notes the vivid manner in which Ariosto manages with a simile to represent the rise and fall of Alcina's breasts due to her respiration (pp. 100 and 156), while on the other hand, he grumbles because the eyesight of Tasso's Erminia could not possibly be sharp enough to allow her to distinguish individuals in the Christian army all the way from the battlements of Jerusalem, with a cloud of dust rising from the skirmish underway and with a distance intervening of about a mile by his own estimate—an estimate based, of course, on evidence supplied by the text (p. 85). Such concerns appear on almost every page of the *Considerazioni* and the *Postille,* leaving no doubt that the literal imagery has at least as much importance to Galileo as any thematic values that might be attached to it. Furthermore, it is clear that Galileo expected the images to render faithfully the things they describe. Good poets "transmute themselves into the things to be represented," while the bad poet "transmutes the things he describes into things familiar to him"; hence Tasso confuses the winds of Palestine with those of Lombardy (p. 128). Galileo's objectivity leads him to make some humorous comments, as when he ridicules in Tasso the underwater visit to the sorcerer of Ascalona, likening the knights' return to the world to the rising of ravioli from the bottom of a boiling pot (p. 134), and it also leads him to disgust over the imagery Tasso uses to describe Armida's face: "I have never seen perspiration grow white, except on the testicles of horses" (p. 142). In fact, the former observation provides occasion for his sanctions against the kind of allegory that distorts the literal level of a narrative in the manner of anamorphoses. Although, in this place, he voices the conventional dictum that nothing of the forced or otiose should be introduced into a narrative for the sake of allegory, the preponderance of his observations deny altogether any serious taste for the technique, no matter how well it might be executed.

It is startling, if one stops to think about it, that Galileo's criticism could have achieved so much freedom from allegorical interpretation in an age when an edition of the *Orlando Furioso* would scarcely have been considered respectable unless it carried a full complement of allegorical appendages, and it is also startling that if Galileo had read Tasso's own allegory of the *Gerusalemme Liberata* (which seems more than likely), he himself leaves us no solid evidence of the fact. He was certainly aware of the vogue for allegorical interpretation of Ariosto's work. In fact, the observation about Alcina's breasts appears to have been written in defense of their real beauty against an allegorist who would have interpreted Ariosto's passage in such way as to render them flabby and repulsive in conformity with whatever vice he believed the character to represent. For the most part, Galileo appears to have ignored the allegorists, or else to have solidly opposed them, and his observations steadily indicate that verisimilitude, decorum, and internal consistency were the highest criteria by which he judged a narrative and its characters. In one of his rare laudatory comments on the *Gerusalemme Liberata,* he states,

> In my opinion, these three stanzas are very beautiful, and represent admirably that which the poet has undertaken to depict. And in this placing before our eyes that which he depicts, he acquires something of the divinity of Ariosto (pp. 135–36).

There is no need to belabor the point that this divinity does not reside in any theological or philosophical rectitude of precepts or ideas attaching to the poet's imagery—here, an aerial view of the port of Gaza. Galileo qualifies as divine the poet's ability to reflect vividly a marvelous world, to make it familiar, to place it before the reader's eyes so that the narrative appears to be recording a reality, not weaving a tissue of "pure finzioni" (p. 106).

"Pure fictions" is the term Galileo reserves for Tasso's heroes, who regularly do violence to his sense of reality with their "madrigalesque" speeches. He complains constantly that no captain, woodcutter, or lookout would ever have used the words that Tasso places in his mouth, and in the tone of these animadversions there is something that reminds one very strongly of Tolstoy expressing his disdain for the artificiality of opera. In the realm of character, Galileo's demand for the real is a demand for the representation of human beings as they appear in ordinary life, and this leads him to perceptions, such as the one concerning Orlando's taciturnity and distractedness, that have a peculiarly modern cast. In fact, one twentieth-century student of Galileo's aesthetic thought goes quite far in his admiration of this note on Orlando:

> Much more profitable and precise are Galileo's progressive, gradual, coherent, and wonderfully insightful observations on the psychological portraiture of Ariosto's heroes. It is precisely his well-justified admiration for that type of spiritual inquiry which proceeds without hesitation to illuminate

new aspects of the protagonists' consciousness that wrings from Galileo some of his most acute and ingenious comments—possibly the only ones in which there is manifested an attempt, perhaps unconscious, but happily successful, at introspection of the most modern kind. The summit, in the sense of revolutionary newness, of his aesthetic criticism seems to us in fact to be attained in the following highly subtle sentence . . .[7]

If this sounds fulsome or anachronistic or a trifle self-congratulatory in a "modern" essay, let it, at least, suffice to say that Galileo's perceptions, extraordinary in themselves, may shed some light on what was unusual about the *Orlando Furioso* in its time and also on the new direction it may have established for narrative fictions. When we find Galileo making demands of the *Orlando Furioso* that would be appropriate if they were applied to the works of Fielding, and when we find him satisfied that his demands have been fulfilled, we are compelled to wonder if Ariosto, instead of Cervantes, should not be considered the progenitor of the novel.

Galileo's view of character differed considerably from the views of his immediate predecessors in the Ariosto-Tasso controversy, and the exact way in which it differed accounts for its compatibility with modern critical approaches to character. His predecessors, for the most part, adapted to their polemical purposes the conventional sense attaching, in their time, to the first of Aristotle's four requisites for character; that is, they assailed or else praised the *Orlando Furioso* on account of the moral goodness or badness of Ariosto's characters, who were either exemplary types or gratuitously evil. Hence, on the one hand, Camillo Pellegrino could say that

> Ariosto introduces into the *Orlando Furioso,* not only wicked, but base persons, and these in great number, and a nastiness of behavior in them which he should not have portrayed, and he does so unnecessarily and without verisimilitude and without any usefulness whatsoever to that poem,

while his adversary, Lionardo Salviati, disagreeing with his conclusions, could not only agree with him in principle, but even suggest that characters in an epic should conform to a moral scheme of poetic justice:

> What provides a worse example in any kind of literature, or story that is listened to or presented before us, than to see virtue go without a reward or vice go unpunished? And in what else besides the example consists the profit of an epic poem? For what other purpose than for the sake of the example to be drawn from them by their audience do poems have introduced into them precepts and laws regarding excellence of characterization?[8]

Galileo's contribution to this aspect of the Ariosto-Tasso controversy was precisely what one would expect it to be. With the same razor he applied to allegory, he excises the first of the four Aristotelian requisites for character, leaving the other three in its former position of paramount importance: propriety, trueness to life, and consistency.[9] This means that characters must, in his opinion, exhibit traits conformable to their circumstances, must not violate common-sense dictates of verisimilitude, and must remain internally consistent, even in their inconsistencies, throughout a narrative. To determine whether these requisites have been fulfilled, Galileo proceeds inductively, setting aside much of the critical dogma of his age in favor of a scrutiny of the *Orlando Furioso* and the *Gerusalemme Liberata* as phenomena, like celestial bodies, whose guiding principles lie open to comprehension through direct observation of the relations among their parts. And hence his criticism seems, and *is,* more modern than the criticism practiced by his contemporaries and his immediate predecessors. In the realm of character, at least, he might be considered to be among the earliest of readers of the novel, even though the novel itself, as we know it, did not exist in his time.

Galileo had to satisfy himself with the *Orlando Furioso,* or else perhaps it would be truer to say that, in responding to the *Orlando Furioso,* he learned how to read fiction in a way that was new in his time. According to his earliest biographer, he considered himself a literary disciple of Ariosto:

> And when people honored him for the clarity and the perspicuity of his works, he responded with modesty that if those qualities were to be found in them, he owed it all to his repeated readings of the *Orlando Furioso,* in which he perceived the true property of excellence, that is, that no matter how many times he reread it, he always discovered its wonders and its perfections to be greater than he had thought. He confirmed this with two verses from Dante adapted to his meaning: "I have not yet read it so many times that I fail to find in it new beauties."[10]

Still, whether Galileo's disposition as a reader was developed before or after his readings of the *Orlando Furioso,* his defense of Ariosto's work is carried out along empirical lines, and hence it is new, bearing at least as much resemblance to Fielding's "Preface" to *Joseph Andrews* as to anything in the Ariosto-Tasso controversy in the past. Like Fielding, Galileo considered "the true excellence" of epic narrative to consist in "the exactest copying of nature," and he would have agreed with Fielding that characters should be drawn from the author's "own observations and experience." Hence, he would have disagreed with most approaches to the *Orlando Furioso* to be found in modern narrative theory, for it was not at all the abandonment of historicity and verisimilitude that he saw in the *Orlando Furioso,* but it was precisely on account of Ariosto's retention of narrative's mimetic features that he valued the *Furioso* as highly as he did, and perhaps saw in it an antidote to the various literary, social, and religious dogmatisms that beset his age. The extent, then, to which we are able to trust Galileo's perceptions of the *Furioso* can be considered a measure of the *Furioso's* closeness to the novel.

An example of a specific doubt on Galileo's part as to whether the *Furioso* has fulfilled his demands for "costume," for decorum, verisimilitude, and internal consistency, is illuminating in this regard. There is a note on two stanzas (62 and 63) of canto 7, in which Melissa, disguised as Atlante, is busy persuading Ruggiero of his error in dallying with Alcina. She has already reminded him of his allegiances to Agramante, to Bradamante, and to his own reputation, and now she is offering him the enticement of that glorious progeny he is to beget in union with Bradamante. All goes well enough, in Galileo's opinion, until Melissa launches into the two stanzas in question, which consist of barefaced flattery of Ippolito and Alfonso d'Este, Ariosto's employers. Galileo comments that Ariosto should be contented to see these two stanzas dropped, because the exaggeration is drawn out and winds up attenuating the fervor of the speech as a whole. He continues, "And besides, I do not know how consistent it is that Atlante, who has sought nothing other than to remove him from France, should be discoursing to him about his lineage. So perchance Melissa is taking the risk of shooting too high in the air" (p. 157). The archery metaphor suggests that Melissa may fail of her purpose by using too many arguments, especially arguments that are not consistent with the character she has assumed. Galileo seems to think Ariosto is, in this instance, guilty of one of Tasso's major faults: "the poet ever continuing to propose many things which afterwards slip from his mind and get lost inside his pen" (p. 104). However, this note presents a slight problem, assuming that Galileo believes Melissa to be in danger of betraying herself to Ruggiero by using arguments that to him would be suspicious coming from Atlante. At first glance, Galileo appears to be guilty of a lapse in his memory of the text, since there is no indication in the *Orlando Furioso* before canto 7 that Ruggiero should be aware of any motives on Atlante's part to remove him from France. It is true, of course, that this is

Atlante's sole concern, but there is no hint in the text that Ruggiero is aware of it. So it would seem that Melissa should have nothing to fear and that Galileo is the one who has shot too high. This opinion holds up, all except for one important missing element: the *Orlando Innamorato*.

In Boiardo's work, of which Ariosto poses as the ingenuous continuator, Ruggiero is made well aware of Atlante's desire to keep him away from France. When Galileo jotted down his misgivings, he was probably recalling two passages in the *Innamorato:* one (2.16.35) in which Atlante tries to dissuade Ruggiero from leaving the protection of his mountaintop to view Agramante's tournament by telling him he is doomed to die, betrayed in battle, and another (2.21.53–60) in which Atlante, having witnessed the knighting of Ruggiero by Agramante, delivers on the spot a prophecy concerning Ruggiero's Estensi progeny and warns in greater detail of the betrayal on the part of the House of Maganza. Ruggiero's reply in the earlier passage is to remind Atlante that no one can escape the destiny charted in his stars. So Galileo has sufficient reason to suspect Melissa of having overplayed her part, and it would also appear that he has caught Ariosto in a lapse from the consistency of his pose as the *Innamorato*'s continuator.

However, the significance of this note lies not so much in the justice—which remains to be seen—of Galileo's observation as in the line of thought it represents. It could not be clearer that his first concern is with Ruggiero, Melissa, and Atlante as characters possessing ordinary human qualities, and this is noteworthy since the passage under examination is in the heart of the most allegorical episode in the *Orlando Furioso*. The very edition in which Galileo was scribbling his notes probably contained a full set of allegories covering each of the forty-six cantos, and he might have read in a section entitled "Annotationi et avvertimenti" that Ariosto drew for this appearance of Melissa to Ruggiero upon book 4 of the *Aeneid,* in which Mercury, sent by Jove, orders Aeneas to leave the kingdom of Dido. In the allegories themselves, swollen with the influence of their predecessors Christianizing the *Aeneid,* he could have read that the Island of Alcina signifies sensual pleasure luring the human spirit into earthly befuddlement; that Atlante is the name given to Love that imprisons its votaries; that Melissa represents the grace of the Divine Love descending to help us see our errors and to deliver us from vice; that Ruggiero represents the perfect upholder of matrimonial fidelity overcoming temptation with the aid of grace and reason (Logistilla) only to find his way into the arms of Bradamante, the ideal wife; and so on and so forth.[11] No doubt Galileo did read some version of this edifying story, and he may have read much more than we know, but it is equally certain that he ignored all of it in favor of a personal interpretation that attached much greater importance to character as representing the behavior of real people than to character as a vehicle for moral precepts, and it is much to his credit that he stuck to his interpretation in the face of overwhelming opinion to the contrary.

In the case of the allegorical episode in question, most modern readers would have to agree that Galileo's instincts served him well, for if ever there was an allegory designed to self-destruct in the faces of its unwary admirers, it is this one. Atlante, like Prospero in another romantic comedy, has extraordinary powers at his command, but his sole motive in deploying them is so human that it defies abstraction. Whether protection of an adoptive child or revenge for a usurped dukedom be the magician's motive, his magic becomes an expression of his uncategorizable humanity. Even Alcina, though a very menacing female, who brings out the worst in men with a certain mechanical regularity, cannot be summed up under an abstract heading, for her encounter with Ruggiero changes her. Like Circe and Kalypso, she loses her malign powers to a man whom she loves, and when Ruggiero deserts her, she reacts with the fury of a scorned woman. However, it is left to Ruggiero himself to detonate the allegorical contraption beyond reclaim. When he flies off from Logistilla's palace of wisdom on his newly bridled hippogryph (held by one allegorist to represent the natural appetites)[12] and finds Angelica tied to a rock as prey for the sea monster, he rescues her and whisks her off to the nearest lonely spot in order to rape her, failing in the attempt only because his armor will not come off before she makes herself invisible with the magic ring. This is the consequence of Melissa's exhortations and Logistilla's instruction, and we cannot help thinking that he might be just as well off if he were back with Alcina. The characters of the *Orlando Furioso* refuse to submit to allegorical interpretation. Instead, allegory gives way to parody, and the entire episode in question becomes a lesson that the absolutes upon which allegory is predicated have only a limited power to describe human nature, which always turns out to be ambiguous and elusive.

The major characters of the *Orlando Furioso* regularly evoke a complex response from the reader, and this is because heroes behave at times like villains and villains like heroes. It is extremely difficult to grade them on any moral scale except that which they create themselves out of their own words and deeds and interrelationships, and perhaps it is pointless to try, because Ariosto's use of tradition is always an assertion of independence as vigorous as even Galileo himself could require.

When these characters are put through the paces of an allegorical pageant, the result is what one would expect: histrionic. They become actors in a theatrical event of such spectacular proportions that they cannot possibly carry it off. Their inflated roles force them to commit the deadliest sin of all acting, that is, to rivet their audience's attention not on the parts they are playing, but on the lines and wrinkles of their all too real and human faces. The pageant gives way to the Ridiculous, as Fielding understood the term. The characters in it appear to be the victims of affectation arising from vanity or hypocrisy, and hence they reduce the solemn Platonic formalism of allegory to tatters.[13]

It is no wonder that Galileo has misgivings about Melissa's overplaying her part. The very fact that she comes riding on stage in her Atlante costume mounted on a black stallion that has one red hoof would be enough to create suspicion. This is one red hoof *de trop.* She is affecting something that she cannot be. But when she quotes Anchises from book 6 of the *Aeneid* as a prelude to her flattery of Ippolito and Alfonso d'Este and forgets in the process that she is stepping out of character, we find ourselves ready, along with Galileo, either to make some cuts in the script or else to bring down the curtain on her altogether. And yet we know that this would spoil the fun, because Ariosto, in his role as playwright and stage manager, has designed her performance to be just as self-deflating as the entire episode in which she appears. It is well that she gives Ruggiero the magic ring without too much delay and stops acting, for otherwise her eulogy of Ferrara's rulers might reveal itself too clearly as fustian. Although we would probably not agree with Galileo that the two stanzas should be cut, we must sympathize with his judgment of Melissa's acting, and we must recognize that his line of character analysis accords well with the design laid out by the author of the *Orlando Furioso,* who escapes any arraignment for a lapse in his narratorial pose as Boiardo's continuator. Galileo may not have recognized all of the implications of his note on Melissa, or, if he did, he may have consigned his thoughts to a manuscript now lost; however, the note as it stands represents a perception of character that leads to a productive reading of Ariosto's text.

While Galileo's doubts about Melissa are concerned with the requisite of consistency, there is another note, involving Charlemagne, that concentrates more on decorum. In canto 14 Charlemagne offers a prayer for the survival of Paris in which he argues that God should look out for His friends, for if He allows them to perish, His enemies will take heart and the false law of Babel will drive out His religion. Galileo comments, "I would prefer that Charles contented himself with praying to God, without going on to admonish and advise Him" (p. 164). Is Galileo's tone ironic, and is he appreciating an irony in Ariosto's text, or is he seriously suggesting that there is a flaw in Ariosto's representation of the emperor of the Franks? Numerous are Galileo's complaints about Tasso's kings and generals. Aladino turns his scepter over to a perfect stranger in Clorinda (p. 77), and Goffredo is gullible in giving arms and soldiers to Armida (p. 102). "These are things that savor but little of experience, and do not befit the elderly soldier or courtier" (p. 102), says Galileo. Neither behaves, according to him, in a manner befitting his rank, his circumstances, and his experience. So perhaps Galileo is genuinely disturbed that Ariosto's emperor of the Franks is addressing God in the manner of an Italian petty potentate appealing for military aid from another not-so-petty potentate. But even if he is disturbed, his comment illuminates the essential feature of Charlemagne's prayer: it is the prayer of a Charlemagne who has undergone dislodgment from his mythic throne. Galileo's comment measures the displacement undergone by Ariosto's emperor in the direction of Fielding's concept of the Ridiculous. Of course, it follows very sensibly that the prayer itself should set in motion the celestial Punch and Judy show that ends with the Archangel Michael pounding Discord over the head with a crucifix. If such prayers are to be answered, this is the sort of answer they deserve. If Galileo's comment is indeed ironic, then it matches well the irony of Ariosto's passage.

Galileo is quick to perceive Charlemagne's pedestrian qualities, and he is also quick to perceive that the character of Angelica contains a study of a certain kind of feminine behavior. In canto 12, Angelica is deliberating over the difficulties of returning home to the Orient without a protector when she happens conveniently upon Atlante's palace of illusions, which she is able to enter with the help of her magic ring. There she finds Orlando and Sacripante pursuing her feigned image. Feeling compelled to choose one of them to be her escort, she chooses the weaker man because she knows that she will be able to discard him when he is no longer needed; the stronger man might dominate her. Galileo comments, "Female behavior admirably described, and this is one of the reasons that women, it seems, generally prefer men of meager parts to persons of great estimation" (p. 161). Here we find Galileo focusing on the trueness to life, instead of the decorum or the consistency, of one of Ariosto's characters. It is telling about Angelica that she sacrifices the greater security of Orlando's protection in order to preserve her freedom, and it is telling about Ariosto's narrative that Angelica seeks a companion at all when she has the magic ring with which to make herself invisible. Galileo, who is indefatigable in uncovering inconsistencies and contradictions in the *Gerusalemme Liberata,* never mentions this apparent contradiction in Ariosto's text. It is tempting to conclude that he showed favoritism to Ariosto, but such a conclusion would imply that the magic ring occupied, in his opinion, as important a place in the narrative as Angelica's very human motives for behaving as she does. Galileo does not note the contradiction for the simple reason that he must not have believed there to be one. In his reading, the magical paraphernalia of romance evaporates when exposed to any realistic representation of human behavior.

The question as to whether such a reading should be accepted will always occur to anyone who thinks seriously about the *Orlando Furioso.* The temptation to dismiss the hippogryph and the rest of his super-natural friends will always tease the reader who, like Galileo, is struck with Ariosto's complex delineation of character and led thereby to ponder over a real world that he perceives to be reflected and to be interpreted in Ariosto's narrative. However, this temptation must be resisted, if only for the obvious reason that it distorts the *Orlando Furioso* beyond recognition. Without the dazzling shield, the horn of horrible sound, the palace of illusions, and most of all the hippogryph, we would be missing the very iconography with which we identify the *Furioso.* Galileo's total submission to the lure of the real should not, however, be regarded as an invalidation of his criticism, even though it does set a clear limit to its reliability. Fantasy and reality coexist in Ariosto's narrative in a delicate balance, the mythical elements never yielding completely in interest to the purely representational, even though comprehension of them depends almost entirely upon scrutiny of the latter.

In the present case, Angelica's possession of the magic ring qualifies her choice of companions in an important way. It points up, not a contradiction in Ariosto's narrative, but an ambiguity in Angelica's character. With the magic ring she is perfectly free to do without a companion, and yet this alternative never enters her mind. Not wanting to be dominated, and yet unable to act independently, as Bradamante does, Angelica chooses the lesser of two evils—the weaker of two men for whom she feels nothing. Although she feels nothing for Sacripante, she prefers the illusion of dependence upon him to an acceptance of freedom along with its responsibilities. It comes as no surprise later that she bestows her love on the weakened, prostrate figure of a man near death. Possession of the ring complicates Angelica's character, render-ing her much more psychologically intriguing than she would be without it as merely a coquette or a virgin in distress. The ring emerges from its mythic shell to provide an important thematic nuance to this episode by stressing Angelica's freedom. While Galileo is correct in avoiding the attachment of transcendent values to Ariosto's imagery and in focusing on the mimetic aspect of character, his approach tends to ignore the possibility that the mythic elements of the *Orlando Furioso* may become symbols whose meanings emerge and develop within a plot generated by a complex and realistic interpretation of character. Still, what remains is that Galileo's eye, like Ariosto's, is focused on the trueness to life of Angelica's behavior.

With proper reserve, and with a distinction held firmly in mind between the allegorical symbol and the symbol whose manifold meanings emerge as the text becomes more and more familiar, it should be possible now to move on and to examine the characters of the *Furioso* using Galileo's approach. His observations about Orlando, Melissa, Atlante, Charlemagne, and Angelica all illustrate his concentration on the mimetic and on coherency. He also concentrates on the demands of a continued narration upon the development of character, and in doing so he poses his greatest challenge to modern Ariosto criticism. In order to use Galileo's approach, it is necessary to examine each appearance of a character in light of all of his other appearances. In reading, as Galileo did, any particular episode of the *Orlando Furioso,* we must stand with a telescope that enables us to see in the distance all that has already happened and all that is yet to come. In other words, we must strive for the memory we expect of the ideal reader of novels, and the first thing we must remember as we analyze the characters of the *Orlando Furioso* is that we may be witnessing the novel already on its rise into being.

2
Homo Prudens or "Gran Pedone"?

s one of the more talkative characters in the *Orlando Furioso,* Rinaldo of Chiaramonte has attracted some attention from the critics. In canto 4, stanzas 63–67, and canto 43, stanzas 6–8, he delivers speeches that appear noteworthy for their common sense. The first one, occurring in the Ginevra and Ariodante episode, has for its ostensible subject the equality of men and women. As soon as Rinaldo is finished the narrator assures us that Rinaldo receives "il consenso universale" of his listeners, who, in this case, are the monks who have been endeavoring with materialistic arguments to enlist him in Ginevra's defense. The second speech occurs in the episode involving the magic goblet, which spills if a cuckold tries to drink from it. Rinaldo gives his reasons for refusing to undergo the trial of the goblet, and his host, having heard these reasons, lavishes compliments on him. Both speeches stand out from the whole narrative context. They appear to have been designed to attract attention, and, coming as they do at the beginning and the end of the *Furioso,* they also have the appearance of an exordium and a peroration to all that comes between. It is no wonder that much has been made of them.

These speeches have sources and analogues in the writings of ancient authors and in those of Ariosto's contemporaries. Predictably, Ariosto gives these sources very free-handed treatment, developing a line of thought beyond the point to which it was taken before, or else applying it to a case that is altogether new. The natural consequence has been to regard the character to whom Ariosto gives these extraordinary speeches as voicing the philosophy of life of which Ariosto approves. According to one interpretation of the magic goblet episode, this philosophy is essentially Horatian. Rinaldo becomes the proponent of *aurea mediocritas,* counseling his forlorn host not to ask too much of life and not to seek painful knowledge that will leave him worse off than if he had remained ignorant. Human beings have limitations, and they

17

must respect these limitations if they are to lead the good life. Rinaldo is seen as providing the answer to a condition of human life in which "we have exceeded the mean and proved once again that we love our own desires and illusions beyond the bounds of common sense or sanity."[1] As the peroration to a text in which a deluded hero goes mad for love of a girl, Rinaldo's speech poses a heavy attraction, and yet perorations and exordia, speeches and all other statements of a discursive nature, no matter how convincing, can rarely be granted final authority in narrative fictions.

In another, and far more detailed, interpretation, Rinaldo assumes the proportions of the *homo prudens* as described by the humanist Giovanni Pontano in his *De prudentia*. This, of course, is the interpretation of Mario Santoro, who first presents it in his essay "L'Astolfo Ariostesco: *Homo Fortunatus*" and then develops it in a subsequent piece entitled "Rinaldo ebbe il consenso universale."[2] The interpretation deserves close attention because it reveals certain qualities exhibited by Rinaldo throughout the *Orlando Furioso,* even though it focuses for the most part on his colloquy with the monks in canto 4. According to Santoro, the part of the episode involving the forest of Caledonia has undergone a demythologization, by comparison with the treatment of similar episodes in earlier romances, and Rinaldo is a hero "degradato," reduced from an abstract typology of heroism to human dimensions. (Northrop Frye's term *displacement* would furnish a good translation of Santoro's meaning.)[3] The colloquy itself takes place in a "clima antieroico." Hence, irony develops as Rinaldo behaves in unexpectedly human ways. Santoro takes note of his worldly common sense and his habit of pausing to deliberate before he comes to a decision. Rinaldo suspends judgment about Ginevra's innocence, refusing to be influenced by the monks. He has insufficient evidence to reach a conclusion, so he prefers to assume a detached, critical posture toward their arguments. The remainder of Santoro's essay is devoted to a demonstration that Rinaldo, in his discourse to the monks against the law of Scotland and in his refusal to try the magic goblet, "offers an emblematic measure of his awareness of the relativity and fallibility of nature, of the limit placed by experience upon absolute and abstract principles and values."[4] Ariosto's full approval of Rinaldo's speeches is taken for granted, along with his approval of the character.

Santoro's perception that Rinaldo exhibits the characteristics of the prudent man as these are described in a contemporary humanist tract is of great value, as is his conclusion that Rinaldo's association with the defense of women theme is not accidental, but offers him a wide arena for the display of his prudence. Santoro's line of approach is particularly interesting in its tendency to regard Rinaldo has having undergone demythologization and as having acquired a number of realistic traits; however, it is precisely at this point that a disturbing paradox looms up. Whether we come from Horace or Pontano to a view of Rinaldo as the typically prudent man, we find that we have not advanced much further than the sixteenth-century interpretation of Orazio Toscanella: "Rinaldo is the name given to travail and to the experience of many things."[5] Despite the brevity of Toscanella's utterance, it covers the ground traversed in more detail by his modern colleagues. The difficulty with all three interpretations is that they attach a static value to the character, leaving unanalyzed the permutations this value undergoes as the character travels through the narrative landscape and becomes involved with other characters. Once having declared Rinaldo a hero "degradato," Santoro fails to pursue the implications of his statement. The hero who departs from the realm of myth in order to join the real world cannot be judged by a single action or a single speech. Instead, his function within a narrative and the author's estimate of him can only be determined through a patient weighing of all of his words and acts against one another. His significance, then, emerges from an intricate set of relations and retains the complexity and ambiguity of the real.

Galileo's approach to character, which stresses psychological coherency, affords an escape from the paradox of interpretations that emphasize Rinaldo's awareness of practical limits to the validity of abstract principles, and yet place him firmly within the straitjacket of a single, abstract, allegorical significance. Galileo's approach requires that Rinaldo's two major appearances be judged in light of his less noteworthy activities, and it defines the whole psychological portrait designed by Ariosto, whose viewpoint, as a result, becomes discernible. Furthermore, Galileo's approach provides a better understanding of the *Furioso's* unity, at least with respect to the episodes involving Rinaldo. Santoro's view of Rinaldo as *homo prudens,* far from being invalidated, is reinforced with the exception that Rinaldo as *homo prudens* becomes a creature primarily of Ariosto's invention, and not of Pontano's or Horace's. Nor does this approach detract from the significance of the placement of Rinaldo's two major appearances near the beginning and the end of the *Furioso.* However, it deemphasizes the speeches themselves and focuses on the character as a totality, lending Rinaldo the significance of a foil or a frame-character in contrast with whom the

Furioso's true protagonists reveal their salient qualities. This approach helps to explain Rinaldo's peculiar prominence in the narrative despite his being, by most standards, a minor character.

If, however, one begins a systematic reading in the first canto, problems arise immediately with the *homo prudens* interpretation. Our first vision of Rinaldo is of a "gran pedone," a big foot-soldier, chasing his horse through the woods, and the narrator compares him with a half-naked peasant running for a prize in a race. This does not bode well for a figure who is to assume prominence for his intellectual powers; nor is our first impression much improved when the narrator assures us that his horse is favored with "intelletto umano" and only wishes to lead him to his desired Angelica. These few details of Rinaldo's early exploits are unforgettable and must serve later to qualify any extreme enthusiasm on the reader's part for those speeches containing so much fine common sense. Rinaldo's entry into the narrative stamps him indelibly with marks of the Ridiculous.

In the opening canto, we also have the first example of Rinaldo's prudent reasoning. In the middle of his combat with Ferraù, it dawns on him that they are laboring in vain since Angelica has taken advantage of their encounter in order to flee. He convinces the pagan to lay down his arms and to join him in pursuit of her; otherwise they would injure each other for nothing. They can recommence their battle once they have caught and secured her. Although both warriors come freighted with heroic epithets and Ferraù has dashed bare-headed into the fight, neither shows any concern with the glory-for-its-own-sake to be won by the victor in such a combat. Instead, the two enemies form a temporary alliance in the interest of expediency. Ariosto's audience among the ruling class of Ferrara must have seen many such alliances come and go in a period when Italy was in the throes of invasion and every petty state was out to protect its interests at any cost. Thanks to Rinaldo's prudent reasoning, the narrator is able, as the two knights of different faiths ride off together on the same horse, to declare with caustic irony, "O great goodness of the knights of old!" [Oh gran bontà de' cavallieri antiqui!] This single phrase then becomes the measure in the *Orlando Furioso* of the disparity between any mythic realm of romance and the real world its narrative attempts to reflect.

Although Rinaldo is the *homo prudens,* he is certainly not exempt from infatuation, even if it is only temporary. The narrator impresses this fact upon us from the instant that Rinaldo first appears in the text. What is particularly interesting about this condition is the ambivalence ensuing from it. The alliance with Ferraù is a good example of pragmatism shading off into opportunism, and throughout the narrative one has difficulty distinguishing practical wisdom from cynicism in Rinaldo's words. Both are present, the one contaminating or else mitigating the other. The reader need only establish the degree to which one is established at the expense of the other, and this can be accomplished by comparing Rinaldo's actions with his words. With Angelica in the near vicinity, it is not difficult to resolve the question. Cynicism and opportunism prevail in canto 2 as Rinaldo dashes off on his captured horse toward Paris, where he believes Angelica to be. He leaves Sacripante in the dust, and the narrator notes that it never crossed his mind to extend to Sacripante the same courtesy of a ride that he himself had received from Ferraù. One is reminded of the Machiavellian dictum that princes should enter alliances and maintain them solely as circumstances demand.

Rinaldo dashes off toward Paris, only to be dispatched against his will to Britain in search of reinforcements against the Saracens, who have recently defeated Charlemagne and laid siege to his city. In narrative terms, Rinaldo is dashing into the long novella that begins at the end of canto 4 and ends at the beginning of canto 6, the episode functioning very much like a subplot linked to the main body of the *Furioso* by the mission in behalf of Paris and, more distantly but perhaps not less significantly, by the character Zerbino. The story of Ginevra and Ariodante is complex enough in itself that it would seem only decent not to heap on further complications. However, this is impossible, since Rinaldo, due to the quick, deft strokes lent his character in cantos 1 and 2, enters the story as a psychological force to be reckoned with. The very extent of his involvement in the rescue of Ginevra is problematic, along with the accuracy of his view of the issues raised by her predicament.

At the risk of allegorizing and oversimplifying, it would be well at the outset to sketch these issues. In the plainest possible terms, the story is about the assault of force and fraud on faith. Polinesso devises an elaborate fraud in order to undermine Ariodante's faith in Ginevra. Deceived as well, the violent Lurcanio takes Polinesso's scheme a step beyond its original purpose by invoking the law of Scotland when he hears the false report of Ariodante's suicide. Faith has a moral truimph over Polinesso's fraud and Lurcanio's truculence when Ariodante champions Ginevra despite his having reason to believe that she has betrayed him. However, were it not for Rinaldo's sudden appearance, this would be exclusively a moral triumph, and a bitter one at that. By itself it might leave Polinesso unpunished, and it would certainly bring death for Ariodante or else the murder of his brother. Furthermore, if

Ariodante died, Ginevra would die as well. The story would become a *guignol* of suffering innocence and of evil performed with impunity and even limited success.

At this point, Rinaldo enters the lists very much like a *deus ex machina*. However, the opinion of the allegorist Porcacchi, that Rinaldo represents justice sent unexpectedly by God, simply will not do, unless we are disposed to regard Rinaldo as an instrument of forces beyond his control or understanding. If Rinaldo is an arm of Providence, he is embarrassingly innocent of the fact.[6] The best we can say for him is that he comes upon this adventure in Scotland by accident, gets involved in it for the wrong reasons, learns the truth through no mental effort of his own, and brings a resolution to Ginevra's dilemma that would be most unsatisfactory were it not for the extraordinary resolution provided by Ariodante. If matters were left exclusively to Rinaldo (or indeed to anyone else who happened to drop out of the sky), it is true that Polinesso would be exposed and punished, that Lurcanio would receive a just reproach for his violence, and that Ginevra's life would be saved; but it is also true that Polinesso's original evil purpose—the destruction of Ariodante's faith—would be accomplished. Only Ariodante in solitude, in the privacy, and despite the confusion, of his spirit, can insure that *fraude* will not prevail over *fede*—*fede* not in any religious sense of the word, but in its range of meanings from trust to loyalty.

Only through a fortunate confluence of events does the tale of Ginevra and Ariodante end in unmitigated happiness for its major characters, and since similar good fortune proves to be rare, but significant, in the *Furioso* as a whole, this instance of it deserves a leisurely examination. Rinaldo's participation in the story begins in canto 3 when he sets sail for Britain. We are told that he is so anxious to complete his mission and return to the pursuit of Angelica that he sets out in threatening weather against the advice of experienced sailors. When a storm ensues, he gets blown off course, and his imprudent decision ends in his washing up accidentally in Scotland. There he determines, with a resourcefulness already exhibited in his dealings with Ferraù and Sacripante, to make the best of his bad luck. Since he finds himself in the forest of Caledonia, he decides to add to his glory by performing a deed worthy of his noble predecessors in romance mythology. The mission in behalf of Paris is, ironically, forgotten, and so is the pursuit of Angelica, as Rinaldo, the opportunist, goes off to stray self-indulgently through the woods. Nor will this be the only time that we find him tarrying in a landscape far from the one where he knows he is needed. The combat on the island of Lipadusa will await him in vain while he lounges in comfortable quarters listening to edifying stories and exhibiting his Horatian good sense. We may briefly wonder at his abandoning the pursuit of Angelica, but we learn soon enough that this passion was always of the breakable kind, and if we compare it with Orlando's passion for the same girl, we find ourselves sympathizing with the intensity and abandonment in Orlando's behavior that is missing altogether from Rinaldo's. If making the best of one's folly is prudence, then perhaps Rinaldo is prudent.

By the time Rinaldo reaches the abbey where he delivers the first of his famous speeches, the reader has had considerable experience of him, and most of it is not of the sort that inspires confidence. At the abbey commences the narrative proper of Ginevra and Ariodante, and before proceeding any further with Rinaldo, it is necessary to note the structure of that narrative, because it is strongly marked and because Rinaldo's behavior must be viewed in light of it, as well as in light of the theme of faith under assault by fraud and force. The story falls into three distinct parts: the episode at the abbey, the episode narrated by Dalinda, and the trial by combat in the city of St. Andrew. The movement from episode to episode progresses clearly from the general to the particular, from the abstract to the concrete, from the detached perspective of the outsider to the perspective of the impassioned participant, and it culminates in an account of the intimate thoughts and feelings of Ariodante. Rinaldo's participation throughout is strictly limited: he decides to become involved in the first place, he rescues Dalinda, and he defeats Polinesso in battle. Otherwise, he listens, in all three parts, to accounts of events that have already occurred, and reacts only in word or thought. He is, for the most part, a passive bystander who suddenly finds himself, due to his misunderstanding of the issues, involved in a dilemma that goes beyond his depth.

In the first episode of the story, the monks do little more than present Rinaldo with a general case, the general case of all romance: the virgin in distress. Ginevra has been accused of fornication and stands to suffer death because of a certain grim law of her people. One would expect the monks to argue heatedly in her defense, but they do not. Instead, they try to lure Rinaldo with fame, with the power and riches of the king, and with the beauty of the girl, and their attempts have the natural effect of diminishing belief in her innocence. Nor do they ever say that they themselves believe her to be innocent. The best they can do is declare that Lurcanio has accused her "perhaps out of hatred more than for good reason" and that she is a paragon of chastity "according to popular opinion" (4.58, 62). This "perhaps" leaves much to be desired, as does the support she has received from the populace. After all, she is a king's daughter, which may also account for the partisanship of the monks. So Rinaldo makes a cautious reply, tabling altogether the question of her innocence and exhibiting common sense enough insofar as it proves that he knows his audience:

Sia vero o falso che Ginevra tolto
s'abbia il suo amante, io non riguardo a questo:
d'averlo fatto la loderei molto,
quando non fosse stato manifesto.
Ho in sua difesa ogni pensier rivolto:
datemi pur un chi mi guidi presto,
e dove sia l'accusator mi mene;
ch'io spero in Dio Ginevra trar di pene.

Non vo' già dir ch'ella non l'abbia fatto;
che nol sappiendo, il falso dir potrei:
dirò ben che non de' per simil atto
punizion cadere alcuna in lei;
e dirò che fu ingiusto o che fu matto
chi fece prima li statuti rei;
e come iniqui rivocar si denno,
e nuova legge far con miglior senno.

S'un medesimo ardor, s'un disir pare
inchina e sforza l'uno e l'altro sesso
a quel suave fin d'amor, che pare
all'ignorante vulgo un grave eccesso;
perché si de' punir donna o biasmare,
che con uno o più d'uno abbia commesso
quel che l'uom fa con quante n'ha appetito,
e lodato ne va, non che impunito?

Son fatti in questa legge disuguale
veramente alle donne espressi torti;
e spero in Dio mostrar che gli è gran male
che tanto lungamente si comporti.

(4. 64–67)[7]

I care not whether it be true or false that Ginevra has had a lover. I would praise her highly for having had one if only it had not come out in the open. My every intention is to defend her, so quick, give me someone to guide me and lead me to her accuser. I trust in God that I shall deliver Ginevra from her suffering. I would certainly not say that she has not done it, for without firsthand knowledge, I might speak a falsehood. However, I will say that no punishment at all should befall her for a deed the like of that, and I will say that the man who first framed these wicked statutes was unjust or insane and that they ought to be revoked as iniquitous and a new law made with better judgment. If the same ardor, if an equal desire, inclines and impels both one sex and the other to that sweet consummation of love which to the ignorant herd seems a grave excess, why should a woman be punished or blamed for having done with one man or even more than one that which men do with as many women as they have a taste for and come away praised, much less unpunished? Truly, manifest wrongs are committed against women under this unequal law, and I trust in God that I shall demonstrate it to be a great evil that it has so long been complied with.

Far from upsetting the expectations of these faithless monks, his reply follows very sensibly from their own argument, only developing it one stage beyond where they have taken it. The monks' explicit appeal to the opportunistic in Rinaldo leads him to explicit cynicism. He argues, with charming straightforwardness, that the law of Scotland should be abolished because women should have the same right as men to fornicate with impunity. Sexual partners, no matter what their condition, should suffer no punishment at all, much less death, provided only that their desire be mutual. At first glance, Rinaldo's opinions appear to represent a refreshing antidote to the indiscriminate cruelty of Scotland's law, and also a recognition of feminine rights, but upon consideration, they reveal themselves to be an expression of a laissez-faire cynicism of which Scotland's law is little more than the opposite extreme.

In order, though, to get some measure of Rinaldo's cynicism, it might be useful to make a brief excursus into another area of Ariosto's *opere*. The *Cinque Canti* contains the startling history of Medea, who, in her advanced years, develops wisdom sufficient to overcome a problem that has always plagued her. She decides that the cause of her grief has always been her obstinate attachment to one man at a time. She wishes to eliminate passion from her life, but she knows that she cannot live chastely. Her solution is to divide her love among multitudes, so that "if one man were about to drag her into pain and irritation, there would be a hundred ready to restore her enjoyment."[8] With this outlook, she easily makes herself the queen of Bohemia, and during her reign the country undergoes a marked increase in population, not only for the obvious reason, but also because neighboring peoples flock to her borders in admiration of her "alta dottrina." She builds a temple where, six out of every ten days, her citizens gather to ask forgiveness from their gods for every pleasure they have neglected since they last came together. Then they form two groups according to sex and blow out the lights. Brothers pounce on sisters and mothers on sons in the melee. At this point, the narrator cries, alas, that Medea had to go to Bohemia and not to Italy where she could have cured everyone's jealousy. Medea's reign continues until the birth of Christ somewhat arbitrarily ends her orgy and she must go back into the woods.

Rinaldo may not advocate incest in his speech to the monks, but he certainly does make himself the proponent of a kind of love that obviates commitment and places the greatest emphasis on sensual pleasure; this, despite any critical effort to whitewash the fact, is hedonistic. That "consenso universale" which he receives when he finishes speaking may be granted him by Ariosto only with considerable irony, perhaps with precisely the same irony that accompanies the popular admiration accorded Medea's "alta dottrina." In the *Furioso's* world of instability and uncertainty, *fede*—whether it be translated as faith, trust, loyalty, or commitment— is essential, or else human relations deteriorate. However, in this world, in which the exclamation "behold human judgment, how often it errs" [ecco il guidicio uman come spesso erra] voices the only certainty, it is perilous to trust anyone or to commit oneself to anyone else. Disillusionment, madness, and despair are too often the rewards of one's trust. Hence, it might be considered prudent to live a life entirely in circumvention of faith, that is, to avoid whenever possible circumstances that require the placing of one's trust in anyone else. This, of course, is precisely the solution adopted by Rinaldo and Medea, and it is also, paradoxically, the solution posed—or imposed—by the law of Scotland. The law, in attempting to enforce faith, misses altogether its essence in voluntariness, while Rinaldo's cynicism merely ignores the necessity of faith in human relations. The reader is left to choose between opposite sides of the same coin: between the circumvention of faith by means of compulsion or by means of avoidance, by means of forced abstinence or of hedonistic promiscuity. Of course, the choice, if these were the only two alternatives, would be simple. The draconian cruelty of the law makes Rinaldo's permissiveness look like prudence: a great evil makes a lesser evil appear to be good. So the reader gives his consent to Rinaldo out of repugnance toward the law, and like Rinaldo, feels quite satisfied with himself until, and only until, Rinaldo's prudence is exposed for what it really is.

In the next episode Rinaldo learns from Dalinda everything of which he was unaware when he spoke to the monks. The case in the abstract becomes concrete, and it is noteworthy that Rinaldo has nothing to say after Dalinda has finished speaking. Instead, he is encouraged in his mission by the discovery that Ginevra is innocent. This represents a great change in his view of matters. Previously, he had been concerned only that she had let herself be caught. Now, her innocence makes a difference in light of the new facts he has learned, and chief among these is the oath that Ginevra "had sworn both in speech and writing," to Ariodante "that she would never be anyone's spouse but his" (5.33). Were Ginevra guilty, she might not deserve execution, but she could hardly avoid, what amounts to the same spiritually, a sentence of ostracism from the company of those among her fellow human beings who attach the highest value to *fede*—trust, loyalty, and commitment. Ginevra pledged her faith to Ariodante, and this fact alone renders Rinaldo's point of view irrelevant to her case. In a sense, Rinaldo learns from Dalinda that he was as much off course in his disquisition to the monks as he was in the first place when the storm blew him to Scotland. So he does the only tactful thing in the circumstances. He remains silent after she has finished speaking.

Rinaldo's silence at the end of Dalinda's story may also be accounted for by his having learned of Polinesso. If Ginevra's oath tends to make Rinaldo's cynicism appear slightly fatuous, Polinesso's satanic evil makes the arbitrariness of Scotland's law appear naive and even more dangerous than it had seemed before. What reader would wish to see Dalinda executed for having succumbed to Polinesso's seduction? If ever Rinaldo's laissez-faire morality can be held to be salubrious, it is in cases such as hers. Polinesso is a monster, perhaps Ariosto's most convincing representation of evil. Saturated with malice, yet endowed with a superior knowledge of human nature and an ingenuity in the commission of evil bordering on the artistic, he brings to mind Iago. A master of illusion, he provides Ariodante with the "ocular proof" of Ginevra's infidelity, creating an impression of certainty where there can be none. In him, Ariosto represents a force that renders prudence impotent and the law a servant of its vicious purpose. It can be destroyed only by its own fierce energy. Rinaldo is nothing more than the immediate cause of Polinesso's destruction. The ultimate cause lies in Polinesso himself, in his own total lack of the very quality he desires most to obliterate in others: *fede*. Dalinda pinpoints the issue (and also measures unwittingly the degree of her former infatuation) when, with sarcasm, she declares of him, "as a reward worthy of my faith he murders me" (5.74). Incapable of trust or loyalty himself, he cannot see how anyone else can be loyal, even to him, so he orders the murder of Dalinda and creates the condition that makes possible Rinaldo's discovery of his evil. In effect, he orders his own misfortune, and evil ends up working in behalf of the good: *pro bono malum*.

The same is true of Lurcanio, whose wrath, we learn in the final episode of the story, brings Ariodante to Ginevra's defense. We know enough about Lurcanio to be reasonably certain that his thirst for revenge is augmented by a violent disposition and by an ingrained misogyny. If Polinesso is a figure of *fraude*, Lurcanio embodies violence, or *forza*. The assault of these two on the *fede* of Ginevra and Ariodante defeats itself. From the moment of Lurcanio's open accusation of Ginevra, Polinesso's scheme gets out of control. When the king commences to interrogate Ginevra's ladies-in-waiting in order to test the truth of Lurcanio's charge, Polinesso sees no security for himself except in the murder of Dalinda. Evil generates evil at an uncheckable rate until the process flies out of control and demolishes itself. Ariosto appears to be commenting on the inherent incompatibility of the two major forms that evil takes, the one incapable of concealment and the other impossible without secrecy. It seems that the Lurcanios and the Polinessos of the world are on a collision course. If it is not a Rinaldo who steps in to hurry the process along, it will be someone else— perhaps someone, as the narrator suggests at the opening of canto 5, for whom the cruelty per se of hired assassins or of Scotland's law is a sufficient motive for action.

In the third episode of the tale of Ginevra and Ariodante, we breathe fresh air for the first time in our journey through the realms defined by the moral vision of Ariosto-Dante.[9] We have visited the circles of fraud and violence, and we have witnessed in Dalinda a victim of blinding incontinence, but with Ariodante's description of his torment resulting from Polinesso's fraud, we enter the true purgatory of the *Orlando Furioso*, beyond which Ariosto, unlike Dante, would postulate no other realm. After the simple instinct for self-preservation has deterred Ariodante from carrying his despair into suicide, he learns that Ginevra has believed an erroneous report of that suicide and that she has almost died of grief as a consequence. With this new information, Ariodante enters the state of every man to whom it is important to know another's feelings: uncertainty, from which no amount of evidence or reason serves as an escape. At first glance, it would appear that he must choose to believe or not believe in Ginevra's innocence, or else, like Rinaldo, attempt to sidestep the question of faith entirely. However, Ariodante does something more admirable than adopting any of these alternatives. He adopts the same course of action that later will be adopted by

Bradamante when she hears the false report of Ruggiero's betrothal to Marfisa. He chooses to risk his life in opposition to the cruelty of his brother and of the law and in confirmation of his own integrity. He loves Ginevra despite the conflicting evidence about her chastity, so he must defend her or be untrue to himself. By refusing to let appearances come between him and his strongest feelings, he achieves a momentary victory over the instability of his world and makes himself the true adversary of Polinesso. In the city of St. Andrew, he engages fraud and violence in a battle against the faith and the selfless commitment that he himself has exhibited throughout his courtship of Ginevra, and in asserting the primacy of his faith despite the appearance that Ginevra has broken hers, he becomes the proponent of a principle far nobler than any law or line of reasoning that common-sense prudence could ever extract from the world of appearances in which he moves. Morally, the spirit of transcendence prevails over the spirit of denial, asserting the superiority of the irrationally loyal and altruistic self over the predatory egotism and the cold logic of the self that exploits human weakness by taking advantage of the world's instability and of human nature's proneness to accept false illusions as promises of certainty and security. In Ariodante, Ariosto creates a moral standard with which to judge the behavior of the *Furioso's* major characters.

Of course, Rinaldo, by virtue of his mere presence on the scene, but particularly on account of his involvement in Ariodante's affairs, must come in for judgment before anyone else. If Ariosto intended his readers to see Ariodante, Dalinda, Lurcanio, and Polinesso as figures in the pattern of a moral vision similar to Dante's what place in the pattern, we must ask, does Rinaldo occupy? Is he good or evil, and to what extent can he be said to be the one or the other? However, if—as Ariosto would seem to desire—we take the assertion or denial of *fede* to be the major criterion for answering these questions, we find ourselves in a dilemma. Rinaldo has neither asserted nor denied the importance of faith; instead, he has blandly ignored the possibility that faith might be an issue in the tasks he has undertaken. It is true, on the one hand, that he has recognized from Dalinda's confession how important Ginevra's innocence is to her defense, and for this he deserves some credit, just as he deserves credit for recognizing Ariodante's nobility and for supporting him at the conclusion of the adventure. On the other hand, it is also true that he has nothing whatsoever to say about the reformation of Scotland's law, even though he had promised from the start that reform would be his purpose. His silence on this score at the end of the story strongly suggests that he is unable to articulate any position other than the one he adopted in his speech to the monks, and this despite everything he has learned in the interim. If, with the name Ariodante, Ariosto desired to signal a thematic affinity with Dante in his tale of Ginevra and Ariodante, perhaps the reader should regard Rinaldo as one of those spirits at the threshold of hell who follows the swirling banner of him who made "the great refusal." Rinaldo, and all that he stands for, appears to be neither good nor evil. He has never made a choice between the two as Ariodante and Polinesso have. So if we look for his figure in the tapestry of Ariosto's moral vision, we are likely to look in vain unless we search the borders for a design contrasting with all of the good and the bad within.

The *homo prudens* deliberates, reasons, suspends judgment, is critical of received opinion, weighs evidence, and by a law of nature coeval with humanity, reduces the world in the crucible of his identity to that nugget of gold most pleasing to his own view. This alchemy, in Rinaldo's case, has the power to burn away from experience all that is beneath and beyond reason, all intense love and hatred, all of the very best and the very worst of life. Self-destructive evil and selfless good evaporate under his scrutiny. Rinaldo may seem attractive when he advocates a comfortably equal distribution of life's pleasures, but his outlook is unmistakably pedestrian. In Ariosto's opinion, the *homo prudens* reveals himself to be a "gran pedone," earthbound and restricted in his vision to an image of the world not very different from that image of his horse's rear end which he was pursuing through the woods when he began his fictional life in the *Orlando Furioso*. In the tale of Ginevra and Ariodante, Rinaldo's character receives from his profoundly mistaken point of view the poignancy of all well-intentioned, but obtuse, irrelevancies. Perhaps Ariosto's judgment of the *homo prudens* is that his admirable detachment is both harmless and useless in a world in which nothing can be accomplished if not at the risk of one's sanity. Rinaldo is distinctly unheroic in a field of action that calls for perilous choices.

In a different context, Ariosto concisely demonstrates the pointlessness of Rinaldo's reasoning. In canto 16.32–38, the baron delivers a speech that has attracted much less attention than those in the Ginevra and Ariodante and the magic goblet episodes, even though it is perfectly consistent with those speeches in revealing the severe limitations of the *homo prudens*. This is an exhortation to the reinforcements from Britain. Before setting out against the Saracens besieging Paris, Rinaldo tells the reinforcements that they are fortunate to have it in their power to earn a debt of gratitude, not only from Charlemagne, but from all of Christendom. Conversely, if defeated, they stand to lose, he tells them, not only Paris but their homelands as well. When the narrator adds, in the next stanza, that Rinaldo was able with these and better arguments to stir the troops, "and it was, as they say in the proverb, a case of applying the spurs to a charger already running fast," the effect is humorous. Anyone who thinks self-interest requires encouragement deserves ironic undercutting. Furthermore, it is difficult not to remember this exhortation of Rinaldo's when, soon thereafter, Dardinel appeals to the loyalty of his "faithful friends," his troops, whom he is trying to rally (18.49–51). If the comparison is invidious for Rinaldo, so is the fact that his major accomplishment during the battle of Paris is the slaughter of Dardinel. While the real peril, Rodomonte, rages inside the walls of Paris, Rinaldo is literally the outsider, scurrying from one encounter to the next with adversaries who pose no serious threat, until finally he butchers the one Saracen who deserves a long life.

The narrative logic of the battle of Paris episodes is impeccable in its development of the ironies already attaching to the *homo prudens*. In light of everything we know about Rinaldo by the time he enters this battle, we can interpret his killing of Dardinel as the killing of that which he cannot comprehend or does not wish to comprehend. It is an act worthy of Rodomonte, whose adversary he is even less morally adequate to be than he was to be the adversary of Polinesso. How should a person who cautiously deprecates the role of *fede,* of altruism, in human affairs be a worthy adversary of such invulnerable and crushing egotism as Rodomonte represents?

In specific narrative terms, the battle of Paris episodes also set the stage for Rinaldo's most important failure in the *Orlando Furioso.* In the midst of Rinaldo's night attack on the Saracen camp (31.89–110), Ariosto revives the old dispute from the *Orlando Innamorato* between Rinaldo and Gradasso over the horse Baiardo. While this dispute has its own significance, to which we shall return, it is also very important for the specific expectation it establishes. In defining a special rivalry between Rinaldo and Gradasso, it looks forward to the combat on the island of Lipadusa. If—and as we shall see, this turns out to be a very big "if"—Rinaldo had arrived at Lipadusa in time for the combat, he would have been Gradasso's logical opponent there, and Brandimarte, that man of "so much faith and so much love" [tanta fede e tanto amor], would have been spared. Orlando shares the responsibility for Brandimarte's death, because Gradasso administers it with Durindana, the sword abandoned by Orlando in his fit of madness; but at least Orlando is present on Lipadusa where, and when, he is supposed to be, even if his motives for being there are not attractive. It is largely his fault that the Saracens are better armed and mounted than he and his cohorts, but at least he suffers on Lipadusa, albeit uncomprehendingly, the consequences of his madness. If we are able to hold Orlando solely responsible for the death of any of the faithful in the *Orlando Furioso*, it has to be that of Zerbino, cut down in a dramatic duel with Mandricardo, the cruelest of the Saracens, who might have perished without Durindana. Mandricardo's seizure of the sword in the very place of its abandonment by Orlando and his immediately subsequent murder of Zerbino make Orlando exclusively culpable for this loss, which is rendered doubly poignant by its timing at just the point when Zerbino and Isabella have become reunited and by the fact that it was Orlando himself, through his rescues of them, who brought about the reunion. In this case, Orlando's madness nullifies the good that he has accomplished. On the other hand, in Brandimarte's case, we cannot help but feel that Orlando is entitled to assistance that he never receives, and since Gradasso not only wields Durindana but is mounted on Rinaldo's horse, Baiardo, there can be no doubt as to who the bringer of that assistance should be. When it does not come, the reader may be excused for asking why— even though there has been nothing in the reader's experience of Rinaldo up to this point to suggest that there should be any cause for surprise over his absence.[10]

Ariosto is extremely precise in his timing of Rinaldo's late arrival on Lipadusa:

> Giunse ch'a punto il principe d'Anglante
> fatta avea l'utile opra e gloriosa:
> avea Gradasso ucciso et Agramante,
> ma con dura vittoria e sanguinosa.
> Morto n'era il figliuol di Monodante;
> e di grave percossa e perigliosa
> stava Olivier languendo in su l'arena,
> e del piè guasto avea martire e pena.
>
> (43.151)

He arrived at just the moment in which the prince of Anglante had performed his useful and glorious work. He had slain Gradasso and Agramante, but the victory was harsh and bloody. Dead was the son of Monodante, and Oliviero lay languishing on the sand with a grave and perilous wound. From his injured foot he suffered pain and torment.

Just an instant too late to be of any use whatsoever, Rinaldo's arrival is the opposite of Orlando's "utile opra." In choosing the word *utile* to describe Orlando's deed, Ariosto is implying that its opposite, *inutile,*

Figures in Ariosto's Tapestry

describes whatever it was that delayed Rinaldo for the few crucial hours that would have made the difference between life and death for Brandimarte and would perhaps have spared Oliviero his wound. The naturalistic detail of the wound in the foot intensifies the pain occasioned by Rinaldo's absence, just as the epithet "il figliuol di Monodante" intensifies the loss of Brandimarte by recalling his origins in the *Orlando Innamorato* and thereby causing the reader to reflect on his long history of faithful service to Orlando before the *Furioso's* narrative even commenced. What inglorious and useless adventure was it that detained Rinaldo?

The narrative provides a precise answer to this question. On the eve of the combat on Lipadusa, Rinaldo arrives at the banks of the Po, where he is accosted by a Mantuan knight who asks him if he is married. When he replies in the affirmative, the knight invites him to take lodging in his palace for the evening, at the same time promising to show him something that everyone who has a wife should wish to see. Forgetful of his purpose,

> Rinaldo, sì perché posar vorrebbe,
> ormai di correr tanto affaticato;
> sì perché di vedere e d'udire ebbe
> sempre aventure un desiderio innato;
> accettò l'offerir del cavalliero,
> e dietro gli pigliò nuovo sentiero.
>
> (42.72)

> Both because he was fatigued by now with so much hurry and wanted to rest and because he had ever had an innate desire to see and hear of adventures, Rinaldo accepted the knight's offer and set out behind him on a new path.

This "new path" leads directly to the trial of the magic goblet and also, of course, to that other famous speech by Rinaldo. Narrative timing and structure demand that Rinaldo's speech in denial of the goblet should be judged in light of the Lipadusa episode, for the time he takes to deliver this denial would otherwise have been spent in the useful work of fighting Gradasso and sparing Brandimarte. However, his susceptibility to creature comforts and his "desiderio innato"—his curiosity—to hear about new adventures distract his attention from more important concerns. The reader is reminded of Rinaldo, at the outset of the Ginevra and Ariodante episode, filling his belly in that "badia-ristorante," as one critic calls it,[11] and reminded also that Rinaldo would never have become involved in Ginevra's rescue had it not been for his curiosity about the forest of Caledonia and his desire to win fame there. Fortuituosly and paradoxically, in this earlier episode, Rinaldo's temporary neglect of his responsibility to raise reinforcements for Charlemagne leads to a prolongation of life for the faithful. However, his similar neglect in canto 42 leads directly to the destruction of *fede* in the person of Brandimarte.

Nor is it illogical that the time it takes to deliver another speech in deprecation of faith should be time crucially lost to the preservation of the faithful. The major premise of Rinaldo's second prominent speech is the same as that of his first: human beings (not just women) are too unstable to be trusted. Hence, it is wise to expect the worst of them, and even wiser, when it concerns someone close to oneself, to shut one's eyes to the possibility of unpleasant realities:

Pensò, e poi disse: "Ben sarebbe folle
chi quel che non vorria trovar, cercasse.
Mia donna è donna, et ogni donna è molle:
lasciàn star mia credenza come stasse.
Sin qui m'ha il creder mio giovato, e giova:
che poss'io megliorar per farne prova?

Potria poco giovare e nuocer molto;
che 'l tentar qualche volta Idio disdegna.
Non so s'in questo io mi sia saggio o stolto;
ma non vo' più saper, che mi convegna.
Or questo vin dinanzi mi sia tolto:
sete non n'ho, né vo' che me ne vegna;
che tal certezza ha Dio più proibita,
ch'al primo padre l'arbor de la vita.

Che come Adam, poi che gustò del pomo
che Dio con propria bocca gl'interdisse,
da la letizia al pianto fece un tomo,
onde in miseria poi sempre s'afflisse;
così se de la moglie sua vuol l'uomo
tutto saper quanto ella fece e disse,
cade de l'allegrezze in pianti e in guai,
onde non può più rilevarsi mai."

(43.6–8)

He thought, and then he said, "That man would be a fool for certain who looked for the thing he did not wish to find. My wife is a woman, and every woman is pliant. Let us leave my belief where it has stood. Till now my belief has served me, and it still serves. What advantage can I derive from testing it? It could help but little and do harm aplenty, for

Figures in Ariosto's Tapestry

sometimes God disdains to be tested. I know not whether in this I be wise or foolish, but I do not want to know more than befits me. Now let this wine be removed. I have no thirst for it, nor do I wish any to overtake me, because God has prohibited this kind of certainty more than he did the tree of life to our first father. For just as Adam, after he had tasted the apple which God from His own lips had forbidden him, took a fall from happiness to weeping, whence he suffered misery ever after, so it is that if a man wants to know all there is to know about what his wife says and does, he will fall from cheerfulness into weeping and misery whence he will nevermore be able to pick himself up."

If this speech appears to be a model of prudent reasoning, and if Rinaldo's host leaps up to embrace him, it is for the same reason that his speech in canto 4 has that appearance and receives "il consenso universale" of the monks—as well as the approval of many unwary readers. Just as Rinaldo's first speech appeared to represent a refreshing antidote to the cruelty of Scotland's law, his second speech seems to be the answer to the Mantuan knight's destructive quest for certainty. However, like its predecessor, it is only the opposite extreme of the moral condition with which it is juxtaposed. Out of fear of practicing *fede,* the Mantuan knight attempts to know everything. Not even success in the trial of the goblet is enough for him; he has to push his knowledge to the point of omniscience by creating a temptation that will assure him of his wife's fidelity, not only for the present and the past but for the future as well. On the other hand, Rinaldo is content to know nothing, or else to know only as much as it suits him comfortably to know. For Rinaldo the trial of the goblet is much too much, not because he prefers to practice faith, but because his belief that "every woman is pliant" convinces him that ignorance and self-deception are safe and pleasant and reasonable. Ariosto's irony in Rinaldo's allusion to Genesis is vitriolic. Rinaldo would have us avoid the forbidden fruit, not out of faith and obedience, but out of fear of disabusing ourselves of comfortable illusions. Between Rinaldo and the Mantuan knight, the kind of faith Brandimarte always exhibited in his relationships with Orlando and Fiordiligi becomes as extinct as Brandimarte himself.

Besides our knowledge of the grim outcome of the combat on Lipadusa, other plot elements cast doubt on the worth of Rinaldo's prudent words. In the first place, it is startling to learn that Rinaldo has a wife. It is true that Clarice was mentioned some twelve and a half cantos earlier in the text, but nothing was made of her, and the reader could excusably have forgotten her existence by the time of the Mantuan knight's arrival in the narrative. From this minor detail, one gets the impression that Rinaldo may not have very much at stake in the trial of the goblet and that his words may cost him very little effort. If his perception of the ideal marriage calls for a life of tranquil self-delusion, this may be explained by the tepidness of his feelings toward Clarice and by his adulterous passion for Angelica. However, even of this passion, one distinguished Ariosto scholar was prompted to make the following observation: "Take away the beginning and the end of the epic, along with a few other places that almost escape our notice, and no one would realize that Rinaldo has drunk from the fountain of Merlin and is therefore in the grip of an irresistible passion."[12] In truth, it appears to be eminently resistible. After its brief, but frenetic and memorable, introduction in cantos 1 and 2, we hear very little about it until we are informed in canto 27 that Rinaldo has been wandering about in search of Angelica ever since the defense of Paris in canto 18. In canto 30, when we next meet him, he is again on his way to Paris, this time with his brothers and cousins. He will remain in Charlemagne's service until canto 42, when Malagigi reveals to him Angelica's union with Medoro and their departure for Cathay. At this point, there occurs the allegorical pageant in which Disdain conquers the monster, presumably, of Rinaldo's own jealous rage. Then Rinaldo drinks, from the fountain of Merlin, an abiding antipathy toward Angelica, whom he regards henceforth as unworthy of his attention. How easy this seems by comparison with what Orlando has gone through! When Rinaldo faces the trial of the goblet in the next canto, it is safe to conclude that he is free of any infatuations that may earlier have held him feebly and sporadically in their grip. In this respect, he is very different from the Mantuan knight, who remains far more captivated by his lost wife than Rinaldo appears ever to have been by Angelica. So Rinaldo's words in denial of the goblet must be regarded as those of one who is utterly detached from the immediate problem, and for this reason alone, they should be considered subject to the corrosive irony that we expect of Ariosto. Once again Rinaldo is out of his depth.

If the magic goblet episode portrays Rinaldo as prudent, it does not suggest that Ariosto held prudence in very high esteem. Instead, it brings to mind a distinction we sometimes make between a reasonable man and a man of reason. The latter is passionate in his commitments, struggling to improve himself and his surroundings by applying, often at material sacrifice to himself, the conclusions of reasoned discourse to his circumstances. On the other hand, the reasonable man, though subject to infatuation, is not passionate at all. Like Rinaldo, he seeks an accommodation with circumstances and generally does so out of self-

Figures in Ariosto's Tapestry

indulgence. Not only does reason not lead him to any vision of the way things ought to be as opposed to the way they are, but it fails to acquaint him with the broader implications of issues and events in which he happens to be immersed. The reasonable, or prudent, man is myopic in his wary concentration on details and on appearances, and this ironically justifies Ariosto's establishment of Rinaldo as the adversary of Gradasso, the character more concerned than any other in the *Furioso* with accumulating the accoutrements of honor—so concerned with these objects, in fact, that he is willing to purchase a horse or a sword with his own dishonor. The objects he seeks as embellishments expose his corruption, just as the issues in which Rinaldo becomes involved expose his inability to understand or to experience the committed behavior of an Ariodante, a Brandimarte, a Zerbino, or a Dardinello.

Rinaldo's combat with Gradasso in canto 33 perfectly mirrors his combat with Ferraù in canto 1. Whether the dispute is over a horse or a girl the result is approximately the same. When the horse or the girl disappears, a truce ensues in the interest of expediency so that the combatants can go and round up their prize, without which they—like that "half-naked peasant" of canto 1 running for the "red cloth"— would consider their combat meaningless. In his concentration on the object under dispute, Rinaldo misses the significance of the dispute itself, ignoring the real honor to be achieved by defeating Gradasso (or earlier Ferraù) and ignoring also his responsibility to the faithful. When, with an ironic twist, Ariosto in canto 33 has Gradasso play a trick of horse thievery on Rinaldo that strongly resembles Rinaldo's discourtesy to Sacripante in canto 2, we suddenly realize that more was being described than mere bravery when Rinaldo and Gradasso met to begin their combat:

> Poi che l'un quinci e l'altro quindi giunto
> fu quasi a un tempo in su la chiara fonte,
> s'accarezzaro, e fero a punto a punto
> così serena et amichevol fronte,
> come di sangue e d'amistà congiunto
> fosse Gradasso a quel di Chiaramonte.
>
> (31.110)

When one from one side and the other from the other side had arrived at the clear spring at almost the same instant, they embraced each other and showed expressions every whit as mild and amiable as if Gradasso and he of Chiaramonte were joined by blood and friendship.

They are quite definitely joined in a brotherhood subject to devastating irony on account of its failure to value correctly the objects of its concern. If Gradasso's materialism is consciously harmful to others and therefore uglier than Rinaldo's cautious self-indulgence, this should not blind the reader to the fact that the Saracen and the Christian are similarly inadequate to the tasks they undertake and are therefore caught in a process of self-deflation culminating on Lipadusa, where both are defeated. Is it worse, one wonders, to lay down one's life in repayment for the evil one has committed, or to live on after having been exposed as a moral non-entity?

"In sum, the story of Rinaldo is a story of missed opportunities," says one interpreter of the *Orlando Furioso,*[13] while others claim that Rinaldo is a model of prudence. Although there appears to be a glaring conflict between these opinions, actually none need be held to exist at all. The history of the *homo prudens* in the *Orlando Furioso* is a history of failure. If, in the course of the entire poem, Rinaldo never vanquishes a single Saracen hero, it is not because he does not have the opportunity, but because he barters his opportunities for a horse or a girl, or for whatever else at the moment seems more important to him than his service of a cause that transcends the self. However, the subject of Ariosto's poem is irrational man, as the title suggests, and the events of the narrative, having causes beneath and beyond reason, must repeatedly expose the prudent, the reasonable, the dispassionate, the unimaginative man as either naive or cynical. Paradoxically, this *homo prudens,* the possessor of practical wisdom, will always find himself isolated from the urgent concerns of life. In a sense, he is imprisoned within himself, and a major postulate of the *Orlando Furioso* is that, if one wishes to become involved in life at all, as opposed to merely surviving, one must risk one's sanity along with everyone else. Even the narrator of the poem announces in his exordium that he may not tell his story as well as he would like, because he, too, is on the verge of madness, owing to his passion for a mysterious lady.

Although this ironic portrait of Rinaldo was complete in 1516 in the *Furioso's* first edition, Ariosto may have wished to stress the symmetry of its design. This motive would help to explain his use of Rinaldo in the Leone episode added in 1532. The combat on Lipadusa had brought Orlando, for all of his shortcomings, into favorable contrast with the *homo prudens,* but there was still the *Furioso's* second hero to be dealt with. In the 1516 edition, Ariosto, it is true, had already arranged an ironic confrontation between Rinaldo and Ruggiero in that single combat called to determine the outcome of the entire war between the pagans and the faithful. Rinaldo, the complacent cynic who had repeatedly deserted Charlemagne's cause into order to pursue an infatuation, found himself flying the colors of the Faith, and he was too puffed up with the dignity of his position ever to doubt his worthiness to occupy it. On the other hand, Ruggiero, paralyzed by the conflict between his private pledge of faith to Bradamante and the public trust conferred on him by Agramante, found himself in the absurd position of championing the enemies of the Faith. Appearance and reality in this episode of the 1516 edition had already undergone total ironic inversion; however, Ariosto may have wished to involve the *homo prudens* at the conclusion of the narrative in circumstances similar to those in which he had placed him at its beginning, and in doing so to stress an analogy between Ruggiero and Ariodante.

In the Leone episode, Rinaldo, championing the cause of Ruggiero and Bradamante, has come full circle from his involvement earlier with Ginevra and Ariodante. However, if his presence proved to be of benefit, albeit accidental, in the earlier adventure, this is certainly not the case in the later one. Here, the reader is led to wonder if Ruggiero, with Rinaldo as his friend, needs adversaries. Rinaldo's father courteously defers his final decision concerning a marriage between Bradamante and Leone until he has at least had the opportunity to mention it to his son. However, Rinaldo, failing to return the courtesy, marches into Paris with the news that he, Rinaldo, has already, before witnesses, promised his sister to someone else. In comparing Rinaldo to her parents, Bradamante may be able to declare that he "is many, many times more prudent than they, nor has excessive age taken away his brains" (44.46), but the reader is likely to have formed a different impression. Rinaldo's behavior may not be senile, but neither is it prudent. Juvenile it might be, in its glaring lack of diplomacy, but in any case it does indisputably exacerbate the dilemma of the lovers by infuriating Amone. Moreover, this particular dilemma, unlike the one in which Ginevra and Ariodante found themselves, should be surmountable for a reasonable man such as Rinaldo. In fact, the practical wisdom of a *homo prudens* should be well suited to smoothing over the objections of Amone and Beatrice to Ruggiero, based, as they are, on practical considerations of wealth and social position. However, even in this field of action, Rinaldo fails to be of any use, and the lovers are left to solve their problems by themselves, just as Ariodante had no alternative but to champion his own cause if he wished to remain constant in the faith he had always exhibited toward Ginevra. With the milder difficulty Ruggiero faces, Ariosto appears to be emphasizing, at least insofar as Rinaldo is concerned, the inefficacy of prudence in matters involving faith. The solution to any assault whatsoever on faith is faith itself, not practical wisdom or common sense.

Ironically, at the end, it is Leone, Ruggiero's erstwhile adversary, and not Rinaldo, his friend, who persuades Amone to change his mind, and also "persuades him not to refuse to go in person and beg Ruggiero to pardon him and to accept him as father and father-in-law" (46.64). When the narrator declares that Leone "knew very well how to speak," the reader agrees, and in doing so, tacitly expresses a final doubt concerning Rinaldo's speaking ability. Ariosto's skepticism—the same that may have led Montaigne to list the *Orlando Furioso* among his favorite books to be read for amusement—is far-reaching in his representation of Rinaldo. Besides prudence, eloquence itself comes under scrutiny. Just as, with Polinesso, Ariosto represents a natural fascination with illusion as the common denominator between artistic creativity and fraudulence, in Rinaldo he creates a symbol of the ambiguity of eloquence, a double-edged instrument, which may assist in the creation of a self and the discovery of truth, or else separate its possessor from himself and the humanity surrounding him. Rinaldo, the talker, the *homo prudens,* is very much the hero "degradato" of Santoro's judgment, so much so, in fact, that even the judgment of Luigi Pulci's Brunoro in *Il Morgante Maggiore,* a work whose influence on the *Furioso* is perhaps underrated, seems perfectly accurate when applied to Ariosto's Rinaldo and his kind:

> Se la ragione aspetta che costoro
> l'aiutino, in prigion se n'andrà tosto,
> S'avessi più avvocati, argento o oro,
> O carte o testimon, che fichi agosto.

> (3.41)

> If the right waits for these men to aid it, it will soon wind up in prison, even if it has more lawyers, more silver or gold, more documents or witnesses, than August has figs.

However, Ariosto's Rinaldo, unlike Pulci's version of the character, upsets our expectations, because he combines the attributes of the *homo prudens* with traditional features of the scapegrace he always was in the Italian romances. The result is a "gran pedone," an Ariostan critique of pure prudence divorced from its conventional analogy in the microcosm of man with Providence in the macrocosm of God. Rinaldo becomes a complex, ambiguous, ironical character who causes us to look forward, along with Galileo, to the novel for similar developments in characterization within the narrative form.

3
Rodomonte

ccording to Italo Calvino, "Rodomonte is a co-
lossus with a sensitive spirit."[1] The author of *Il
cavaliere inesistente* perceives the essence of Rodomonte's character, despite his ferocity in battle and
his defiance of everything sacred, to be in his limitless mortification over the defeats dealt him by
Doralice, Isabella, and Bradamante, one after an-
other. Agreement with Calvino's point of view is easy to find in recent
Ariosto criticism. One interpreter notes how "Rodomonte grows human going mad, as opposed to Orlando, who goes mad and becomes
bestial" while another calls attention to Rodomonte's merciful rescue of
Brandimarte after Fiordiligi moves him to pity her in the name of the
dead Isabella and in the name of any love he may ever have experienced
(31.73–75).[2] On the one hand, recent Ariosto criticism projects a rather
sentimental image of Rodomonte as the mortified, remorseful giant,
maladroit in one amorous mishap after another, and yet capable of
compassion if he is appealed to in the name of unfortunate love. On the
other hand, there looms the judgment of Arnoldo Momigliano, with its
neat distinction between Rodomonte as the epic hero of the *Furioso* and
Orlando as the sentimental hero.

According to Momigliano, the most pathetic moment of Rodomonte's existence has nothing to do with love at all, but occurs instead
when he looks back at Paris with regret on account of his failure to
accomplish total destruction there (18.24–25):

> That savage melancholy and that remorse over destruction he has failed to
> achieve say more about him than the ruin sown by his sword. All of Rodo-
> monte is in that incendiary look and in that sigh; Ariosto has found for him
> the very thing that would be sought in vain for so many other characters of
> the epic: the attitude that defines him—a thing different from the customary
> declining falls of the Ariostan music and the customary enchantment of
> colors blending into each other—the voice of the soul.[3]

For Momigliano,

> Everything about physical force that could have provided Ariosto with poetic inspiration—the body's monumental postures, its agile, irresistible motions, unconquered resoluteness of spirit, coldness, courage, ferocity in confronting and exterminating the enemy, slaughter on an immense scale—is gathered into the figure of Rodomonte in its most pronounced and violent forms (Momigliano, *Saggio,* p. 248).

Accordingly, Rodomonte becomes a combination of Achilles, Turnus, and Capaneus—an embodiment of sheer force and defiance. The purpose of this chapter is not to take sides, either with Calvino and current Ariosto criticism or with Momigliano, but to confront the problem posed by such contradictory views. The contradictions are due to the critics' propensity to dwell on textual evidence narrowly selected to support their hypotheses and also due to the subtlety of Ariosto's characterization of Rodomonte. Ariosto made this most dangerous of Charlemagne's enemies a complex, paradoxical human type. What follows is an attempt to outline the paradox by following Rodomonte through his whole history in the *Furioso* and by briefly examining his origins in the *Orlando Innamorato.*

From the beginning of his existence in Boiardo's poem, Rodomonte promises to be an interesting personage. He leaps into being at the opening of book 2 of the *Orlando Innamorato,* where he gives the impression that Boiardo has invented him as a replacement for Agricane, the ferocious king of the Tartars, slain by Orlando in book 1. However, Rodomonte is from the start more colossal than his predecessors. Unlike Agricane, whose sole objective is Angelica, and unlike Gradasso, who places his entire kingdom in jeopardy to obtain Durindana and Baiardo, Rodomonte seems impelled by an urge to subject the entire cosmos, natural, supernatural, and human, to his will. When Agramante declares his intention, not only to conquer Charlemagne, but to subjugate the entire world and then to make war in paradise, Rodomonte swears, "Into heaven or hell I will always follow King Agramante, or I will go there ahead of him" (2.1.65),[4] the last phrase expressing exactly the truth of events to come. When the first expedition to find Ruggiero's mountaintop hiding place fails and the pagan army is delayed in its passage to France, Rodomonte declares his disbelief in the prophesy concerning Ruggiero's importance to Agramante's enterprise and expresses his contempt for all prophets and for the gods whose human voices they claim to be. At the same time, he

Figures in Ariosto's Tapestry

delivers a credo that defines his character throughout the rest of the *Orlando Innamorato* and throughout the *Furioso* as well:

Se egli è alcun dio nel cel, ch'io nol so certo,
Là stassi ad alto, e di qua giù non cura:
Omo non è che l'abbia visto esperto,
Ma la vil gente crede per paura.
Io de mia fede vi ragiono aperto
Che solo il mio bon brando e l'armatura
E la maza ch'io porto, e 'l destrier mio
E l'animo ch'io ho, sono il mio dio.

(2.3.22)

If there is any god in heaven (for I have no certain knowledge of him), up there on high is where he stays, and he does not bother with what happens down here. No man has actually seen him, but the common people believe in him anyway out of fear. I give you an open account of my faith: only my good sword and my armor and the mace that I bear and my warhorse and the spirit in me are my god.

However, Agramante, dismayed by the death of his prophet at the very moment the prophet himself had predicted, decides to continue the search for Ruggiero, whereupon Rodomonte stalks out of his presence muttering that he will see whether heaven "has power enough to prevent me from crowning myself in France" (2.3.35).

Having challenged the gods, as well as Charlemagne and the Saracen council, he makes his next appearance in the port of Algiers, where he challenges nature in the shape of storm winds impeding his fleet from setting sail for France:

Soffia vento—dicea—se sai soffiare,
Ché questa notte pure ne vo' gire;
Io non son tuo vasallo e non del mare,
Che me possiati a forza retenire;
Solo Agramante mi può comandare,
Et io contento son de l'obidire:
Sol de obedire a lui sempre mi piace,
Perché è guerrero, e mai non amò pace.

(2.6.4)

"Blow wind," said he, "if you know how to blow, for tonight I intend to set forth anyway. I am not your vassal or the sea's, that you can detain me by force. Only Agramante can command me, and I am content to obey him. Only to obey him pleases me always, because he is a warrior and never loved peace."

The irony of this oath of obedience to Agramante is apparent enough even without the condition Rodomonte tacks on at the end. However, the crescendo of challenges reaches its climax when an old Moroccan sea captain tells Rodomonte that he, for his part, would not set sail in such weather even if Muhammad assured him in person that his death would not come from drowning. Rodomonte replies, defying death itself,

> O morto o vivo,
> Ad ogni modo io voglio oltra passare,
> E se con questo spirto in Franza arivo,
> Tutta in tre giorni la voglio pigliare;
> E se io vi giongo ancor di vita privo,
> Io credo per tal modo spaventare,
> Morto come io serò, tutta la gente,
> Che fuggirano, et io serò vincente.

(2.6.10)

Dead or alive, no matter how, I intend to cross over, and if I reach France with this spirit in me, I will seize the whole place in three days. And even if I come there deprived of life, I believe that by that means, dead as I shall be, I will frighten all the populace, who shall flee, and I will be victorious.

The word *rodomontade* takes its definition from this kind of speech. Boiardo's description of subsequent events—the crossing in the storm, the landing on the seashore of Monaco, and the slaughter of Charlemagne's forces there—heightens the image of Rodomonte as an embodiment of the sheer force of defiant will coupled with massive physical strength. Interlaced with the fable of Orlando's confrontation with Fortune in Falerina's garden, these events acquire by contrast an immediacy surpassing reality itself. Rodomonte has no need to seize Fortune by the forelock, because his own audacity is enough to overcome even those misfortunes he draws down on himself. In the *Orlando Innamorato*, Momigliano's Rodomonte is already alive in every detail, and Ariosto pays homage to Boiardo's mammoth creation, surpassing it at the same time, when he chooses to introduce Rodomonte into the *Orlando Furioso* in canto 14 in the midst of the assault on Paris.

On the other hand, the other Rodomonte—Calvino's Rodomonte—does not make himself felt quite so strongly in the *Innamorato*. The first octave Boiardo allows his character to speak achieves an elegiac note that promises, in its context within the Saracen debate over whether to invade France, to broach questions of high epic seriousness, but this quickly sinks into the bathos of an accusation of senility directed against Agramante's elderly and more experienced advisors:

Levossi in piede e disse: "In ciascun loco
Ove fiamma s'accende, un tempo dura
Piccola prima, e poi si fa gran foco;
Ma come viene al fin, sempre se oscura,
Mancando del suo lume a poco a poco.
E così fa l'umana creatura,
Che, poi che ha di sua età passato il verde,
La vista, il senno e l'animo si perde."

(2.1.53)

He rose to his feet and spoke: "Everywhere that a flame is ignited, for a time at first it remains small, and afterwards it grows into a great fire, but as it nears its end it becomes dimmer and dimmer losing its light little by little, and so it is with the human creature, for once he has passed the green time of his age, eyesight, mind, and spirit fail."

There is, however, a surprising moment of reflectiveness when Rodomonte experiences his first setback in France. He goes in search of Rinaldo, the first member of Charlemagne's forces to stand up to him in battle,

Dicendo: "Questo dono il ciel mi faccia,
Pur che ritrovi quel baron valente,
O ch'io l'occida, o torni seco in graccia;
Ché, essendo morto, in terra non ho pare,
E se egli è meco, il cel voglio acquistare.

Né creder potrò mai che 'l conte Orlando
Abbia di questo la mera bontate.
Io l'ho provato, e di lancia e di brando
Non è il più forte al mondo in veritate.
O re Agramante, a Dio ti racomando,
Se tu discendi per queste contrate!
Essendote io, come serò, lontano,
Tutta tua gente fia sconfitto al piano.

Come diceva il vero il re Sobrino!
Sempre creder si debbe a chi ha provato.
Or, s'egli è tale Orlando paladino
Come costui che meco a fronte è stato,
Tristo Agramante et ogni Saracino
Che fia di qua dal mar con lui portato!

Io, che tutti pigliarli avea arroganza,
Assai ne ho de uno, e più che di bastanza."

(2.15.28–30)

Saying, "May heaven grant me this boon if I find that valiant baron again, either that I may kill him or that I may come back with him in amity, for if he is dead, I will have no peer on earth, and if he is with me, I will conquer heaven. Nor will I ever be able to believe that Count Orlando possesses the sheer excellence of this man. I have made trial of him, and in truth there is no stronger man in the world with sword and lance. O King Agramante, I commend you to God if you descend into these territories! I being, as I shall be, far from your side, all your troops will be routed in the field. How truly did King Sobrino speak! One should always believe a man who has had experience. Indeed, if Orlando the Paladin is like this man who has stood face to face with me, bad is the lot of Agramante and every other Saracen who is carried with him to this side of the sea. I, who had the arrogance to take on all of them, have had enough, nay, more than enough, to do with one man."

The various contradictions woven into this speech suggest that more is involved here than any momentary confusion on Rodomonte's part over a single unexpected setback. First, he invokes heaven to help him obtain the ally he needs to conquer heaven. Then he pronounces Agramante's cause to be lost against two such warriors as Rinaldo and Orlando together unless he is present to lend assistance, but at the same time he acknowledges that one of them alone might be more than enough for him to handle. At this very moment, of course, he is declaring his intention not to assist Agramante at all should the effort get in the way of his own urgent need to mend his self-esteem by fighting Rinaldo single-handedly. For a similar reason, near the end of the *Furioso,* Agramante will indeed find himself deserted by Rodomonte. Finally, Rodomonte exposes the contradiction within the position he took in the Saracen council much earlier: he had heaped scorn upon Sobrino and Branzardo for arguing from experience against the expedition to France and then he himself argued that the gods should be disregarded because they cannot be experienced. One hesitates to attempt the summation of chaos; however, the Rodomonte Boiardo gives us here has potential vulnerabilities and enough sensitivity to reflect upon them even though his understanding may be feeble.

Possibly, the image Boiardo intended to create is of the egotist reflecting on the evidence of his own insignificance, but at the same time pretending that nothing has changed. If this is the case, all that is wanting is for a big enough ax to fall, and then the madness of that limitless mortification to which Calvino refers might be let loose to run its course. As it is, Rodomonte's worst moment of mortification in the *Orlando Innamorato* arrives when, knocked unconscious by Ruggiero, he drops his sword and wakes up later to find his life spared because Ruggiero had scorned to take advantage of his helplessness. Here, he becomes "almost mad" with shame, swearing fealty to Ruggiero, who may henceforth command him "as the stronger may his inferior." Then he rides off vanishing from sight "in less time than it takes to boil a cabbage" (3.5.11–14). Ariosto may reserve for him a nobler end at Ruggiero's hands and a nobler desperation, but a certain "anima sensibile," like the *anima violente,* has already been planted in Rodomonte and cultivated by the author of the *Innamorato.*

The most obvious direction for Ariosto to take in the development of Rodomonte's character was to sharpen that ax left hanging over his head by Boiardo and to let it fall—and, of course, Ariosto did sharpen it to a razor's edge, letting it fall again and again with the help of Doralice, Isabella, and Bradamante. However, even for this line of development, Ariosto had a suggestion from Boiardo. In the *Innamorato,* Rodomonte, searching for Rinaldo in the forest of Ardennes, finds instead Ferraù, who happens in the course of casual conversation to mention that he is just returning from Granada, "where for a long time he had loved a certain lady, and how she was named Doralice and was the daughter of King Stordilano" (2.15.35–36). No sooner has Rodomonte met his match in battle with Rinaldo than he discovers a threat, worded vaguely enough to leave open the worst possibilities, to his pre-eminence as Doralice's knight. No other character, in his passage from the *Orlando Innamorato* to the *Furioso,* including Ruggiero, makes clearer Ariosto's debt to Boiardo than Rodomonte does, and yet Ariosto's Rodomonte has a prominence and a fascination that Boiardo's character never achieves. Ariosto tones down the bombast of Rodomonte's speeches, tests the limits of the "anima sensibile" with successive shocks and humiliations, and intensifies the already developed spirit of defiance, thereby deepening the paradox of Rodomonte's nature and raising the character to the stature of a protagonist in the *Furioso's* world, where he competes, often successfully, with Orlando and Ruggiero for precedence in the reader's interest.

For all of its liveliness and perspicuity, Boiardo's treatment of Rodomonte ceases at a certain point to be the exploration of a character's psyche and develops instead into a blustering pageant of the rise and fall of *Superbia* and *Ira.* In his last appearance in the *Orlando Innamorato,* Rodomonte tumbles to the ground from the top of a ladder he has erected against the battlements of Paris (3.8.26–32); in his first appearance in the *Orlando Furioso,* he requires no ladder, nor any assistance other than his own might. No sooner has he forded the moat than "he has felt the battlements beneath his feet" (14.121), and after a brief delay to carve out a passage for his followers, he leaps over that second moat inside the walls:

> Poco era men di trenta piedi, o tanto,
> et egli il passò destro come un veltro,
> e fece nel cader strepito, quanto
> avesse avuto sotto i piedi il feltro.
>
> (14.130)

> It was little less than thirty feet across, or perhaps just that much, and
> he passed over it with the agility of a greyhound, and in landing he made
> no more noise than if he had had felt beneath his feet.

With the eerieness of this silent landing, Ariosto lends Rodomonte in a single stroke greater horror and more awesome strength than the character manages to acquire in one spectacular scene after another throughout the cantos of his prominence in the *Innamorato.* However, Rodomonte's power in the *Furioso* depends more than anything else on his place within a greater, more poignant, and more finely articulated moral-philosophical scheme of the world than Boiardo had ever entertained. Ariosto's Rodomonte can be understood only within the context of the *Furioso*'s most important themes.

That *fede* is the principal theme of the *Orlando Furioso* and that this faith is exercised by the *Furioso*'s characters in an unstable world separated from Divine Providence are matters now established in Ariosto criticism.[5] Commitment, dedication, loyalty, trust—faith under all of its reassuring names, as it applies to relations between persons but not between God and man, is subjected to mordant criticism in episode after episode of the *Furioso;* however, the severity of Ariosto's secular vision has its sanction at the fountainhead of Christian literary tradition. The meaning of faith in the literature of Christianity emerges from those harrowing words of Matthew (10:34–39) that begin with Jesus' declaration that he came "not to send peace on earth . . . but a sword" and conclude with the chilling paradox: "He that findeth his life shall lose it: and he that loseth his life for my sake shall find it." The quest for selfhood requires self-abandonment through faith, and this is the quest of the majority of the *Furioso*'s characters, with Orlando and Ruggiero especially prominent. However, Ariosto's world is radically different from the world of the gospels. Ariosto's world is so unstable that the

Christian recompense for self-sacrifice—fullness of being in another existence—is no longer felt to be available. In the *Furioso*'s universe, humans still experience the impulse toward faith, but that is all it is, an impulse bound to their nature, no longer the gift of a beneficent Creator. Hence, the *Furioso*'s characters, to attain selfhood, must create gods out of the material of their uncertain surroundings and then run the risk of sacrificing themselves to these idols of their own creation. To justify and to assert their creations, they bring the force of their beings—the force of their swords. If Rodomonte's sword is particularly trenchant, it may mean that his deity is one of the more powerful and dangerous ones in the *Furioso*.

Ariosto's Rodomonte inhabits a universe where the impulse toward faith surviving despite uncertainty, the creation of deity, the fanatical dedication of the self on the altar of this deity, and then more often than not the bitter disillusionment over a god that fails are the elements of a pattern or the throbbings of a rhythm pervading every man's life.[6] One minor character after another—like those mowed down by Rodomonte's sword—represents a variation of the pattern. After telling Orlando, in words echoing those of the gospel, that she has sacrificed her father and brothers, her kingdom and all her worldly goods, for the sake of Bireno, Olimpia concludes,

> Se dunque da far altro non me resta,
> né si truova al suo scampo altro riparo,
> che per lui por questa mia vita; questa
> mia vita per lui por mi sarà caro.
>
> (9.50–51)

If then nothing else remains for me to do, nor any other means for his rescue is found, than for me to lay down this life of mine for him, it shall be precious for me to lay down for him this life of mine.

When her god, Bireno, fails her, she collapses upon a rock overlooking the sea, "nor does she seem to be less like a stone than a true stone seems" (10.34). Two millennia conserve the revenge of the women of Alessandretta against men, those gods who failed when their female ancestors, "leaving behind their fathers and sons and brothers and having stripped their homes bare" (20.18), abandoned themselves to a troop of pirates led by Clytaemnestra's bastard son. Like Olimpia, these legendary females, when deserted by their gods, stand like "motionless statues on the shores of the sea" (20.22) sending their prayers and recriminations into the void, but their resourcefulness soon helps them to a slightly more accommodating deity, *la Vendetta,* to whom they build a temple and abandon themselves with just as much zeal as they had exhibited in their former devotion. Even Marganor's grotesque cruelty is mitigated because his blind worship of his sons improved his nature for a time. If the death of those sons brings on a furor as blind as his former worship, it is only because he becomes the implacable enemy of the murderers of his gods, sacrificing them over the tombs of his sons and converting their admirers "over the consecrated host" and with the sword to an everlasting hatred of the female sex (37.84–85). The pervasive religious imagery of the Marganor episode underscores, as does all of the religious imagery of the *Orlando Furioso,* Ariosto's concern with the destiny of man's impulse toward faith when it is exposed to an antagonistic, uncertain, or indifferent universe. The grand cause of the *Furioso*'s protagonists is to create or to discover gods in whom one can believe without going mad, without lapsing into fanaticism or cynicism, without making a fool of oneself, and without rendering oneself vulnerable to the cruellest of the *Furioso*'s evildoers who consciously exploit their fellow man's impulse to be loyal and trusting. Throughout the *Orlando Furioso,* Ariosto seems to be asking whether it is possible to live in the world and exercise faith, or whether one must, like Dalinda of the Ginevra and Ariodante episode, grow fed up with the world and renounce it for a convent or a monastery.

Rodomonte's answer to this question is as sweeping and decisive as his performance in battle. He renounces the existence of any god external to himself, whether it be in the form of an idea, another person, or a material object. For Rodomonte, the self is God, and all else exists only in the realm of contingency. In the paradox of Matthew, Rodomonte is the man who has found his life, and in the course of the *Furioso,* he loses it gradually, dying at the conclusion a more desperate blasphemer than ever, the death of his god coinciding with the death of himself. Rodomonte's open assertion of his belief in nothing but himself lends him a grandeur surpassing that of most of the *Furioso*'s other characters, including Charlemagne, whose pious posturing gives rise to the burlesque of the Archangel Michael and Discord. In light of such cavortings in heaven and in light of the uncertainty of his universe, Rodomonte's choice of deity is understandable, and he defends it bravely and without conscious hypocrisy. If there is no God and no orderly Providence for whose sake to sacrifice oneself, why should one not have faith only in oneself? What else is there?

Ariosto's answer to the first question lies in his development of Rodomonte's character; his answer to the second question is nothing less than all of the *Orlando Furioso.* If the great antagonist of the *Orlando*

Furioso is Uncertainty itself, Rodomonte, like Orlando, deserves to be considered a protagonist who fails, and even if his failure is greater than Orlando's, he at least recognizes the immensity of his antagonist and attempts a defiance of equal proportion. The impression we develop from the start—in reading Boiardo's poem and in observing Ariosto's care to remain in conformity with Boiardo's characterization of Rodomonte—that Rodomonte is consciously engaged in a rebellion against the human condition itself, not only rescues the character, despite the bestiality of most of his deeds, from the contempt we reserve for such evildoers as Polinesso and Gabrina, but elevates him in our esteem above a host of other characters. If the Good were apparent in Ariosto's world, which is beset with illusion, Rodomonte could be regarded as a Miltonic Satan, but since it is not, he must be regarded as exhibiting the blindness understandable in many tragic figures of Renaissance and classical literature. The Good is so elusive in the *Furioso*'s world that even the best of men, Ruggiero, required forty cantos to attain it in the 1516 edition, and then later, upon Ariosto's further reflection, forty-six.

Unlike Mandricardo, Gradasso, Ferraù, Agramante, or any of the other Saracens, Rodomonte enters the *Furioso* with no delusion that victory lies in the acquisition of a horse, a sword, a woman, or a kingdom, or in the accomplishment of any specific act of revenge. The solution he seeks to the instability of life is its total submission to his will—a solution that dwarfs him as soon as he attempts to put it in practice. His assault on Paris makes clear in the bluntest possible way the inevitability of failure. The population of Paris, much less the whole world, is too large to be subdued by one man:

Dei cavallieri e de la fanteria
tanta è la calca, ch' a pena vi cape;
la turba che vi vien per ogni via,
v'abbonda ad or ad or spessa come ape;
che quando, disarmata e nuda, sia
più facile a tagliar che torsi o rape,
non la potria, legata a monte a monte,
in venti giorni spenger Rodomonte.

(18.16)

Such is the press of horsemen and infantry that it can scarcely be contained there. The crowd converging on that spot from every street grows thicker and thicker, like a swarm of bees, so that even if, disarmed and naked, it were easier to cut through than turnips and vegetable stumps, Rodomonte would not be able to extinguish it, piled up in heaps, in twenty days.

Even if the world were peopled with turnips instead of men, there would still be more than one man could slice. The irony is acerbic here because people are getting sliced, not turnips, and as if to emphasize this point, Ariosto has already made a connection, at the opening of the previous canto, between Rodomonte's carnage in Paris and the foreign invasions of Italy contemporary with his writing. The opening of this canto, with its linkage to Rodomonte, suggests not so much that Providence is at work in current events punishing Italy for her sins, as that, by an irony of human nature exemplified by Rodomonte, men who subjugate others make themselves worse than their victims, no matter what their victims have done to cause their own suffering, until the victims themselves rise to dominate, debasing themselves in their turn in an endless, wasteful ebb and flow of blind aggression. The immensity of Rodomonte's failure in the *Furioso* derives from the fact that Ariosto also considers it a failure of human history. The misery of the failure is that human beings get sliced up on account of it as if they were turnips.

The paradox of Rodomonte's nature is that self-deification leads to self-debasement. The struggle for omnipotence ends in impotency, for omniscience in myopia. The tragic law of Rodomonte's character is that the assertion of the self as God against the uncertainty of everything else only increases the chaos. Unstable conditions provoke a response that worsens them. To stress the futility of Rodomonte's efforts in Paris, Ariosto interlaces their description with the panorama of Astolfo's fabulous travels through the Orient and Grifone's adventures in Damascus. Paris is reduced to the size of a speck and Rodomonte to much less. In the 1532 version of the *Furioso*, the effect is intensified by stanzas 18–36, which were added to canto 15 to praise Charles v. To the broadening of the spatial dimension is added the sweep of centuries. Andronica prophesies the discovery of new worlds and the coming of a successor to the Charlemagne against whom Rodomonte is wasting his energy, a successor who will be more pleased to reward his loyal captains than to conquer a new empire. The reflection upon Rodomonte is obvious no matter what Ariosto may have thought of Charles v. The world is large enough to make those who would like to subjugate even a part of it seem infinitesimally small.

Ariosto must have wished to create a similar effect with his abrupt return in stanzas 73–80 of canto 17 from the Grifone episode in Damascus to a scornful overview of those French, German, Spanish, and Swiss ravagers of Italy whom he had already compared to Rodomonte at the opening of the canto:

Dove abbassar dovrebbono la lancia
in augumento de la santa fede,
tra lor si dan nel petto e ne la pancia
a distruzion del poco che si crede.

(17.74)

Where they should be lowering their lances in augmentation of the holy
faith, they give it to each other instead in the chest and the guts, to the
destruction of what little there is to believe.

Just as Rodomonte is diminished by juxtaposition with a boundless
world, so too are the European powers who are busy destroying Italy
and each other as if such destruction could end in their glorification.
Nothing so clearly reveals and so certainly fosters the nearsightedness of
men as their impulse to subjugate others, and nothing so certainly
diminishes their stature as the struggle for self-glorification. For Ariosto, the figure of Rodomonte inherited from Boiardo serves as a means
of analyzing contemporary political disasters from a psychological
standpoint. The extent to which Ariosto takes pains to understand
Rodomonte and to explain his ways is a good measure of the poet's
generosity toward the barbarians of his time and also a measure of the
urgency he attached to understanding the mentality responsible for the
wars going on all around him. Ariosto's care to understand a certain
phenomenon has perhaps given rise to the sentimental image of Rodomonte that one finds in some recent criticism, where Ariosto's analytic
penetration is mistaken for an excess of sympathy.

Ariosto's labor of understanding is carried out in the episodes involving Doralice, Isabella, and Bradamante. The love theme enters not so
much because Rodomonte is capable of experiencing love in the same
way Orlando and Ruggiero do, as because it helps determine the limits
of Rodomonte's ability to deal with other people one at a time. It defines
his psychological limitations. By means of it, the vast disparity between
his concept of himself and the concept others have of him, along with
the uses to which they put him and he puts them, can be treated in a
wide range of ways, from the ridiculous and the grotesque to the tragic.
Rodomonte's dealings with Doralice are consistently ridiculous, because Ariosto depicts her as the most ordinary of women. Rodomonte
makes a great deal more of her than she is because, as he sees it, his
consort must possess attributes of a goddess. In Rodomonte, there is
some of the world-distorting self-absorption of Shakespeare's Troilus,
and in Doralice the practicality and earthiness of Chaucer's Criseyde. If

Doralice deserts Rodomonte for Mandricardo, she has had good reasons all along for doing so. Terrified at first by the spectacle of Mandricardo's slaughter of her entire armed escort with a bludgeon left over from a broken lance, she is swiftly put at ease by his courtesy and his flattery. Her relief turns to interest, and she adjusts her feelings to her radically altered circumstances. If her adjustment seems to require little effort, that may be, not because Doralice is fickle but because Ariosto has never described her as having had any particular feelings toward Rodomonte in the first place. Nor has Ariosto depicted Rodomonte as attaching any value to Doralice save as a symbol of his own mightiness to be borne aloft on a banner, even though Doralice herself is not a person to value symbols greatly.

Rodomonte's first words upon catching up with Mandricardo and Doralice reveal no concern at all over her well-being:

> Incominciò gridando il re d'Algiere,
> ch'a penitenza gli faria tornare,
> che per un temerario suo piacere
> non avesse rispetto a provocarsi
> lui, ch'altamente era per vendicarsi.

(24.97)

> The king of Algiers began by shouting that he would reduce him to penance for not having had, on account of a rash whim of his, the respect to avoid provoking one who was highly prepared to avenge himself.

The reflection of Mandricardo's act on his own reputation is all that concerns Rodomonte, and one must wonder how this sits with Doralice, who had just ventured aloud to Mandricardo that Rodomonte would hold it a great injury to have lost her. Her earlier susceptibility to Mandricardo's flattery suggests that she would be only too sensible now of the difference between what she had thought would be Rodomonte's sense of injury over having lost her and what turns out to be his resentment that someone had so little respect for him as to provoke him for the sake of mere enjoyment. If Doralice were to feel uncomfortably put off by this, the reader should probably not be surprised, even if he were not to learn soon enough that this same Doralice cannot understand why Mandricardo would jeopardize his possession of her by risking his life in a duel over an eagle painted on a shield (30.31–45). Mandricardo, in his most generous moment in the *Furioso*, must patiently explain to her that it is not the painted eagle, but his honor, that concerns him. Furthermore, it is likely that Doralice senses the insult implicit in Rodomonte's firmness about keeping his oath to delay the settlement of his

Figures in Ariosto's Tapestry

quarrel over her with Mandricardo until Agramante can be rescued from Charlemagne. Of all the Saracens who quarrel with each other, Rodomonte is the firmest in keeping his oath. If he wavers at all in his resolve not to quarrel, it is when Ruggiero demands that he immediately relinquish custody of the horse he has stolen from him and fight for ownership later (26.92–97, 113–119). This Rodomonte refuses to do, even though he has been magnanimous about deferring the question of who should have custody of his wife, Mandricardo or himself. If Doralice had any doubts as to which were more important to her husband, herself or a stolen horse, it would be no wonder, nor is it any wonder, that when she is given the opportunity later to choose whom she will have, she chooses Mandricardo over Rodomonte.

Worth considering in this context is the irony of Ariosto's last words in the *Furioso* concerning Doralice. The Saracen camp is celebrating Ruggiero's mortal victory over Mandricardo, whom Doralice was unable to prevent from fighting, even though she had prevailed upon him to the extent that he had agreed not to reject another offer from Agramante of a peaceful solution. However, the battle begins before Agramante can intervene, and Ruggiero wins amid universal rejoicing:

Né di tal voluntà gli uomini soli
eran verso Ruggier, ma le donne anco,
che d'Africa e di Spagna fra gli stuoli
eran venute al tenitorio franco.
E Doralice istessa, che con duoli
piangea l'amante suo pallido e bianco,
forse con l'altre ita sarebbe in schiera,
se di vergogna un duro fren non era.

Io dico forse, non ch'io ve l'accerti,
ma potrebbe esser stato di leggiero:
tal la bellezza e tali erano i merti,
i costumi e i sembianti di Ruggiero.
Ella, per quel che già ne siamo esperti,
sì facile era a variar pensiero,
che per non si veder priva d'amore,
avria potuto in Ruggier porre il core.

Per lei buono era vivo Mandricardo:
ma che ne volea far dopo la morte?
Proveder le convien d'un che gagliardo
sia notte e dì ne' suoi bisogni, e forte.

(30.71–73)

Nor were the men alone thus disposed toward Ruggiero, but the ladies as well who had accompanied the troops from Africa and Spain to the confines of France. Even Doralice herself, who was weeping with sorrow over her wan and pallid lover, might perhaps have fallen in with the rest, if shame had not been a stiff restraint. I say "perhaps," for I would hesitate to make you any assertions, but still it could have come about easily enough, such was the beauty and such were the merits, the manners, and the countenance of Ruggiero. She was, as we have already seen, so prone to change her mind that she would easily have been capable of giving her heart to Ruggiero in order not to see herself deprived of love. For her, Mandricardo was good while he was alive, but what could she do with him dead? Her nature it was to furnish herself with someone valorous day and night in her needs, and strong.

Supposedly "we" have seen the evidence of Doralice's fickleness, that is, her choice of Mandricardo over Rodomonte in canto 27. However, we had better ask ourselves what indeed we have seen, or else we are likely to find ourselves, through a too complacent acceptance of the narrator's invitation to join in with his congenial "we," the objects of Ariosto's humor. It is the reader, not Doralice, who is in danger here of feeling the bite of Ariosto's irony. All that we have seen of Doralice is that she has made one choice of a man, Mandricardo, that she had her reasons for making it (some of the better ones provided by Rodomonte himself), and that she has done everything to make a go of it with Mandricardo. We have no evidence at all that she is promiscuous. She is merely an ordinary woman with ordinary common sense, and no vainer than the rest of us, and if we confuse her sensuality with promiscuity or fickleness, we run the risk of associating ourselves with that afflicted bull of canto 27 who stalks away bellowing his disdain for the whole female sex because it is intolerable to him that one female could find him inferior to another bull. The reader's safest response to the narrator's sly "perhaps" would be a sly "perhaps" of his own, because the narrator has either lost his wits at this point, as he has said he, like Orlando, often does, or else he has opened a back door through which to lead the sluggish reader into company with Rodomonte.

Doralice understands Rodomonte's character as well as she must. For two reasons, Ruggiero's horse and Agramante's peril provide more compelling motives for Rodomonte to act than does her abduction: first, they offer him better occasions for self-exaltation through beating someone in battle, and second, despite her abduction, he has no doubt that she is his. He considers himself so mighty that she can do nothing less than declare herself his. He has no need to consider her feelings about the matter because she, to his way of looking at things, is no more independent of his will than any mere creature in the presence of God. Of course, he has no conception whatsoever of how she has been impressed by what she has recently seen of him, and she has seen him battered by Mandricardo (24.95–107) and justly accused by Ruggiero of stealing a horse from a defenseless woman (26.91–97). One only hopes that she has managed to comprehend the insult added by Mandricardo to his previous injuries of Rodomonte when he undertakes the battle for possession of Marfisa so that he can turn her over to Rodomonte in compensation for Doralice (26.70). Rodomonte's unawareness of Mandricardo's motive for fighting Marfisa only adds to the foolishness of his pose of Olympian reserve and righteous indignation in the face of the discord all around him. He has no idea that his position, from Doralice's point of view, might appear signally ungodlike, so his astonishment is no less profound than everyone else's when she finally chooses someone who has neither insulted her nor comported himself quite so ridiculously on his own account.

To his credit, Rodomonte does realize that he has been disgraced before the entire Saracen camp and that there is nothing he can do about it, but he has no conception of his own contribution to the disgrace. All he can do is desert his king and accuse him of ingratitude and curse all womankind in the terms of a barnyard Petrarca addled with grief. Furthermore, in this moment of his greatest impotence, he can solace himself only with a fantasy of omnipotence in which, all by himself, he rescues Agramante from ruin. Not only does he not begin to comprehend Doralice's motives, but he fails to understand that Agramante's sole objective, in light of his recent peril, has been to compose all of the quarrels among his captains with the least damage possible. Rodomonte's mortification at this moment is as extreme as even Calvino could wish, but the image Ariosto presents is of a crushing failure of the imagination to recognize the otherness of other people and to recognize, as a result, one's own responsibility for how one is treated by them.

The figure sketched by Boiardo of a Rodomonte suffering from the evidence of his own insignificance and yet pretending that nothing has changed is brought to its clearest realization by Ariosto in this episode of the *Furioso*. Ariosto's great contribution at this point is that his character does not go mad and run amok. Rodomonte has felt the ax fall on his neck, but he does not realize that he has been beheaded. He merely wanders off to a place where it will be easier to think of himself as the only god in his universe. On the way, he gets badly cut, though he does not realize this either, by one of those turnips who had proved too much for him when he was in his glory inside Paris. The innkeeper who tells the story for which the *Furioso* may be most notorious deserves all of the credit he has received over the centuries. "Il buon ostier," we are told,

> fu dei diligenti
> che mai si sien per Francia ricordati,
> quando tra le nimiche, e strane genti
> l'albergo e beni suoi s'avea salvati.

(27.132)

The good innkeeper [we are told] was among the most diligent on record throughout all France, considering that he had held on to his inn and his belongings in the midst of foreign and hostile peoples.

It is possible that Rodomonte has left the field of battle populated with kings and barons only to find himself confronted with a type of person much more formidable, if in a different way.

According to one recent critic the story told by the innkeeper, ostensibly to soothe Rodomonte's colossal woe, "extracts from the relish of everyday life a taste of the *Decameron* in the thoroughly worldly love of Fiammetta, who, lavishing herself upon a kitchen-boy, mocks the mighty ones already humiliated by a page and a dwarf." The same critic draws attention to Rodomonte's new surroundings: "first a landscape with a river after a Flemish painting, crowded with boats and boatmen, merchandise and cargoes, then the inside of a hostelry at the conclusion of a generous supper . . . in the company of good ordinary folks."[7] These are the turnips who proved too numerous for Rodomonte's sword in Paris, and the story told by the shrewdest of them is no less detrimental to Rodomonte than it is to its two heroes, equally as infatuated with themselves as he is with himself. The *querelle des femmes* theme enters only as the familiar Ariostan red herring. In fact, whenever Ariosto's narrator points to this theme as his major concern, the reader should look in the opposite direction for the sense of the narrative. The wise old man who takes issue with what he perceives to be the story's insult to women is just as dense (though in a much more congenial way) as Rodomonte, who stupidly declares at its end,

> io credo ben che de l'ascose
> feminil frode sia copia infinita;
> né si potria de la millesma parte
> tener memoria con tutte le carte.

(28.75).

I can well believe that there is an infinite abundance of hidden female frauds; nor would it be possible to preserve a memory of the thousandth part of them with all the sheets of paper in existence.

More than a shrewd, satirical thrust at the *amour propre* of a ruling class the innkeeper has every reason to detest, the story is a parable of faith. The ability of Astolfo and Iocondo to find a faithful woman is inversely proportionate to their self-infatuation. Faith, they learn, cannot be purchased with good looks or money, much less exacted by force. What they fail to learn, and what Rodomonte has failed to learn from Doralice, is that faith has to be freely given by another person, whose character must be considered. However, this is obviously a consideration outside the scope of people who recognize no one besides themselves as worthy of consideration. The penalty, then, of electing oneself to the station of deity is that one must also serve as one's only worshiper.

The unfolding of Rodomonte's story from this point in the narrative until the end moves in the direction of ever more isolation. Wandering off from the inn, Rodomonte passes many populous cities without entering them until at last he comes upon an appropriate place to stay.

Verso Acquamorta a man dritta si tenne
con animo in Algier passare in fretta;
e sopra un fiume ad una villa venne
e da Baco e da Cerere diletta,
che per le spesse ingiurie che sostenne
dai soldati, a votarsi fu constretta.
Quinci il gran mare, e quindi ne l'apriche
valli vede ondeggiar le bionde spiche.

Quivi ritrova una piccola chiesa
di nuovo sopra un monticel murata,
che poi ch'intorno era la guerra accesa,
i sacerdoti vòta avean lasciata.
Per stanza fu da Rodomonte presa;
che pel sito, e perch'era sequestrata
dai campi, onde avea in odio udir novella,
gli piacque sì, che mutò Algieri in quella.

(28.92–93)

He kept on toward Aigues-Mortes to the right, with the intention of crossing over in haste to Algiers, when beside a river he came upon a village, the delight of Bacchus and Ceres, which had been abandoned owing to the frequent injuries it had sustained from soldiers. On one side was the great sea, and on the other he saw in sunlit valleys golden ears of wheat rippling. There he found a little church built recently on a hill, which the priests had left empty when war broke out in the neighborhood. It was appropriated by Rodomonte as a lodging. On account of its site, and because it was sequestered from the fields of battle, whence he hated to hear news, it pleased him so much that he made it his substitute for Algiers.

Ariosto's entire conception of Rodomonte is contained in this passage. Nature, producing wheat and grapevines, fecund and creative, undulating in the sunlight, reproaches the sterility and destructiveness of human nature. The town and the little church have been emptied by war and are now the perfect residence for Rodomonte, the man whose choice of deity creates desolation. Here he might have a shrine to worship himself in without interference; however, Isabella's arrival proves that the impetus of such a nature as his cannot find peace in a world remaining obstinately populated and fertile.

It has been said that Rodomonte exhibits inconsistency throughout the episode involving Isabella, first in his attraction to her despite his professed hatred of women, then in his spouting of Ovidian topics of wooing, and finally in his apparently surprising eagerness to achieve invulnerability.[8] However, to the extent that these are inconsistencies, there is also an Aristotelian consistency within them that demands emphasis if the more colossal ironies of the Isabella episode are to be appreciated. Rodomonte may try to behave as if he were a god and faultless, blaming the whole female sex for the consequences of his own boorish treatment of Doralice, but he is still only a man subject to his "blind appetite" (29.12), the blindness being the main consequence of his self-exaltation. Ordinary human sexual desire is all that impels Rodomonte toward Isabella, though it is assisted, the narrator notes, by the Saracen's opinion that she is a person "most worthy in whom to locate his second love, and with whom to extinguish the first, just as one nail is knocked out of a board with another" (28.98). He values her, as he did Doralice, according to the usefulness to him of her outward appearance, both as an emblem of his might and now as a tool to repair his damaged ego. The narrator is also careful to note that the Ovidian topics of wooing are merely "words that go together" (29.8)—naturally, since Rodomonte's sensibility is insufficient to lend them any feeling. He is no more able to think of Isabella as an independent being than he was able to think of Doralice as such, despite the signs—a corpse slung over a warhorse and a bearded monk giving consolation—that this time such consideration would be wise. Instead, with his Ovidian platitudes he only draws attention to the vacuity of his sentiments and to the irony of his being compelled, like lions, bears, and serpents, to seek out a desolate place, while Isabella has chosen her solitude.

As for Rodomonte's sudden desire to achieve invulnerability, is it really so inconsistent with what we might expect him to desire at this point? The language describing his retreat from Paris much earlier is unmistakable:

> Al pagan, che non sa come ne possa
> venir a capo, omai quel gioco incresce.
> Poco, per far di mille, o di più, rossa
> la terra intorno, il populo discresce.
> Il fiato tuttavia più se gl'ingrossa,
> sì che comprende al fin che, se non esce
> or c'ha vigore e in tutto il corpo è sano,
> vorrà da tempo uscir, che sarà invano.
>
> (18.17)

To the pagan, who cannot see his way to the end, that sport begins to grow unpleasant. Making the ground around him red with the blood of a thousand or more diminishes that populace but little. All the while his breath is growing thicker and thicker, so that he realizes at last that if he does not retreat now, while he has the strength and his body is sound in every limb, he will soon wish to depart but it will be in vain.

He has to retreat from Paris, because he is growing weaker and might be killed. On the one hand, as he thinks himself a deity, he must obliterate anything or anyone who opposes him; on the other hand, the Paris adventure has made him vaguely aware that he has taken on more than he can handle. So it is no wonder that rendering his body invulnerable might appeal to him. Rodomonte's sensibility is limited, never to the point that he does not know that he has been disgraced or defeated, but specifically limited in that he always blames others for his failures. The major irony of the Isabella episode is that Rodomonte has already achieved a kind of invulnerability, with no one's help but his own, long before he ever encounters Isabella. The simile that most effectively describes Rodomonte's nature, of all the similes used to describe him in the *Furioso,* enters the text at the moment he is grappling with Orlando on the bridge he has built ostensibly to honor the memory of Isabella:

> Simiglia Rodomonte intorno a Orlando
> lo stolido orso che sveller si crede
> l'arbor onde è caduto; e come n'abbia
> quello ogni colpa, odio gli porta e rabbia.
>
> (29.46)

Grappling with Orlando, Rodomonte resembles the stubborn bear who thinks to uproot the tree he fell from and, as if it bore all the blame, vents his rage and hatred on it.

Like the bear, he is invulnerable to any awareness that he is the cause of his own repeated downfalls, and instead he lashes out at whatever seems immediately threatening, and this gradually becomes nothing less than the whole world. In a flash of superior intuition, Isabella, as befits a sensibility profounder than Doralice's, reads Rodomonte's character more deeply than it has thus far been read, and she offers him what he thinks he needs most: invulnerability to the attacks of his universal enemy. Consequently, the blow she delivers him with his own hand, martyring herself at the same time to the god she has chosen in Zerbino, has a powerful effect, not of changing him or broadening his field of vision, but of reducing him to a caricature of himself.

The transformation Rodomonte works upon the landscape in building his monument to the memory of Isabella turns it into a stereotypical setting of Arthurian romance, and Ariosto punctuates this fact by concluding his description with the sentence "the world contained no peril the like of that one" [Ugual periglio a quel, non avea il mondo] (29.36), practically a formula in the *Orlando Innamorato*, where the reader never believes it because he knows he will see it again as soon as Boiardo invents or embroiders yet another of his stupendous perils. However, in its new context in the *Furioso*, where it has not been used as a formula, the sentence has the opposite effect: the reader wonders if it might not be true. The image of the narrow bridge, in its new context, also acquires a certain freshness and unexpected explanatory power. It is the image of a place where only one man can stand, which is, of course, the state to which Rodomonte would like to reduce the world. Perversely, Rodomonte's intention to erect a monument to Isabella's memory turns into an excuse for him to continue asserting his claim to deity and to continue punishing the world for being so large that there is room for more than one person in it. Isabella's monument becomes a compulsive, mechanical repetition of the behavior that destroyed her. We may well ask what greater peril the world contains than such madness as this, so absurdly at odds with reality that it can be represented only by a literary cliché. However, we do not have to ask if it had crossed Ariosto's mind that the repeated invasions of Italy during his lifetime had been instigated by men who had fallen victim to the identical madness. He had already established that connection when Rodomonte first entered the *Furioso,* and now, as a result, it is difficult not to regard that narrow bridge as a gruesome symbol of what the warring madmen of his time, whom Ariosto detested so much, were trying to make out of Italy.

The madness of Rodomonte's course is only clarified by his confrontation with Bradamante and by the absurd condition he imposes in case of his victory:

Ma s'a te tocca star di sotto, come
più si conviene, e certo so che fia,
non vo che lasci l'arme, né il tuo nome,
come di vinta, sottoscritta sia:
al tuo bel viso, a' begli occhi, alle chiome,
che spiran tutti amore e leggiadria,
voglio donar la mia vittoria; e basti
che ti disponga amarmi, ove m'odiasti.

Io son di tal valor, son di tal nerbo,
ch'aver non dèi d'andar di sotto a sdegno.

(35.46–47)

But if it touches you to go under, as it is more suitable, and as I am certain it will turn out, I do not will you to leave your arms here, nor do I will your name to be written down among the vanquished. To your beautiful face, to your beautiful eyes, to your hair, which all exude love and gracefulness, I wish to dedicate my victory, and it is enough if you dispose yourself to love me, though you hated me before. I am of such valor and of so much strength that you must not be indignant about going under.

Bradamante, accurately appraising his behavior, has already asked him, "Beast, why do you want the innocent to do penance for your own sin?" (35.42) However, it is not to be expected that Rodomonte should now be susceptible to the truth when his recent butchery of Isabella did nothing but harden him in his invulnerability to it. Furthermore, it is difficult to discern any pathos in his speech. Much more obvious are its arrogance, its scurrility, and its stupidity in suggesting that love can be forced. The magic lance with which Bradamante topples Rodomonte into the river only calls attention to the futility of Rodomonte's position. Fall he must, because the world is too great for him and because love and faith cannot be exacted by force, but the sorrow and the pity of his determination is that he must make so many human beings fall with him, punishing them for his own failure.

Orlando's brief encounter with Rodomonte (29.39–48), occurring very soon after the bridge is built, calls more attention to Orlando's failings than to Rodomonte's, and so does not have to be treated at length in this chapter. However, the reader of the *Orlando Furioso* cannot help but feel that the responsibility for much of Rodomonte's carnage rests on Orlando's shoulders, if only because Orlando was absent during the assault on Paris when he, as Charlemagne's strongest warrior, would have been the logical opponent of Christendom's fiercest enemy. On a grand and public scale, the assault on Paris resembles the more personal catastrophes of Zerbino's and Brandimarte's deaths under the sword Durindana abandoned by Orlando in his madness. Now, when the mad count meets the equally mad, though consciously and methodically destructive, Rodomonte, the reader cannot help but be reminded of the terrible results of the failure of Orlando's own gods and his subsequent madness. Orlando's gods, the chivalric and courtly Petrarchan conventions of Ariosto's Italy, disable their worshiper when reality intervenes to shatter them. While Orlando, witless and naked as the day he was born, thrashes about looking for something he has lost, though he does not remember what it was, those who never worshiped anything but themselves are free to lay waste the land. After Orlando dashes off to give Angelica's horse a ride, Rodomonte pulls himself out of the water and goes back to business as usual: the slaughter of the faithful and the innocent. Fiordiligi's successful appeal to him in behalf of Brandimarte may represent a break in the pattern, and Bradamante may stop him for a year, a month, and a day while he does penance in a hermit's cell for having transgressed against his own mightiness by allowing a mere woman to get the best of him, but he returns at the end of the *Furioso,* more faithful to himself than ever (and certainly at least as faithful to himself as Ruggiero has been to Bradamante) to accuse Ruggiero of disloyalty to Agramante and to threaten him with the same fate suffered by Zerbino and Brandimarte. The reader has by this time so often seen the reward of good turn out to be ill that Bradamante's fears as Ruggiero prepares to meet Rodomonte must seem very real to him. It almost seems as if the *Furioso* will end with the grief of another Fiordiligi, despite all those prophesies of an illustrious progeny to issue from the marriage of Ruggiero and Bradamante. It seems as if Orlando's madness will share the responsibility for yet another and graver destruction of what little there is to believe [distruzion del poco che si crede].

In fact, the *Furioso* ends on a prayer. Rodomonte returns as colossally self-indulgent as ever, and the narrator emphasizes this point:

Quest'era il Re d'Algier, che per lo scorno
che gli fe' sopra il ponte la donzella,
giurato avea di non porsi arme intorno,
né stringer spada, né montare in sella,

fin che non fosse un anno, un mese e un giorno
stato, come eremita, entro una cella.
Così a quel tempo solean per se stessi
punirsi i cavallier di tali eccessi.

Se ben di Carlo in questo mezzo intese
e del re suo signore ogni successo;
per non disdirsi, non più l'arme prese,
che se non pertenesse il fatto ad esso.
Ma poi che tutto l'anno e tutto 'l mese
vede finito, e tutto 'l giorno appresso,
con nuove arme e cavallo e spada e lancia
alla corte or ne vien quivi di Francia.

(46.102–3)

This was the King of Algiers, who had sworn, on account of the
humiliation done him by the damsel on the bridge, not to put on armor,
take sword in hand, or sit in a saddle until he had spent one year, one
month, and one day in a cell like a hermit. So it was in those days that for
the like excesses knights were accustomed to undertake their own
punishment. Though he heard during this interval of all that befell
Charles and the king his own lord, he took up arms, in order not to break
his oath, no more than if the news had had nothing to do with him.
However, now that he sees the whole year and the whole month elapsed,
and the whole day as well, he betakes himself there to the court of France
with new arms and a new horse, with a new sword and a new lance.

The irony of the last two lines of the first stanza is more scorching even
than the irony of their proverbial counterpart at the opening of the
Furioso, when Rinaldo and Ferraù ride off together on the same horse to
seek Angelica: "Oh gran bontà de' cavallieri antiqui" (1.22). The repetition in the second stanza of *giorno, mese,* and *anno* stresses the narrow-
minded punctiliousness with which Rodomonte has placed his own
need to compensate for a blow to his self-esteem before his duty to his
king, as if Agramante's destruction had nothing whatsoever to do with
him. Nonetheless, he dares to accuse Ruggiero of disloyalty to Agramante, and he is ready to punish Ruggiero with death for an act of which
he himself is guilty. The ferocious, but for Rodomonte, characteristic,
absurdity of this would be astounding even if Ruggiero were not the
Furioso's embodiment of the struggle to achieve altruism. Ruggiero has
suffered repeatedly on account of his conflicting loyalties, to the extent
that he has been on the verge of losing everything for Agramante's
benefit. The battle that ensues represents the clash of two opposing
human types, and Ruggiero wins only because, as the narrator suggests,

he has "fortune by the forelock" (46.135) and because "by right he had to win" (46.127).

Luck and the will of Ariosto, his creator, produce Ruggiero's victory. The reader has seen too much slaughter of the faithful to believe that right alone is enough to produce a victory over the insane ferocity represented by Rodomonte. Rodomonte breaks his sword, and this time Ruggiero, unlike the Ruggiero who fought Rodomonte in Boiardo's poem, holds his own sword tightly. Ariosto arranges it so that the man whose faith embraces others destroys the man whose faith denies their right to exist. In a sense, right must conquer if the reader is to be reassured that a future exists beyond the narrative rapidly approaching its end; however, Ariosto uses Rodomonte's broken sword as a harsh reminder that in reality circumstances cannot always be contrived, as in a narrative, to produce a moral victory and to insure a future. The contrast of this battle scene with the close of the *Aeneid,* to which it alludes, is chilling. In Ariosto's world, Ruggiero does not have the strength of Aeneas to vanquish furor. Rodomonte is more powerful than Turnus, because he draws his strength tragically from the same conditions as those from which Ruggiero draws his, conditions described by Boiardo in yet another anticipation of his harder-minded successor: "It is said that God creates men, and then they find themselves together by themselves" (2.24–43). In response, one man egotistically erects a god inside himself, another man altruistically discovers gods in other selves, and the outcome of the clash between the two will always be uncertain. Ariosto, the demiurge of the *Orlando Furioso,* merely decides matters as he fervently wishes them to be decided. Pity and fear accompany whatever other responses we have to the descent of Rodomonte's spirit into Hades, because Ariosto has enabled us to understand his error and recognize our own vulnerability to that bitter despair.

4
Ruggiero

riosto's Ruggiero is among the most exasperating characters in Renaissance literature. A kind of Aeneas in reverse, he repeatedly postpones his destiny in order to fulfill more immediate commitments. However, the word *commitment* is often unfitting, unless one wishes to dignify the character's urges with a generous euphemism. Confused and indecisive much of the time, on occasion thoroughly benighted, Ruggiero seems a most unheroic hero, and yet his many perplexities, considered together, form the pattern that organizes Ariosto's immense tapestry more than any other pattern, including those of the war and Orlando's madness. As we read the *Furioso,* we are tricked at first into believing that Ruggiero's every deed is momentous because it contributes to the fulfillment of a destiny similar to Aeneas's. However, even after Ariosto's ironies have shed doubt on the similarity, we do not cease to take Ruggiero seriously. Instead, we continue to attach as much importance to his actions as if we remained deceived. We laugh at ourselves for having taken something seriously while we continue to take it seriously. Perhaps the best explanation of this peculiar response is provided by Italo Calvino, whose commentary on the *Furioso* is sometimes as amusing as the poem itself:

Having a destiny is a hard destiny. The predestined man advances, and his steps can carry him nowhere but to that place, to the point of arrival the stars have fixed for him, or to successive points of arrival, propitious or unpropitious, in a case like Ruggiero's, where the planets have decreed for him a marriage for love, a glorious progeny, and yet, alas, a premature end. Still there can succeed, between the point at which he now finds himself and the fulfillment of his destiny, ever so many vicissitudes, so many obstacles can interpose themselves, so many impulses of the will can enter the field to resist the will of the planets: the road the predestined man must run can be, not a straight line, but an interminable labyrinth. We know, of course, that all of the obstacles will be vain, that all extraneous wills will be defeated, but there remains with us the doubt as to whether that which really counts is the distant point of arrival, the final goal fixed by the stars, or else whether it is the interminable labyrinth itself, the obstacles, the errors, the vicissitudes, that give form to existence.[1]

While the image of an endless labyrinth may be too dizzying to describe the pattern of Ruggiero's behavior, Calvino's perception that the many points along the way are what give meaning to his existence, and not the faraway destiny itself, provides the premise upon which this chapter is based. Ariosto's ironies may erode his tribute to the Este dynasty, but in doing so they focus the reader's attention on Ruggiero as a figure undergoing a development marked by stages that assume the significance of a destiny in their own right. At first, nothing exists for Ruggiero beyond his own imaginings; subsequently, he attempts to organize his life by devoting himself to a principle; finally, principles give way to personal commitments and he discovers the object of his faith. The first stage of this development ends in canto 22 with Astolfo's destruction of Atlante's palace of illusions, the second ends with Ruggiero's baptism in canto 41, and the third, culminating in the destruction of Rodomonte, consists mainly of the Leone episode, much maligned in recent Ariosto criticism, and much misunderstood.

If to suffer and develop while in the quest for a trustworthy purpose in life is Ruggiero's destiny, his greatest obstacle is treachery in all of its forms, from the treacherousness of an unstable world to self-betrayal and to betrayal by evil people. Before Ariosto and even before Boiardo, the name *Ruggiero* had been used when the Este family, charged by Ferrara's enemies with descent from the traitorous Maganza clan, needed to invent a legendary progenitor who would be a paragon of loyalty.[2] In the *Innamorato,* at the outset of the first canto of book 2, the first thing we learn about Ruggiero is that he will eventually meet his death after being betrayed by members of the House of Maganza. He has scarcely begun his existence as a fictional character before we learn that treachery will spell his destruction. At the same time, however, we are told that he will survive just long enough to set in motion a sequence of events leading to a golden age in the remote future. In the *Furioso,* Ariosto retains and reinforces these givens of the character's destiny. We may rapidly learn to doubt that the reign of Ariosto's employers, Alfonso and Ippolito d'Este, constitutes the golden age for which Ruggiero lived, but we never doubt that he has a purpose. Nor do we ever doubt that he is in a battle with circumstances and in a race with time in order to accomplish that purpose. The weight of the dominant theme of the *Furioso,* the *fede* theme, rests more on Ruggiero's shoulders than on those of any other character in the poem. If Ariosto's characterization of Rodomonte presents an answer to the question as to why a person may not invest his faith solely in himself, Ruggiero's characterization goes further than any other—except Bradamante's—toward answering the more important question as to what there is in the world that a person may believe in. As we have seen, whatever grandeur and humanity Rodomonte possesses stem from his own warped impulse toward faith in something absolute. The same can be said for Ruggiero, except that in him the impulse is not warped, but is repeatedly betrayed. To the extent (and it is a very great extent) that these betrayals stem from Ruggiero's own mistakes and weaknesses, the reader may grow exasperated, but the narrative never permits this exasperation to culminate in rejection. For at the point of greatest self-betrayal Ruggiero always undergoes a symbolic death and rebirth. He emerges at a new stage in his development and the reader's new hopes emerge with him.

To begin to understand Ariosto's Ruggiero, it is necessary to examine Boiardo's rendition of the character. Ariosto was no more the creator of Ruggiero than he was the creator of Rodomonte. He found both characters, along with most of their essential features, already vividly developed in the *Innamorato*. Nor did he take the liberty of changing them in order to make them fit a new story. He adapted the plot and circumstances of his narrative to characters already familiar to his audience. One of the strongest arguments that characterization is the major organising principle of the *Orlando Furioso* is found in the care Ariosto devoted to preserving the essential traits of Boiardo's Rodomonte and Ruggiero. Ariosto's originality may be found in the sharper focus he lends these characters, in the implications he reveals of their behavior, and in the moral perspective in which he places them, a perspective far more profound than Boiardo's. The Ruggiero of the first twenty-two cantos of the *Orlando Furioso,* from his sojourn in Alcina's paradise to his release from Atlante's palace of illusions, is a character struggling to free himself from the legacy of the *Orlando Innamorato.* In these cantos, we watch the youth of the *Innamorato* begin his painful and sometimes embarrassing development into the adult who is able, at the end of the *Furioso,* to take advantage of his good fortune and slay Rodomonte without jeopardizing his own success by making a chivalric game out of the matter. To understand the Ruggiero who lounges in Alcina's paradise, and hence to understand the Alcina episode itself, we must study the young man of book 2 of the *Innamorato* who comes down from his mountaintop hiding place confident that good intentions are all he needs to win honor for himself in the service of others.

Almost as soon as he invented Ruggiero, Boiardo invented Brunello, an embodiment of the confusion that overtakes youths of Ruggiero's nature, "tiny indeed of person, but wondrously full of cunning" (2.3.40), a master of fraud and thievery who can steal a man's horse out from under him. Boiardo could not have conceived of a better means of representing the low comic antithesis of Ruggiero's idealism and demonstrating how a dishonest world can overturn the honorable intentions of trusting persons. It is from Brunello that Ruggiero receives his horse, his sword, and his armor, so the earliest contact of his generous and honest nature with the world implicates him in multiple theft. When Brunello feigns generosity with his offer of the arms, declaring that though they are priceless they are at Ruggiero's disposal if his lack of them is all that keeps him from demonstrating his prowess in Agramante's tournament, Ruggiero trusts him, not only because of his impatience to join the combat but because to him it is natural to attribute to others the generous impulses he regularly feels. As a result, Brunello momentarily gets to enjoy the glory Ruggiero won. When Ruggiero returns the armor and goes back to his hiding place, Brunello is only too happy to use the armor to deceive the combatants into thinking that he, and not Ruggiero, had defeated them. However, Ruggiero's killing of Bardulasto places Brunello in unexpected jeopardy and in need of rescue. Brunello's near disaster on account of his uncontrollable urge to seize the immediate prize even at the expense of his long-range purpose—to get paid opulently for recruiting Ruggiero into Agramante's enterprise—is a clever psychological touch on Boiardo's part. However, the genius of the episode reveals itself in Ruggiero's rescue of Brunello.

When the Ruggiero of book 2 of the *Innamorato* sees Brunello carried off to the gallows and rushes down from his hiding place to rescue him, he brings with him, in rough outline, the essential traits of the Ruggiero in the *Furioso,* who will joust with Erifilla for the opportunity to languish in Alcina's voluptuous domain. He is very much the naive young man as he interposes himself between Brunello and his executioners, declaring that he does not understand why Brunello has come to this pass but that he himself is the one who killed Bardulasto in self-defense. He prepares to take punishment for his deeds in order to rescue the person who stole their glory. Then he sees that no one has the slightest intention of challenging his word or of punishing him:

Il giovanetto, di valore acceso,
Di novo incominciò con voce pia
—Parmi—dicendo—aver più volte inteso
Che il primo officio di cavalleria
Sia la ragione e il dritto aver difeso:
Onde, avendo io ciò fatto tuttavia,
Ché di campar costui presi pensiero,
Famme, segnor, ti prego, cavalliero.

E l'arme e il suo destrier me sian donate,
Ché altra volta da lui me fu promesso,
Et anco l'ho dapoi ben meritate,
Ché per camparlo a risco mi son messo.

(2.21.51–52)

The youth, burning with valor, began anew in reverent tones, saying, "I
believe I have many times heard that the first office of chivalry is to
defend the right and the truth; therefore, I having done that just now,
when I undertook the rescue of this man, make me, I beseech you, my
lord, a knight. And let his arms and his warhorse be granted me, for they
were promised me by him before, and besides I have merited them since,
for I placed myself in danger to rescue him."

Agramante knights him, of course, but not on account of his chivalric
deed, and as for the murder of Bardulasto, Agramante surely would
have knighted Ruggiero even if he had slaughtered two thirds of the
royalty at the tournament. "For Bardulasto," says the narrator, Agramante "felt no grief; if he were dead, that was his problem" (2.21.50).
The defense of rectitude and justice does not interest Agramante, nor
does the truth. What interests him is obtaining the advantage to his
cause prophesied to reside in Ruggiero's right arm. So the young man's
chivalric deed only serves to obligate him to an unscrupulous leader and
to bring about the accomplishment of Brunello's deceitful purpose. For
having delivered Ruggiero into Agramante's hands, Brunello receives a
kingdom, which he enjoys until Agramante in the *Furioso* makes him
pay a bitter price for his insolent treatment of Marfisa in the *Innamorato.* Having used Brunello to obtain Ruggiero's aid in the *Innamorato,* Agramante executes him in the *Furioso* in order to ingratiate
himself with Marfisa (32.7–9). Not even Ariosto could improve upon
Boiardo's depiction of the cynical ruler using men and discarding them
according to his convenience. Brunello's fate in the *Furioso* is another
example of the tribute paid by Ariosto to his predecessor's gift for
strong characterization.

Crime, as Boiardo points out, is relative in affairs of state. A courtly service to one's sovereign is never a crime. Instead, the perpetrator becomes a loyal vassal and his punishment a reward—until the sovereign changes his mind. There is an amusing touch, as Brunello is being carted off to the gallows before Ruggiero's rescue, when everyone laughs at him and calls him unrefined for reminding Agramante of his past services, the proverbial answer in court to such querulous reminders being always, "My good friend, if you served me, I treated you well" (2.21.38). But Ruggiero is not one to forget services received; upon witnessing what is about to become of Brunello, he declares,

> Ancor ch'io dovessi morire,
> In ogni modo io gli vo' dare aiuto.
> Costui mi prestò l'arme e il bon ronzone:
> Non lo aiutando, ben serìa fellone.

(2.21.40)

Even if I should die for it, I will help him in every way. This man lent me his arms and his good horse. I would be criminal indeed not to help him.

Ruggiero's idea of crime may be morally attractive, but it does not equip him to deal with the likes of Agramante or to understand the machinations of the courtly world. Instead, his honesty and his generosity play into the hands of the self-centered, deceitful monarch, and his rescue of Brunello becomes his own enslavement. He is knighted and simultaneously corrupted. As for Agramante, once he has captured his man he loses interest in the expedition to France, where Ruggiero's glory is to be established, and instead leads his army off to Biserta for some feasting and carousing. There Ruggiero's most memorable exploit, a farcical battle with an elephant, turns him into something more closely resembling a circus performer than a valorous knight. Boiardo does a magnificent job of using the callow youth's natural nobility to satirize the cold-blooded manipulations of court, and there his accomplishment stops. Ariosto, on the other hand, seizes upon the propensity of Ruggiero's nature to attribute his own good intentions to others and thereby to make the world over according to his own imaginings; as a consequence, the source of illusion in the *Furioso*'s opening scenes involving Ruggiero becomes Ruggiero himself instead of a corrupt court. In the *Furioso,* we enter the mind of the *Innamorato*'s callow youth.

The way from the fleshpots of Biserta to Alcina's hothouse may be a journey beyond satire, but it is certainly not a journey beyond the courtly atmosphere, even if it is only the frivolity of that atmosphere, and not its cruelty, that serves Ariosto's purpose. Most critical readings of the cantos of the *Furioso* involving Ruggiero's experiences with Alcina and Logistilla end up emphasizing the edifying story of a young man who must learn that all good things are not what they seem to be, that pleasures are often sorrows, and that a person must get control of his passions by distinguishing between illusion and reality. From the sixteenth century to the present day, enough sermonizing has been generated by these cantos to make any further criticism seem pointless. The allegorical contraption erected in cantos 6 and 7 is perhaps the greatest red herring in the *Furioso*. For this beautifully costumed and choreographed pageant to function properly as the solemn moral allegory so many have professed to see in it, its central figure, Alcina, would have to be the "malignant manipulator of illusion" in her encounter with Ruggiero that one twentieth-century student of earthly paradises claims she is.[3] However, she is neither malignant toward Ruggiero nor manipulative; instead, she is the one who is manipulated. We are told by the narrator that Atlante sent Ruggiero to Alcina's island,

> perché obliasse l'arme in quella corte;
> e come mago di somma dottrina,
> ch'usar sapea gl'incanti d'ogni sorte,
> avea il cor stretto di quella regina
> ne l'amor d'esso d'un laccio sì forte,
> che non se ne era mai per poter sciorre,
> s'invechiasse Ruggier più di Nestorre.
>
> (7.44).

so that he would forget about arms in that society, and as a wizard of the highest erudition, who knew how to use enchantments of every sort, Atlante had bound the heart of that queen in love for him with a rope so strong that she was never to be able to loose herself from it even if Ruggiero were to grow older than Nestor.

We are also given Atlante's motive:

> Quel più tosto volea che lungamente
> vivesse e senza fama e senza onore,
> che, con tutta la laude che sia al mondo,
> mancasse un anno al suo viver giocondo.
>
> (7.43)

He wanted him to live a long time without fame and without honor rather than that he should lose a single year of his merry life for all of the accolades in the world.

What we are left with after we have read these lines is the impression that we have just made an immeasurably long journey astride a mythical flying beast only to find ourselves in circumstances remarkable for their banality.

Atlante, we are reminded (for in the *Innamorato* he was always just as we find him here), is none other than the confused parent who has always encouraged his child's aptitudes and yet fears nothing quite so much as he does their consequences, while Alcina is the convenient vamp whose sexiness can be tolerated as long as she keeps the young man from taking risks commensurate with his abilities. Atlante's desire to keep the innocent Ruggiero from being taken advantage of by cynical powers cannot be faulted. We believe with Atlante that there is little honor to be won in becoming the deluded instrument of an unscrupulous king. Ruggiero is no Achilles, and in the *Furioso*'s world no single decision can guarantee undying glory in exchange for an abbreviated life span. However, all of this is not the stuff that allegory is made of. If, to paraphrase Ariosto at the opening of canto 7, one is among those to whom the light of this discourse clear, one senses that the allegorical rigamarole of the Alcina episode is an elaborate joke played at the expense of allegory itself. One also senses that the gist of this episode lies not in the array of moral commonplaces that can be wrenched from it, but in the psychological development it portrays of a young man whose suppositions about the world and about himself will render him a victim of banality unless he learns to change them. However, he must change them without losing the very idealism that adds to his susceptibility.

The main analogy between Ruggiero's recruitment by Agramante in the *Innamorato* and his seduction by Alcina in the *Furioso* involves a paradox. In the *Innamorato,* Ruggiero's honesty and generosity cause him, against any expectation within the range of his sensibility, to become the henchman of a tyrant. His very strengths become his vulnerabilities, and they cause him to become something and to do things that are the opposite of his intentions. The same is true of the Ruggiero of canto 6 of the *Furioso,* to whom the ladies who personify Beauty and Grace appeal against the monstrous Erifilla. The Ruggiero of the *Innamorato* was willing to lay down his life to rescue Brunello; the Ruggiero of the *Furioso* tells his alluring lady friends that they may do with him as they please, because his sole purpose in life is to benefit others.

> Non ch'una battaglia,
> ma per voi sarò pronto a farne cento:
> di mia persona, in tutto quel che vaglia,
> fatene voi secondo il vostro intento:
> che la cagion ch'io vesto piastra e maglia

non è per guadagnar terre né argento,
ma sol per farne beneficio altrui,
tanto più a belle donne come vui.

(6.80)

Not one battle, but a hundred shall I stand ready to fight for you. Do
with my person, for whatever it is worth, just as you please, for the reason
that I don plate and mail is not to earn silver and land, but only to benefit
others, and much the more such pretty ladies as you.

This declaration, along with its fatuous concluding line, is the key to the
Alcina episode. The real source of illusion in this earthly paradise is not
Alcina any more than it is the beautiful, graceful ladies—they really are
beautiful and graceful. They and Alcina are what they appear to be, and
as the narrator says, it would take a "divine eye to pass judgment on
them" (6.69). Although Alcina may have been deceitful in the past, she
is now actually and permanently infatuated with Ruggiero. The source
of illusion in this earthly paradise is Ruggiero himself. His own altruistic
character causes him to mistake Alcina for something that she is not,
and as a result, his generous intentions leave him wallowing in hot self-
indulgence. The impetuous youth of the *Innamorato* again kneels before a deity of his own creation.

What this means for the entire Alcina episode is that the earthly
paradise depicted there must be regarded as a surrealistic, not an allegorical, landscape. The scenes involving Alcina bear as much resemblance to the scenes of a Buñuel film as they do to any form of
allegory predating Ariosto's work. When we read cantos 6 and 7 we are
shown the world as Ruggiero sees it; at the same time, Ariosto notes for
us the distortions that enter Ruggiero's vision. What makes it difficult to
attend to this process is that many of the images Ariosto uses come out
of a traditional allegorical repertory. Consequently, we tend to regard
these familiar stage properties as signs that still refer to certain conventional ideas outside the text. From the sixteenth century to the twen-
tieth, critics have struggled to impose these conventional ideas on
Ariosto's text, always with the same result. Either the ideas manage to
bend the text so far out of shape as to make it unrecognizable, or the
text ends up mocking the ideas. Part of the charm of studying Ariosto
derives from charting this comedy. However, the pleasure of understanding his text derives from realizing that there is no frame of reference for any episode of the *Furioso* as reliable as the text itself taken as a
whole. This is why so many readers over the centuries, like Galileo, have
made rereading the *Orlando Furioso* the project of a lifetime. The frame

of reference for understanding the Alcina episode is Ruggiero's character as Ariosto depicts it throughout the *Furioso* and as we find it depicted in Boiardo's poem.

Why does Ruggiero see Astolfo and the rest of Alcina's past lovers as a collection of trees, fountains, and beasts decorating a formal garden? When Ruggiero hitches his hippogryph to Astolfo, and Astolfo objects in sonorous Dantesque terms, we laugh at the incongruity of the solemn tones with the frivolous story Astolfo goes on to tell. There is something childish about that story so full of fish. Of course, from Astolfo's point of view, the matter is solemn indeed, because he too sees himself as a man who has been turned into a tree. However, we cannot help but smile at his description of Alcina's attractions. Evidently, she can charm every fish in the sea, so it is no wonder that she could charm Astolfo, who is only a man. She gave him the impression, he tells Ruggiero, that she could make him hear the sirens' song, so sweet it can still the violent motion of the waves, and she promised to show him every species of fish, including some that have fur. It is easy to analyze Astolfo's problem in terms less fabulous than those he uses himself. He became infatuated with Alcina when he first saw her, he continued to be so once he got to know her, and he remains so even now that he has been rejected. Once he was a fish, and now he is a tree. His description of their actual love affair reveals his state of mind:

> Io mi godea le delicate membra:
> pareami aver qui tutto il ben raccolto
> che fra i mortali in più parti si smembra,
> a chi più et a chi meno e a nessun molto;
> né di Francia né d'altro mi rimembra:
> stavomi sempre a contemplar quel volto:
> ogni pensiero, ogni mio bel disegno
> in lei finia, né passava oltre il segno.
>
> Io da lei altretanto era o più amato:
> Alcina più non si curava d'altri;
> ella ogn'altro suo amante avea lasciato,
> ch'inanzi a me ben ce ne fur degli altri.
> Me consiglier, me avea dì e notte a lato,
> e me fe' quel che commandava agli altri:
> a me credeva, a me si riportava;
> né notte o dì con altri mai parlava.

(6.47–48)

Once upon a time I enjoyed her delicate members. To me it seemed that in them I possessed all of the good gathered together that is parceled out among mortals in many parts, to one more and to another less and to no one much. Nor do I remember France or anything else. I was forever contemplating that face. My every thought, my every sweet design ended in her, nor passed beyond that mark. I by her was loved as much or more. Alcina cared no longer for others. She had abandoned every other lover of hers, for others indeed there had been before me. She had me beside her day and night, her counselor, and made me the one who commanded others. In me she used to trust, and on me she relied. Nor night nor day did she ever speak with anyone else.

The crescendo of first person pronouns exposes the extreme self-absorption behind Astolfo's claim that he and Alcina were paradises to each other. Having allowed himself to think that he once was everything to Alcina, Astolfo feels himself reduced to nothing the instant she turns her back on him. Alcina herself is essentially innocent of his suffering. It is not Alcina who has reduced Astolfo to his miserable self-conception; Astolfo's own continuing belief in the splendor of his former condition is what paralyzes him. He was the one all along who endowed Alcina with her magic powers, and he continues to do so. The pleasant scenery of which he and the others who share his delusion are a part is only an externalization of his and their self-indulgent pleasure in their own suffering. What finally breaks the spell for all of them is seeing Ruggiero grow tired of deluding himself in time to reject Alcina before she rejects him. When Alcina becomes the jilted lover, it is no longer possible to regard her as having magic powers. Nor is it possible any longer to regard her as a paradise on earth. So the trees, beasts, and fountains return to human form, finding themselves somewhere between the fantastic ecstasies and the fantastic agonies of their former deluded state.

The one piece of wisdom in Astolfo's long warning is revealed at the end when he expresses doubts about Ruggiero's ability to avoid the fate of the others. While Ruggiero is never reduced to the despair these others experience, he does briefly enjoy the same infatuation they had felt. He avoids their despair only because for once Alcina is just as infatuated with someone as he is with her. Ruggiero is merely fortunate. Otherwise, at this point, he is no different from the rest of them. That he sees Astolfo and the others as landscape ornaments in Alcina's garden means that he shares their belief that a woman can be an earthly paradise and that her spurning of a lover can amount to an expulsion of him from Eden into a wooden and deathlike trance. Ruggiero is as blind as Astolfo to his own role in surrounding Alcina with a haze of magic powers. His altruistic nature, moreover, is particularly susceptible to making gods, goddesses, and devils out of other people. Other selves exercise extraordinary power over Ruggiero throughout the *Orlando Furioso,* so it is especially important for him to learn how to separate the influences and the claims he attributes to them from those they actually possess. He must learn to know his gods. In the Alcina episode, he confronts the power of his own sexual passion to distort his vision of other people. If he comes out of this confrontation able to regard women as human beings, not as wicked enchantresses or beneficent goddesses, he will have accomplished a great deal. His union with Bradamante will have entered the realm of possibility. The allusion to the Pier delle Vigne episode of the *Inferno* is serious, insofar as the immobilization of the mind by such delusions as Astolfo's and Ruggiero's can be said to be suicidal. After conversing with Astolfo, Ruggiero may be "expert and instructed" as the narrator says, and he may be "disposed and determined to use every means so that Alcina should not have sway over him" (6.56–57), but it is already clear that none of this forewarning and determination will have the slightest effect. What Ruggiero needs to fear most is not Alcina but his own radically distorted view of her.

When Ruggiero first glimpses the wall surrounding Alcina's territory, it seems to him to be made of gold, and just as the reader is about to pounce on the word "seems" [*par*] and confidently conclude that this wall is not what it seems to be, the narrator intervenes with his own opinion:

> Alcun dal mio parer qui si dilunga,
> e dice ch'ell'è alchimia; e forse ch'erra,
> et anco forse meglio di me intende:
> a me par oro, poi che sì risplende.
>
> (6.59)

> Some depart from my opinion here and say it is alchemy. Perhaps they err, and then again perhaps they are wiser than I. To me it seems to be gold, since it shines so.

It is true, says the narrator, that all that glitters is not gold, but one must remember, he insists, that gold does glitter. So the wall may be made of gold, and even if it is not, does it make any difference? The source of illusion here is not a wall or a woman, but Ruggiero himself. His combat with the horde of monstrosities guarding the exit from Alcina's domain makes this clear immediately. Alarmed by his own distorted perception of Astolfo's state, he regards all those who would urge him to stay and enjoy Alcina's gifts as grotesque, subhuman creatures, emblems of arrogance, lechery, sloth, drunkenness, gluttony, and so forth. Since the world contains many drunks and lechers, Ruggiero's vision is not altogether inaccurate. However, the partial truth of his vision only increases his difficulties, because the evidence the world provides him of the rectitude of his outlook only reinforces his essential blindness. It is much more important for him to realize that the sources of dissipation lie within himself than for him to shudder with horror at the vices of others and to lay all the blame for them on a woman. It is amusing to think of Ruggiero in his battle with these ugly folk as waging a temperance crusade and losing because human nature outnumbers and overwhelms him. A large part of the reason for his eventual submission to the allure of Alcina is his failure to realize that the enticements to lechery are not necessarily ugly, but can be genuinely attractive, just like the glittering wall of gold around Alcina's realm.

When Ruggiero decides not to use the magic shield against this "evil race" (6.66), so great in number it has no need of armor to overwhelm him, the narrator notes that he could easily have triumphed but that perhaps it is just as well that he preferred to use prowess instead of fraud. This is a curious assessment of the matter unless the word *frodo* (6.67) suggests that Ruggiero would have considered himself compromised by any assistance beyond his own abilities. If this is the case, then it is good that he does not use the shield, for using it would prevent him from experiencing the failure that shows him his weaknesses and teaches him how to pass beyond his distorted judgment of woman's power. He must not be shielded, so to speak, against this failure. Evil must win in this instance in order for evil later to be vanquished. Ruggiero will use the shield twice in order to escape from Alcina, but only after he has learned that sometimes it is necessary to use whatever help is available—at least until one has grown strong enough to manage by oneself. The forces ranged against Ruggiero in this scene are the ordinary calamities caused by human nature. Their defeat is not accomplished by identifying them in other people and combating their manifestations outside oneself. The real victory lies in discovering the susceptibility of one's own character to debasement. One of the main lessons of cantos 6 and 7 is that a person makes these discoveries in the school of experience, not by being "expert and instructed" in edifying moral allegories, and certainly not by being shielded from harm.

When the real challenge to Ruggiero's character appears, he is totally unprepared. His naiveté has made him believe that since vice is ugly, the enticements to it must also be ugly. So when Beauty and Grace enter the scene in the form of two young ladies, he is instantly disarmed. The appearance of these ladies does not bring about the ugly, destructive consequences he has attributed to woman's power. Instead, the ladies bring him relief from ugly visions and ask him to protect them from a genuinely ugly female creature, the giantess Erifilla, an emblem of female pride and rapaciousness. These beautiful, graceful ladies give Ruggiero the satisfaction of combating a figure that does correspond to his distorted view of women. Moreover, defeating Erifilla provides him with the satisfaction of thinking that he has fulfilled the promise upon which his very identity depends. He has performed an altruistic act of courtesy, subordinating his own welfare to the claims of someone in distress. However, the real distress of these ladies, in ordinary courtly terms, has to seem rather frivolous. It disturbs them that their pretty world is encumbered by proud, greedy women whose suitors make the very courtship of women seem an ugly business. Perhaps this is what the women mean when they say that the monstrosities Ruggiero was fighting are Erifilla's spawn. When Ruggiero topples Erifilla, his deed amounts to nothing more than a gesture, a snub. The ladies for whom he is fighting prevent his making anything more of the matter because they require nothing more than a gesture. The existence of the likes of Erifilla even has some advantages for them, because they seem all the prettier by comparison. If Ruggiero thinks he has performed a great deed at considerable risk to himself in this courtly pageant, it is only because he has accepted the fiction that there are women who have the power of giantesses to go galloping wolflike through the world and to transform men into wooden apparitions. His defeat of Erifilla completely disarms Ruggiero, for he thinks that he has triumphed over the worst there is to fear when, in truth, he has done nothing.

Ruggiero undergoes his induction into the experience of sensual self-indulgence by mistaking courtliness for courtesy, by confusing politeness with genuine altruism. Hence, he is able to give himself the illusion of difficulty in attaining Alcina. The narrator notes that the road to Alcina's palace is "somewhat difficult and rough" (7.8), the emphasis being on the "somewhat" at the beginning of the line and the diminutive form of "rough" [*aspretta*] at the end. More importantly, Ruggiero is now able to regard the sexual excitation he is soon to enjoy as being of greater significance than it is. Now he can regard it as the fulfillment of his ideal, just as he was able in the *Orlando Innamorato* to regard being knighted by Agramante as the fulfillment of all his hopes. However, he is only another victim of the law of paradox governing the majority of the *Furioso*'s characters. Instead of exercising his prowess nobly to the benefit of others, he winds up exercising it in bed, to his own great satisfaction until the pleasure begins to cloy. One lesson of Ruggiero's escape from Alcina's clutches is that repletion is one of the best antidotes for sexual enthusiasm.

For the time being, though, Ruggiero believes that he has attained the earthly paradise. It will take a while for him to realize that belief in the attainment of such a paradise leads only to blindness and starved cravings. This is the lesson learned by Senapo, that other seeker after the earthly paradise, whom the liberated Astolfo rescues from despair. The true nature of Alcina's realm is described the instant Ruggiero passes through its golden gateway:

Su per la soglia e fuor per le colonne
corron scherzando lascive donzelle,
che se i rispetti debiti alle donne
servasser più, sarian forse più belle.
Tutte vestite eran di verdi gonne,
e coronate di frondi novelle.
Queste, con molte offerte e con buon viso,
Ruggier fecero entrar nel paradiso:

che si può ben così nomar quel loco,
ove mi credo che nascesse Amore.
Non vi si sta se non in danza e in giuoco,
e tutte in festa vi si spendon l'ore:
pensier canuto né molto né poco
si può quivi albergare in alcun core:
non entra quivi disagio né inopia,
ma si sta ognor col corno pien la Copia.

Qui, dove con serena e lieta fronte
par ch'ognor rida il grazioso aprile,
gioveni e donne son: qual presso a fonte
canta con dolce e dilettoso stile;
qual d'un arbore all'ombra e qual d'un monte
o giuoca o danza o fa cosa non vile;
e qual, lungi dagli altri, a un suo fedele
discuopre l'amorose sue querele.

Per le cime dei pini e degli allori,
degli alti faggi e degl'irsuti abeti,
volan scherzando i pargoletti Amori:
di lor vittorie altri godendo lieti,
altri pigliando a saettare i cori

la mira quindi, altri tendendo reti;
chi tempra dardi ad un ruscel più basso,
e chi gli aguzza ad un volubil sasso.

(6.72–75)

Over the threshold and outside among the columns wanton girls run playfully, who would be more beautiful perhaps if they observed more the manners befitting ladies. They were all dressed in green gowns and crowned with fresh, leafy sprigs. With many offers and with good cheer, they made Ruggiero enter that paradise, / for such might well that place be called which I believe was the birthplace of Love. One stays not there save in dancing and playing, and there all hours are spent in festivity. A white-haired thought can lodge itself neither much nor little in any heart there. Death and discomfort enter not, but Plenty remains at all times with her horn replete. / In this spot, where it seems that with mild and joyful countenance gracious April is smiling all the time, young men and ladies are to be found: one, beside a spring, sings in a sweet, delicious manner; another, in the shade of a tree or hillside, plays or dances or amuses himself in some not ignoble way; and still another, apart from the rest, reveals his amorous complaints to a loyal friend. / All about the tops of the pines and laurels, the high beeches and bristly firs, tiny childlike Loves fly in sport, some rejoicing merrily over their victories, others taking aim thence to pierce hearts, and others placing nets. One below tempers his darts in a brook, and another sharpens them on a whetstone.

To youths who are experiencing sexual pleasure for the first time, this is the sort of place the world seems to be. This is a place where love is born, but not where it can develop. The cavortings of the infantile cupids exactly parallel the enjoyments of the young men and women in their perpetual Spring. These enjoyments inflame a never-changing emotion that breeds itself upon itself in a closed, incestuous circle. The absence of discomfort, want, and the cares of age marks the fragility of this paradise. No developing human being could remain in the condition it represents without eventually becoming grotesque even in his own eyes. Ruggiero has no need of being rescued from Alcina by outside intervention. It is enough for him to languish awhile and to grow tired of having "more than one tongue in his mouth" (7.29). Like all of her interventions in behalf of Bradamante throughout the *Furioso,* Melissa's fantastic rescue effort signifies nothing more than a movement of human nature, though not necessarily a predictable movement, for not all humans develop beyond the life of sexual obsession. In this case, Bradamante is assisted by Ruggiero's own sense of tedium and also, unexpectedly, by the very parent figure whose influence brought Ruggiero to Alcina in the first place.

Despite all of his truck with demons and his magical manipulations, Atlante is one of the most likeable figures in the *Orlando Furioso*. When Melissa appears to Ruggiero disguised as Atlante, she represents the way in which the influence of Atlante's protectiveness is thrown into confusion by the influence of his own paternal pride. On the one hand, more or less like every parent, Atlante has always been anxious to shield his child from the dangers of going into the world and accomplishing things there. A natural fear of mortality has always focused Atlante's attention on the perils his child will have to face upon growing up, and so the magician-parent's influence, still working within the child who is now a youth, tries to override nature's laws and arrest the youth's development by seeking a replica of the childhood state designed to satisfy the biological urges of an adult. This replica is Alcina's paradise, at once a young man's voluptuous interpretation of a parent's impossible wish and a fearfully efficient creator of boy-men and girl-women. However, the other side of Atlante's affection for Ruggiero enables the disguised Melissa to rebuke the boy-man for consenting to be sheltered in the first place:

> È questo dunque il frutto ch'io
> lungamente atteso ho del sudor mio?
>
> Di medolle già d'orsi e di leoni
> ti porsi io dunque li primi alimenti;
> t'ho per caverne et orridi burroni
> fanciullo avezzo a strangolar serpenti,
> pantere e tigri disarmar d'ungioni
> et a vivi cingial trar spesso i denti,
> acciò che dopo tanta disciplina
> tu sii l'Adone o l'Atide d'Alcina?
>
> (7.56–57)

Is this then the fruit I have waited for so long from my sweat? Did I give you your first nourishment from the marrow of bears and lions, did I make you accustomed as a child to strangling serpents in caverns and horrible gorges, to disarming panthers and tigers of their claws, and often to pulling out the tusks of wild boars still alive, so that after such discipline you should become the Adonis or the Atis of Alcina?

These lines echo those of the *Innamorato* (3.5.35–37) in which Ruggiero himself describes his childhood to Bradamante. Like the Ruggiero of the *Furioso,* the Atlante of the *Furioso* is the same character Boiardo created. Consequently, the Ruggiero languishing in Alcina's realm is subject, not only to the parental influence that always sheltered and separated him from the world but also to the influence of the parent who fostered and delighted in his competence to change the world. Within Ruggiero, these conflicting parental influences work like a kind of magic. The one lures him into a condition of arrested development, while the other sickens him with the consequences and drives him out into the world of action and accomplishment. That the latter influence should triumph in Ruggiero is for the most part inevitable and not the product of fortune or of any melodramatic rescue effort from without. Although he has had a proclivity for the juvenile delights of Alcina's paradise, it must be remembered that he would not have succumbed to them in the first place had he not mistaken them for the rewards of valorous conduct.

Bradamante's rescue of Ruggiero from that first enchanted palace in canto 2 could never have proved to be anything but abortive. Although Astolfo's part in restoring Orlando to his senses seems to suggest the contrary, no one can be rescued from himself in the *Furioso* by an outsider. The recollection of Bradamante's love (7.69) does add to Ruggiero's incentive to abandon Alcina, but it is *his* recollection after all. Furthermore, it is not immediately clear how effective that magic ring of reason has been in making Ruggiero reasonable. Spurred by an influence contrary to the one that let him indulge himself to repletion, he now experiences a repugnance as exaggerated as his former enjoyment. Here in canto 7 the ring plays a part similar to its role in Bradamante's inconsequential rescue effort in canto 2. It does not measure the powers of reason so much as it shows reason's limitations.

> Fece l'annel palese ancor, che quanto
> di beltà Alcina avea, tutto era estrano;
> estrano avea, e non suo, dal piè alla treccia:
> il bel ne sparve, e le restò la feccia.
>
> (7.70)

> The ring also made manifest that whatever beauty Alcina had was external, external and not her own, from her tresses to her feet. The beautiful disappeared, and the dregs were all that were left of her.

Now that Ruggiero is driven to abandon Alcina, reason enables him to see that he himself attributed to her all of the attractions she had for him. However, reason does not prevent him from attributing to her a repulsiveness as extreme as those attractions. As the following stanzas

Figures in Ariosto's Tapestry

insist, the ring of reason does not forestall Ruggiero's juvenile reaction against a woman for whom he once had a juvenile passion:

Come fanciullo che maturo frutto
ripone, e poi si scorda ove è riposto,
e dopo molti giorni è ricondutto
là dove truova a caso il suo deposto,
si maraviglia di vederlo tutto
putrido e guasto, e non come fu posto;
e dove amarlo e caro aver solia,
l'odia, sprezza, n'ha schivo, e getta via:

così Ruggier, poi che Melissa fece
ch'a riveder se ne tornò la fata
con quell'annello inanzi a cui non lece,
quando s'ha in dito, usare opra incantata,
ritruova, contra ogni sua stima, invece
de la bella che dianzi avea lasciata,
donna sì laida, che la terra tutta
né la più vecchia avea né la più brutta.

(7.71–72)

Just as the little boy, who hides some ripe fruit and then forgets where he put it and many days later is led back to the place and finds by chance his stores, wonders to see it all rotten and putrid and not as it was when he left it, and though once it was his habit to cherish it and hold it precious, now hates and despises it, finds it disgusting, and throws it away; just so Ruggiero, after Melissa had him return to view the enchantress with the help of that ring which on one's finger prohibits the use of enchantments, found, contrary to his every expectation, instead of the beauty he had left before, a woman so ugly that the entire earth contained not another more foul and decrepit.

By analogy, Ruggiero is the little boy who becomes disgusted upon learning that the precious object he stored away will not keep forever. However, the apple representing Alcina hardly deserves the little boy's disgust. The apple was only being an apple, good for temporary tasting, not for the permanent fulfillment of every desire. Reason, throughout Ruggiero's escape, is a flimsy support. It enters the field only after powerful irrational influences have held sway, then it serves only as a weak second to the stronger of those influences, and in a short time it is consumed by the very process it sought to assist. It would be nice, as the narrator suggests at the opening of canto 8, if we could always wear the ring of reason, but would we then be as well off as the narrator believes?

As a symbol, the magic ring is tantalizing, with its dual powers to grant its owner invisibility and vision to see through false appearances. However, it is impossible to assign it any consistent meaning for all of its uses throughout the *Furioso* or even to assign it a meaning at any particular time unless that meaning is already latent in the circumstances of the text. More often than not the ring underlines a trait, an impulse, or a dilemma of the character who happens to possess it. In the present case, the ring emphasizes that Ruggiero is a youth in the grip of influences mightier than he knows or can control. The conscious and deliberate life is still beyond his reach and will remain beyond him even after his visit to Logistilla. For the moment, however, he has learned caution. He has learned to be wary of projecting his ideals onto unfitting people and unfitting situations. In his exit from Alcina's realm, he employs stealth, having learned temporarily not to place so much trust in the sheer force of his own good intentions. At the boundary of her realm, he again meets a guardian, but this time he sees no horde of monstrosities. Instead, the simple figure of a youth on horseback out hunting with his falcon is enough to alarm him. He is just as comically fearful now of his susceptibility to wasting time in noble pastimes as he was confident before of his ability to rise above the temptations of human nature. So now he shields himself from his slightest weaknesses, fearing that if he does not, he will soon find himself plunged again into a life of squalid self-indulgence. As he advances over "unstable sand" (10.38) toward Logistilla's domain, leaving the earthly paradise farther and farther behind, the world seems more and more desolate to him by comparison until he is again accosted by temptation, this time in the form of three beautiful young ladies relaxing in the shade of an ancient tower. When he refuses their offers of ease, one of them, a "haughty lady" (10.42), charges him with being neither a knight nor a person of noble nature. However, this time, as opposed to his earlier encounter with "haughty Erifilla" (7.2), he remains imperturbable, for "he expects little honor from so vile a contest" (10.42). Honor is not to be found, he has learned, in courtly gesturing and in aristocratic pastimes. This is a considerable lesson, but it is only a negative one; it does not teach where honor is to be found.

Necessity brings about the journey to Logistilla's realm—everyone who escapes Alcina must go there. The narrative simply assumes that this journey from one extreme to another will take place. Although Ruggiero elects to undergo hardship in order to arrive there, he does not elect to go there in the first place. Logistilla's wisdom is acquired on the rebound, not as the result of free choice; hence, it is not likely to leave a very deep impression. What could be more natural than that a revulsion against puerile pleasures should bring on a yearning for the wisdom of age, and what could be more natural than that any wisdom acquired as a result should grow weaker with time as the original revulsion grows less and less intense? There is evidence, moreover, that Ruggiero's vision of Logistilla is just as distorted as his vision of Alcina ever was. The aged helmsman, "wise and learned from long experience" (10.44), who fends off Alcina's forces with the magic shield and carries Ruggiero to the "more stable sand" (10.57) of Logistilla's domain, promises Ruggiero that he will find a love in which desire will have nothing more to seek and will remain forever contented with its object. However, this was the promise of Alcina's paradise, just as it was the promise of the earthly paradise that Senapo went blind and hungry trying to attain. Logistilla's paradise, we discover, is also a place of perpetual spring, maintained with study and care "without need of the supernal motions" (10.63). But human beings, who must eventually contend with the necessities and the vicissitudes of time, can no more remain here than they can remain in Alcina's paradise. Each provides a temporary retreat from the challenges of life but gives no lasting benefits. Even after Alcina, Ruggiero's problem remains the problem of all youths. He is still seeking a permanent fulfillment of his desires, but all he can find is an anodyne for the inevitable disappointments of the quest.

Self-knowledge, the reward Logistilla offers her pupils, is certainly preferable to self-deception, the precondition for enjoying Alcina's bounty. However, self-knowledge by itself, unchallenged by the enticements and the demands of the world, can be a source of illusion in its own right, giving its possessor a sense of aerial detachment from the mishaps to which ordinary mortals are subject. Like the various uses to which the magic ring and the magic shield are put, the bridling of the hippogryph tantalizes the mind to come up with a suitable symbolic meaning. The event and the image seem momentous enough to require a solemn interpretation. However, the consequences of the event, as the text describes them, are surprisingly trivial. The amount of self-control Ruggiero achieves with his newfound self-knowledge is represented by his adventures astride the bridled hippogryph. The first of these, a trip around the world, suggests that Ruggiero has had his eyes opened wide enough to see that there is much of interest in the world. Self-knowledge has broadened his interests, so it has contributed to his development. However, the narrator is quick to note that Bradamante's role in that development has been shelved in order that these travels might take place (10.72), and he also suggests that there is something mildly self-indulgent about them:

Non crediate, Signor, che però stia
per sì lungo camin sempre su l'ale:
ogni sera all'albergo se ne gìa,
schivando a suo poter d'allogiar male.

(10.73)

Do not think, my lord, that therefore he remained aloft on wings all the time throughout such a long journey. He betook himself to an inn every evening, avoiding bad lodgings as best he could.

It is possible that self-knowledge aids in choosing comfortable lodgings, but one hopes that Ruggiero will find a more distinguished use of his new enlightenment.

We see one use to which Ruggiero puts his new knowledge almost immediately—when he stops to view the troops Rinaldo has marshaled in Great Britain to rescue Charlemagne from Agramante's siege. Whether or not Agramante's purposes in general are laudable or his motives concerning Ruggiero pure, Ruggiero has committed himself to Agramante's cause, so to preserve his integrity he must eventually meet the challenge of this commitment. The reinforcements gathering before his eyes are bent on destroying Agramante. Here Ruggiero is confronted with a responsibility to act, a responsibility to himself as well as to the cause he has promised to support. However, his only reaction is the detached amusement of a spectator at a parade. Furthermore, he indulges in a bit of showing off when the English troops express wonderment over his bizarre mount. With a kick of the spurs, he soars into the sky too far above the troops to be touched by anything but the wonderful spectacle he affords the eyes of lesser mortals.

Even before Ruggiero's encounter with Angelica and the orca, it is clear that his visit to Logistilla has been of questionable benefit. As far as Alcina and Logistilla are concerned, Ruggiero is the point at which opposites converge. As a result of Logistilla's guidance, Ruggiero's introspection has led him to frivolous detachment from the world of initiative and responsibility, whereas under Alcina's spell, his altruistic intentions led him to a quagmire of erotic self-indulgence. Obviously, Ariosto regards the domains of both enchantresses as dream worlds, and by choosing to depict them in the allegorical mode, he is suggesting that the absolutes upon which allegory is predicated are dreams. In reality, there is no land of perpetual spring. So Ruggiero's passage from one such land to another amounts to nothing more than his having had two dreams in one sleep. The reader who expects momentous changes in Ruggiero's character to result from his visit to Logistilla has been deceived by a dream. He has mistaken sleeping for waking, madness for sanity. In the Alcina-Logistilla sequence, more than anywhere else in the *Orlando Furioso,* Ariosto achieves the dramatic effect he aims for throughout: implication of the reader in the madness of the fictional characters. To the extent that we are deceived by Ruggiero's adventures with the enchantresses, the very act of reading, during which we think ourselves most alert, inquisitive, and discriminating, becomes nothing more than a period of dreaming from which we, like the dreaming Ruggiero, must be awakened. In an amusing way, the encounter with Angelica and the orca serves as a snap of the fingers, bringing Ruggiero and the reader back to consciousness.

Making this episode amusing and guiding the comedy of it is the double allusion to Ovid and Ovid's allegorizers.[4] The irony of the episode depends largely on the agreement between Ruggiero's deluded view of himself as master of the bridled hippogryph and the allegorizers' view of Ovid's Perseus as a prefiguration of Christ. It also depends on the circumstances of the encounter being purely Ovidian, leaving no room for a Christian moral significance to be attached to the scene. In his exhilaration over his newly acquired self-possession, Ruggiero sees himself as Angelica's savior, as a godlike redeemer unimplicated in the mundane evildoing that has brought her to her present straits. However, Ariosto's customary sympathy with women has caused the narrator to spell out clearly the events leading to Angelica's persecution (8.52–60). In general terms, they comprise a process that first makes women the victims of male pride and lust and then makes them the sufferers who must expiate the crimes committed against them. The orca symbolizes this process. Hence, Ruggiero thinks that he is descending from the clouds into this scene, but from Angelica's point of view, the Ovidian gallantries he uses toward her implicate him in the very evil from which he promises to rescue her. His gallantries suggest that he regards her as an amorous conquest, but she knows that it is not he who will have to suffer the penalties of that conquest. His burlesque battle with the orca suggests that he is not the person to overcome what the beast represents to Angelica and to other women whose nightmares it personifies. After a series of ineffectual assaults, which the narrator compares with those a fly might make against a mastiff on a hot day in August, Ruggiero finds that he cannot tell whether he is flying through the air or swimming in the sea (10.106). His medium and the orca's have become confused. When he is unable to do the creature the slightest harm even after having stunned it with the magic shield, it becomes impossible to regard him as a savior at all. Instead, Ruggiero's use of the shield only emphasizes his incompetence. When Angelica has to tell him to desist from his futile exercise and has to remind him to untie her before the orca wakes up, the reader must conclude that Ruggiero's ineffectiveness amounts to unwitting complicity in the sins represented by the orca. A little later, his attempt to take advantage of the naked girl confirms this conclusion. It was Proteus's rape of the daughter of the king of Ebuda (8.52) that started the train of events leading to Angelica's persecution and to the persecution of a great many other innocent women.

Clearly, Ruggiero can still confuse self-indulgent motives with altruistic intentions. His appeal to Angelica after her disappearance emphasizes the confusion:

> Ingrata damigella, è questo quello
> guiderdone—dicea—che tu mi rendi?
> che più tosto involar vogli l'annello,
> ch'averlo in don. Perché da me nol prendi?
> Non pur quel, ma lo scudo e il destrier snello
> e me ti dono, e come vuoi mi spendi:
> sol che 'l bel viso tuo non mi nascondi.
> Io so, crudel, che m'odi, e non rispondi.
>
> (11.8)

> Ungrateful damsel, is this the reward, said he, you grant me, that you would sooner steal the ring than have it as a gift? Why do you not accept it from me? Not only it, but my shield and my swift warhorse and myself I give you, and you may use me as you please, if only you will conceal from me your beautiful face. I know, cruel one, that you hate me, and you do not answer.

Evidently, this stanza moved Galileo very much, for his note on it exclaims, "O divinissimo uomo," in tribute to Ariosto, whose remarkable consistency in his characterization of Ruggiero merits the compliment.[5] Ruggiero offers himself to Angelica just as he offered himself to the ladies who asked him to fight Erifilla. However, this time the context renders his statement unmistakably comical, since Ruggiero's intention has so clearly been to take something from Angelica, and not give anything, much less himself, away. In fact, this comedy, along with the Ovidian gallantries he used earlier, suggests that Ruggiero may have learned something from Alcina and Logistilla after all. Alcina deserves credit for having taught Ruggiero that sexual gratification per se is more the reward of a game well-played than the fulfillment of a cherished ideal, and Logistilla deserves credit for having endowed him with enough self-possession to join in the game, even if he loses everything at the finish, including his bridled hippogryph. He exhibits the main benefit of his experiences with both enchantresses when he picks himself up after his losses and goes about his business. Instead of remaining infatuated with Angelica, as Orlando has, Ruggiero moves on. No matter how enticing they may be, dreams are insubstantial, and Ruggiero has had his share of imaginary paradises. He has learned that they leave one waving one's arms in thin air offering to barter one's all for a response that will never come.

Mitigating Ruggiero's cruder purposes in his encounter with Angelica, are his desire to be the rescuer and his presentation of the ring to Angelica as defense against the effects of the magic shield. If his intention to rape Angelica had been stronger than his intention to rescue her, it is unlikely that he would have shown so much consideration. The entire episode is morally ambiguous. On the one hand, Ruggiero's urge to play the Christlike savior blinds him to his being implicated in the evil he combats; on the other hand, were it not for his intervention, Angelica would have been devoured by the orca. Unalloyed honor, Ariosto seems to be insisting, can never be the outcome of even the highest services one person renders unto another, for one's relations with others are never simply and clearly motivated. We give and we take with the same gesture. The self that wins honor in the service of others, the altruistic self, may be attainable, but not without constant peril of blind submission to one's baser impulses. Furthermore, a potentially tragic irony hovers over Ruggiero. Narcissism is inescapable in the process of fashioning the self, but it is all the more apparent in the person striving for altruism because of the contradiction it poses. Can a person consciously shape an altruistic self without becoming so self-absorbed as to forget the needs of those he wishes to help?

This question bears directly on that other question of consuming interest to Ariosto as to what there is in the world to believe in. If, in the absence of Providence, self-creation is the lot of man, and if even the best of men cannot shape his identity without falling into a miasma of self-absorption, then faith is impossible unless it takes the form of Rodomonte's self-deification. Through the episodes involving Alcina, Logistilla, and Angelica, Ariosto exposes Ruggiero, his prime example of the man of good will, to challenges that repeatedly prove to be too much for him. At first glance, Ariosto seems to be attempting to convince his readers that there is no point in asking whether anything can be believed in, for even if there is something, men are too obsessed with themselves to perceive it. When Ruggiero wanders off from his encounter with Angelica only to become trapped in Atlante's palace of illusions (again because of his desire to play the knight in shining armor coming to a helpless damsel's rescue), one wonders if betrayal by the Maganza clan, when it finally happens, will not be anticlimactic, considering the repeated self-betrayals that will have preceded it. It seems as if Ruggiero has come full circle, from one palace of illusions to another, despite the apparently momentous events intervening.

Yet there is a change. With his attention focused on Bradamante, Ruggiero has passed from the pursuit of a general, all-consuming, instantaneous fulfillment of his quest for selfhood, from the pursuit of what could only be an anodyne, to concentration on specific responsibilities regarding a specific commitment. Astolfo's liberation of the captives from Atlante's palace of illusions represents for Ruggiero a lucid interval. From the moment of his confrontation with Bradamante in the clearing left by the dissolution of Atlante's palace, he is never again to regard her in generic terms as a damsel in distress. Instead, he treats her as another person whose demands upon his attention and his loyalty may have far more momentous consequences for the formation of his character than the obscure and illusory charms of Alcina, Logistilla, and Angelica. This movement from the general to the particular represents, for Ruggiero, a passage from fantasy to reality, from innocence to experience, from obsession to awareness and judgment. His failures with Angelica and the enchantresses thrust him into a world of other people where he must learn to discriminate among commitments, where he must endure conflict, and where he will never again find a retreat into the solipsism of his former days. The youth who descended from that mountaintop hiding place in the *Orlando Innamorato* has finally come into the open. Ruggiero's experiences throughout the first half of the *Furioso* have brought him to the point where he is ready to begin to profess faith in a world outside himself.

The Failure of Principle

It aids the drama of the *Orlando Furioso* that Ruggiero comes to his senses in the canto preceding Orlando's thunderous loss of wit, making it seem that the cause of those who bear the name of the faithful is truly doomed. With Ruggiero's might added to that of Mandricardo, Rodomonte, Ferraù, Gradasso, and Marfisa, what chance has Charlemagne in the absence of his most powerful knight? For a moment it looks as if

Ruggiero will ride off to baptism and marriage into the Christian cause, but he soon learns that life is not so simple. While in the grip of obsession his mind was free of conflict, but now that the world has entered his consciousness he must find a way to balance the alternatives it forces upon him. He is summoned by Agramante, who finds himself surrounded by his enemies and on the verge of defeat. Ironically, these enemies mainly consist of the British reinforcements that earlier had provided Ruggiero with an entertaining parade as they were mustering. Now they provide the occasion that plunges him into the sophistries and the compromises that are unavoidable to anyone who tries to meet conflicting commitments. Stanzas 86–92 of canto 25 contain the excuses Ruggiero conveys by letter to Bradamante to explain his failure to meet her as appointed at the abbey of Vallombrosa for his baptism. As the one to whom a promise is to be broken, Bradamante is the offended party, but Ruggiero argues that she is as much the cause of her being offended as he is, because now that they are to become one soul in two bodies through marriage, he is more than ever obliged to protect his honor from being stained. Now not only he, but she as well, will receive the blame for any misdeed of his, and blame should in no way be attached to a lady so pure and honest as she. To desert his sovereign in the hour of need would, he trusts she can see, be infinitely blameworthy. So it is as much for her sake as for his own that he must break his promise to her and go off to support the cause of her enemies. Faith can only be kept, Ruggiero implies, by being broken.

If Ruggiero were to let well enough alone at this point and leave his sophistical excuse to sink or swim according to Bradamante's taste or distaste for flattery, he might win her assent, but he would certainly lose the reader's good will. To his credit, he rambles on:

In simili parole si diffuse
Ruggier, che tutte non so dirvi a pieno;
e seguì con molt'altre, e non concluse
fin che non vide tutto il foglio pieno.

(25.92)

In like words Ruggiero poured himself out, so that I cannot tell you them all in full, and he followed with others aplenty, not concluding until he saw that the paper was covered.

Here the narrator suggests that Ruggiero is sufficiently aware of the hollowness of his words to wish to do something to fill the void, if only by supplying more words. However, his continued pleading only makes the hollowness and his confusion all the more apparent. He says that he wishes to silence the ignorant people who will attribute his baptism to expediency if he goes over to Charlemagne while fortune favors the Christian cause. They will say that he never served either Agramante or Charlemagne for any reason but personal gain. Of course, the reader is compelled to ask why Ruggiero should heed the opinion of the vulgar at all if it is the product of ignorance. Would it not be more courageous to disregard public opinion and trust in what one knows to be the purity of one's motives? Ruggiero's rambling words reveal him to be in the predicament of all who seek honor. He wishes to be as highly thought of as possible by other people, but he is concerned about doing what he himself deems right. He is caught in a conflict between appearance and reality, and there is no clear line of demarcation between the two, for honor, in the world of affairs, depends upon the opinion of one's fellow men. He can no more disregard appearances than he can privately neglect to make moral distinctions. He sums up his dilemma when he tells Bradamante that as soon as he has helped lift the siege from the African camp he will seek "convenient reasons, and also just ones" (25.91) to return to her. Reasons convenient for appearance' sake and, at the same time, just by the standard of a personal conviction are likely to take much longer to arrive at than he thinks.

The sophistries Ruggiero uses in order to placate Bradamante are forgivable if one takes into account the difficulty of resolving this conflict. Instead of implicating Bradamante in his decision to delay the baptism, it would have been more honest for him to say simply that he trusted her to understand the sincerity of his motives. An appeal to her faith would have been more attractive than an appeal to her self-interest. However, he has not yet reached that stage of development at which he becomes aware of the complicated mutuality of faith. This is a lesson reserved for the Leone episode. For the moment, it is more important for him to demonstrate his own loyalty to others than to trust in the loyalty of others to himself. Having just emerged from his shell of self-absorbed delusion, he naturally seeks to prove that he is aware of others' need of him and neglects to take into account his own need of them. Consequently, from the moment Astolfo liberates him from the palace of illusions, he becomes involved in a flurry of activity, undoing the unjust law of Pinabello's lady, rescuing Ricciardetto, and going on to rescue Malagigi and Viviano. His decision to go to Agramante's aid only conforms with the trend of his recent behavior. Faith's actives are his main concern, not faith's passives.

The cost of this imbalance is high. For a principle's sake, for honor's sake, Ruggiero compromises in the direction of creating correct appearances. To make demonstrations is more important, for the moment, than to follow the dictates of his conscience. The scene in which he throws the magic shield down a well because it has enabled him effortlessly to defeat the champions of Pinabello's lady emphasizes the cost of too punctilious a concern with appearing honorable. These champions—Sansonetto, Guidon Selvaggio, Grifone, and Aquilante— were coerced by Pinabello into giving their word to execute his lady's vindictive scheme, that of forcing all female travelers through her domain to disrobe and all males to abandon their armor and their steeds. So, on the one hand, these knights are innocent of any wicked intent and are even ashamed of the conditions under which they must gang up on their opponent to finish him off if one of their number alone is unable to defeat him. On the other hand, having given their word, they think it would be dishonorable not to keep it. Their position is absurd. For honor's sake, they dishonor themselves, with never a thought that the circumstances in which they became obligated to Pinabello might absolve them of their oath. However, far from serving as a lesson and a warning to Ruggiero that his obligation to Agramante is neither as binding as he believes nor as ennobling as he hopes, these ridiculous champions provide, in his opinion, a fine opportunity for him to display his prowess. When the shield accidentally becomes exposed and stuns them, Ruggiero reacts with disappointment and shame—a shame no less absurd than his opponents' punctilious concern with their honor. Though foolish in the extreme, they are no more deserving of mortal punishment than is Ruggiero himself for his unexamined allegiance to Agramante. Nevertheless, Ruggiero burns with shame because he has lost the opportunity to bash in their heads for a mistake similar to the one he made when he wrote his letter to Bradamante and took off to defend the African camp.

This scene is a parable whose point is lost on Ruggiero, and the parable cuts surprisingly close, despite its brevity and its apparently casual placement in the narrative, to one of the *Furioso*'s main questions. Is faith in a principle desirable, constructive, or even possible? In the absence of a Providential order, can there be any determinant of a principle besides human judgment (human judgment that so often errs), and can the judgment of the individual ever be free of doubt, doubt that can be allayed only through an appeal to other human judgments? In the *Furioso,* these questions resolve themselves in the dissolution of principles in the acid of human experience. No human being can lead a life of loyalty to a principle without constantly seeking the reassurance of his fellows, to the point where reassurance becomes more important than the principle itself. Appearance becomes more important than reality, public opinion more important than conscience, and subterranean behavior the result of a sincere wish to fulfill a lofty ideal. Besides this unwilled, ineluctable hypocrisy, the individual suffers in his perception of others. Associating promiscuously with those who provide reassurance, he loses the ability to discriminate between wise and foolish, between loving and treacherous, natures. The most distasteful aspect of Ruggiero's desertion of Bradamante is that he values her opinion less than that of the ignorant people. The highest price of honor, or any other principle publicly to be upheld, is paid with this loss of discernment into human nature—a loss that can come perilously close to the loss of faith itself.

Ruggiero's decision to aid Agramante plunges him almost immediately into a Hobbesian war of all against all. No amount of assistance from Ruggiero could solve Agramante's worst problem, his lack of authority over his own strongest warriors, all of whom have private interests more compelling than their allegiance to him. No sooner has Ruggiero set out than he meets Rodomonte, who has stolen his horse from the defenseless lady-in-waiting to whom Bradamante entrusted its care. When Ruggiero asks for it back, he has to suffer a lecture concerning "that which a faithful knight must do in his lord's behalf" (26.96). He would not be so worried about a horse, Rodomonte implies, if he had the interest of his sovereign at heart. He should take his example from Mandricardo, who also happens to be present, and from Rodomonte himself, who have deferred quarrels with each other until they can rescue Agramante. However, the irony of this insult scarcely has time to sink in before Mandricardo notices the white eagle painted on Ruggiero's shield and challenges his right to bear that emblem. Of course, Ruggiero, whose main motive for coming to Agramante's assistance in the first place is to demonstrate his honor, is not about to dishonor himself publicly by abandoning his horse and his shield. So a battle ensues that might easily have ended in his death if the demon injected by Malagigi into Doralice's mount had not sent Mandricardo and Rodomonte galloping off in pursuit of her. From this brief plunge into the discord rampant in Agramante's camp it is clear that Ruggiero has failed to consider the practicability of remaining loyal to a sovereign whose incapacity to command loyalty turns his closest allies into his worst enemies. Nor has Ruggiero considered the dangers of this course.

The great battle with Mandricardo in canto 30 leaves Ruggiero so severly injured, despite his victory, that the reader cannot help but reflect on the probable consequences of the earlier battle with Mandricardo and Rodomonte, and marvel at Ruggiero's sheer good fortune in the battle's breaking up. Furthermore, the victory over Mandricardo in canto 30 casts Ruggiero in a distinctly unpleasant light. Agramante pleads with both warriors at least to defer their single combat for five or six months until Charlemagne can be defeated once and for all, but each refuses because "he deems an accord of that kind opprobrious to the man who gives his consent first" (30.30). Once having compromised in the direction of appearances, Ruggiero becomes caught in a downward spiral. It was for the sake of appearances that he abandoned Brada-mante to go to the aid of his sovereign, and now it is for the sake of appearances again that he refuses to obey and serve that sovereign. Furthermore, the narrator notes in stanzas 43 and 44 that the combat might have been avoided if Ruggiero had not been so quick to rise in the morning and sound his challenge. Doralice had prevailed on Man-dricardo during the night to accept a truce if Agramante asked him again. However, Ruggiero's impatience to fight impels him to sound his challenge before Agramante has a chance to intervene. Here Ruggiero's desire to create the appearance of honor culminates in the utter defeat of what started out as a sincere intention to be honorable and to be of use to others. Mandricardo's ability to wound Ruggiero so severely that the spectators wonder whether Ruggiero has won the battle and wheth-er he is alive or dead suggests that in Ariosto's opinion Ruggiero has sunk morally almost to Mandricardo's level and therefore has almost been responsible for his own destruction. He receives the thigh wound that causes him the most pain the instant after he glories in Mandricar-do's desperate act of casting away his shield to take his sword in both hands:

Ah—disse a lui Ruggier—senza più basti
a mostrar che non merti quella insegna,
ch'or tu la getti, e dianzi la tagliasti;
né potrai dir mai più che ti convegna.

(30.61)

"Ah," Ruggiero said to him, "you have proven once and for all that you do not deserve that emblem, for now you toss it aside, and you slashed it before. Nor will you ever be able to say again that it suits you."

Here his whole attention has been distracted to the point where he focuses on nothing but an eagle painted on a shield.

Far from finding those convenient and just reasons for returning to Bradamante, Ruggiero, being severely wounded, is now obligated to Agramante for the preservation of his very life. Canto 36, in which

Ruggiero finally confronts Bradamante after their long separation, opens on an ominous note:

Convien ch'ovunque sia, sempre cortese
sia un cor gentil, ch'esser non può altrimenti;
che per natura e per abito prese
quel che di mutar poi non è possente.
Convien ch'ovunque sia, sempre palese
un cor villan si mostri similmente.
Natura inchina al male, e viene a farsi
l'abito poi difficile a mutarsi.

It needs must be that a noble heart, wherever it is, will always be courteous, for it cannot be otherwise; from nature and custom it has acquired that which it has not the strength to change. Similarly, it needs must be that a base heart, wherever it is, will always reveal itself plainly. Nature inclines toward evil, and the habit becomes difficult afterwards to change.

Ostensibly, this is written as a compliment to Bradamante for her courtesy toward the knights she has vanquished before the city of Arles, courtesy that contrasts favorably with the vicious behavior of the Venetian mercenaries of Ariosto's day. However, the passage applies equally well, and more ominously, to Ruggiero, who has grown more and more deeply enmeshed in an evil cause. Ruggiero's noble heart may make it impossible for him to change and to espouse evil openly, but Nature inclines toward evil, so that with the passage of time Ruggiero may find it harder and harder to free himself of his obligations to an evil sovereign. And all the while there is the unforeseen. Bradamante has already asked, after reading the letter Ruggiero wrote to reassure her of his return, whether anyone has the power to reassure her that accidents will not prevent him from ever returning, accidents being especially likely in time of war (30.81). By the time Ruggiero confronts Bradamante outside the city of Arles, the worst possible accident that could befall him is in preparation—Astolfo is returning from the moon with Orlando's wits.

Since a clash between Ruggiero and Orlando is inevitable if Ruggiero remains in Agramante's service, the close of canto 36 is especially grim. Atlante's voice, issuing from beyond the tomb, tells Ruggiero in the presence of Bradamante and Marfisa that it was Agramante's grandfather, father, and uncle who had murdered his parents—and Marfisa's parents as well, for we learn here that she is Ruggiero's sister. Upon hearing this, Marfisa upbraids Ruggiero for having lived in the pay of a person upon whom he should have revenged himself long ago. In her opinion, the sins of the father should be revenged upon the son, and she can scarcely wait to make herself Christian like her murdered father and go in quest of Agramante's blood. In contrast to Marfisa's impetuosity, Ruggiero's reaction to Atlante's news seems a model of dilatory and prevaricating diplomacy:

Ruggiero accortamente le rispose
che da principio questo far dovea;
ma per non bene aver note le cose,
come ebbe poi, tardato troppo avea.
Ora, essendo Agramante che gli pose
la spada al fianco, farebbe opra rea
dandogli morte, e saria traditore;
che già tolto l'avea per suo signore.

Ben, come a Bradamante già promesse,
promettea a lei di tentare ogni via,
tanto ch'occasione, onde potesse
levarsi con suo onor, nascer faria.
E se già fatto non l'avea, non desse
la colpa a lui, m'al re di Tartaria,
dal qual ne la battaglia che seco ebbe
lasciato fu, come saper si debbe.

(36.80–81)

Ruggiero answered her adroitly that he had wanted to do this from the start, but through not having understood the issues as now he did, he had waited too long. Now that it was Agramante who had placed his sword at his side, he would be committing an evil deed to put him to death, and he would be a traitor, for he had already chosen him as his lord. Indeed he promised her, just as he had already promised Bradamante, to try every means whereby he might cause the occasion to arise whence he might extricate himself with honor. And if he had not already done it, she should not lay the blame on him, but on the king of Tartary, by whom he was left, in the battle he had had with him, in a condition that everyone should remember.

On the one hand, Ruggiero's decision not to punish Agramante for his father's crimes casts him in a better light than if he were to follow Marfisa's lead. Ruggiero has pledged his faith to Agramante and received benefits in return, not the least of which has been the care he has received for his wounds after the battle with Mandricardo. On the other hand, to blame Mandricardo and the wounds for his not having discovered sooner an occasion for parting company with Agramante is totally specious. His own thirst for honor was as much the cause of those wounds as was Mandricardo's violence. Far from looking for an occasion to leave or trying (as the text suggests) to make one arise, Ruggiero merely played his part in the private quarrels so debilitating to Agramante's cause. He neither kept faith with Bradamante nor served Agramante well. And now he is insisting on returning to the same futile course just when invincible powers are building to destroy Agramante and all of his followers.

After Ruggiero returns to Arles, abandoning Bradamante for a second time, the narrator's lecture on honor in the proem to canto 38 sounds forced and convoluted. The very pains the narrator takes to defend Ruggiero's choice suggest that the choice is not above suspicion. Stanza 4, the heart of the narrator's argument, is full of syntactical contortions:

> Che se l'amante de l'amato deve
> la vita amar più de la propria, o tanto
> (io parlo d'uno amante a cui non lieve
> colpo d'Amor passò più là del manto);
> al piacer tanto più ch'esso riceve
> l'onor di quello antepor deve, quanto
> l'onore è di più pregio che la vita,
> ch'a tutti altri piaceri è preferita.

> For if a lover ought to love the life of his beloved more than his own, or just as much (I speak of a lover in whom Love's not light stroke has traveled deeper than his mantle), he ought also to value the honor of his beloved more than the pleasure he receives, by just so much as honor is of greater value than life, which is the pleasure preferred above all others.

Reading this, one is mesmerized by the workings of a fast and agile tongue. If a lover loves his beloved's life more than his own, or just as much, says the narrator, then he must value his beloved's honor more than his own pleasure by just so much as he deems honor to be of greater value than life, which is the pleasure preferred above all others. These lines say emphatically that Bradamante, if she is a true lover, ought to consider Ruggiero's honor more important than whatever pleasure she hopes to derive from his company. This is plain enough. So why then does the narrator bring in the propositions that honor is more important than life and that life is a mere pleasure, albeit the most delectable of pleasures? If the reader were disposed from the start to think that Bradamante should relinquish Ruggiero's company, then the reader would probably regard these propositions as proofs. However, the circumstances of the narrative up to this point—Bradamante's constancy, Agramante's ineptitude, Ruggiero's near death at the hands of Mandricardo, and worse dangers looming over the horizon—make it most unlikely that the reader will be so disposed. Furthermore, in the proem to canto 38, the narrator assumes that the gentle ladies in his audience are hostile to Ruggiero's decision. (The narrator slyly equates us all with gentle ladies whose judgment may be presumed to be biased!) So why would Ariosto cause his narrator to make so complicated an argument, unless, that is, he wished to call the complicating factors themselves into question? The plainer argument in these circumstances would have been the more effective one. Ariosto clearly wished his narrator's argument to be ineffective.

Ariosto causes us to question whether honor is always more important than life and whether life is merely a pleasure. Since our approval of Ruggiero's departure depends on our consent to these propositions, we hesitate just long enough in granting consent to realize how dangerous they are, to realize how easy it is to throw one's life away for appearance' sake and for the sake of a shibboleth. Life is more than a luxury, we argue, and principles kill. Ariosto makes his point by causing his narrator to argue too extensively against it, and as a result we come away more convinced than ever that Ruggiero's choice is a mistake. We wonder if he has valued his own life and his allegiance to Bradamante as highly as he should have. We wonder if lives are not the important thing and principles often a dangerous luxury. When at the opening of canto 41 the narrator seeks to exalt Ruggiero's honor by comparing it with a fine perfume that lingers in the beard for several days, we realize how fatuous his point of view has been all along.[6]

Subsequent events prove that Ruggiero has overestimated his usefulness to Agramante and underestimated the strength of his attachment to Bradamante. The single combat in cantos 38 and 39 between Rinaldo and Ruggiero to determine the outcome of the entire war ends more decisively than it seems. The real battle is between the principle of honor Ruggiero has invoked all along and his personal attachment to Bradamante, and the latter is the decisive victor. Ruggiero's fear of injuring Rinaldo and thereby alienating Bradamante's affection causes the display of half-hearted fighting that alarms Agramante and induces him to break the truce. Seeing Ruggiero fail him, Agramante deludes himself that Rodomonte will come to his rescue. Of course, Ruggiero's display dishonors him in the eyes of those he most wishes to impress, but in the reader's eyes it redeems him. Finally, there has been a showdown, and loyalty to another person has triumphed over an all too easily corruptible dedication to principle. It is understandable that Ruggiero should still not wish to abandon Agramante altogether. To the degree that he has disappointed Agramante, he shares responsibility for the breaking of the oath, and to the degree that his fighting has appeared timorous, he has reason to fear that his abandoning Agramante "may be ascribed to his cowardice and fear" (40.67). He does, however, maintain his oath to Rinaldo insofar as he refuses to rescue Agramante's troops from the ensuing slaughter, preferring to remain aloof and question witnesses as to which side broke the truce. Hearing from everyone that it was Agramante's side, he should, in order to fulfill the oath completely, transfer his loyalty to Charlemagne. His failure to do so on the spot is not explained, as the narrator declares, by the fact that duty and honor weigh more with him than conjugal love (40.68), but by a motive that has not been mentioned up to this point. "Ruggiero loves Agramante," we read in stanza 65 of canto 40, just as later we read in stanza 74 that Ruggiero loves the Saracen kings he liberates from Dudone. It is not duty or honor but pure compassion that explains Ruggiero's continued attachment to Agramante at this point. From now on personal attachments will dominate Ruggiero's behavior.

Other Persons

Ariosto discounts any religious significance of Ruggiero's baptism on the hermit's island. Ariosto's wise old men, though ever so congenial, almost always miss the point. For Ruggiero, baptism is the most direct means of expressing his strongest emotion, his love for Bradamante, and not an initiation into any formal religious life. His baptism can be regarded as an initiation only inasmuch as it brings him into the fellowship of Bradamante's relatives and friends. His real conversion has already taken place before he meets the hermit. In the storm that overtakes him on his way to Africa, he confronts death, and as a result of that confrontation he is forced to admit the priority of his own strongest feelings over any lingering desire to appear honorable in other men's eyes. In an earlier episode of the *Furioso,* the fear of imminent death by drowning taught Ariodante to trust his own feelings despite appearances, and now Ruggiero is learning the same lesson. Not only does he join the fellowship of Orlando, Rinaldo, and the other Christian warriors, but more importantly, he joins those like Ariodante, Brandimarte, and Zerbino, who have made *fede* their purpose in life. It is no accident that Ruggiero's conversion is simultaneous with Brandimarte's

Figures in Ariosto's Tapestry

funeral, for by the time of his conversion, Ruggiero has evolved into another Brandimarte. Orlando sails from the funeral of his friend, of whom he has told Fiordiligi,

> quei Decii, e quel nel roman foro absorto,
> quel sì lodato Codro dagli Argivi,
> non con più altrui profitto e più suo onore
> a morte si donàr, del tuo signore,
>
> (43.174)

> those Decii, and that man swallowed up in the Roman forum, and that Codrus so praised by the Argives did not give themselves over to death with more benefit to others and with more honor to themselves than did your lord,

only to find a reincarnation of the dead man. Some readers prefer the *Furioso* of 1516, without the Leone episode, to the version of 1532 because the 1516 version more effectively shows the phoenixlike emergence of the new Ruggiero as he replaces that other man of "tanta fede e tanto amor." In the older version, Ruggiero's baptism leads directly to his marriage and his defeat of Rodomonte, a victory that, because of its placement in the text near Brandimarte's death, seems all the more to be a vindication of the dead man's values. Ruggiero, the slayer of Mandricardo, and thereby the avenger of Zerbino, was also the vindicator of Brandimarte's altruism.

We must assume that Ariosto would never have disrupted the earlier *Furioso*'s dramatic conclusion without good reason. Perhaps he felt that the drama, though powerful, lacked substance because Ruggiero's character required further definition. Forty cantos of the *Furioso,* representing all there was in the earlier editions had traced Ruggiero's development through a period of errancy, defining what he was to become chiefly by weeding out of his character all elements antithetical to the goal to be attained. Ariosto must have felt that the goal itself, along with its own special problems, required analysis. Whatever the case, Pio Rajna's observation that the Leone episode and its attendant circumstances represent Ariosto at his most original and most ingenious is truer to the text than the complaints of most other critics that the episode is thematically and stylistically dissonant with the rest of the *Furioso.*[7] One usually hears that the episode attenuates the drama and tone of the narrative by introducing tedious bourgeois themes (conflict between the older and younger generations, between carefree romance and middle-class stability, between love and obedience, and so forth), and one also hears that nothing is added to Ruggiero's character. If a defense is attempted it usually refers to the worn-out humanist debate over Nature and Fortune. Apart from the fact that Bradamante's obedience to her parents in the Leone episode is not so very great at all, and apart from the fact that Charlemagne, venerable for his age, if for nothing else, lends crucial assistance to the young lovers—that is, apart from the facts altogether—a certain perfunctory Marxist slant distorts the Italian criticism of the past twenty years, causing the point of the Leone episode to be missed. Certainly, it raises issues other than those that have been the subject of recent complaint.

The issue of main concern in the Leone episode is the *fede* theme. By the beginning of the episode, Ruggiero has transferred his allegiance from principles to people, but this does not mean that he yet understands how to conduct himself in his new character. The terrible imbroglio that puts Ruggiero on the verge of suicide is not really caused by any ambitious matchmaking on the part of Bradamante's parents. Instead, it is Ruggiero himself who creates the potentially tragic confusion when he dashes off to murder Leone. Despite a written assurance from Bradamante that she will never be anyone else's but his, he fears that she will submit to the coercion of her parents. All of the evidence of resourcefulness and determination she has given throughout the narrative is not enough to allay his fears. When Charlemagne accedes publicly to Bradamante's plea and decrees that she must marry the man who can defeat her in combat, Ruggiero is already half a continent away, at the mercy of a woman whose son he has killed in battle. On account of his rash departure, he loses an easy opportunity to obtain Bradamante's hand and ends up instead beholden for his life to the very man he set out to murder. The point of the story is Ruggiero's lapse of faith. The sequence of events makes it clear that if he had trusted Bradamante, she would have been able to let him defeat her in battle. As it is, his lack of confidence in her turns him into the instrument by which her resourcefulness is undone. From the Leone episode, Ruggiero learns almost at the cost of his life that faith demands passivity: one's faith is defective if it lacks passive trust in the person to whom one is pledged.

Faith in another person, as opposed to faith in one's own delusions or faith in a principle, entails relinquishing autonomy—placing of one's life in someone else's hands and trusting that person to accomplish one's desires. This is the condition, as we have seen, that Rinaldo, the prudent man, studiously seeks to avoid. It is the condition in which Brandimarte dies, having placed his life in Orlando's hands. It is a condition inconceivable to the likes of Rodomonte. The paradox it implies is the scriptural paradox: to find oneself, one must lose oneself. The irony of Ruggiero's plight in the Leone episode is crushing. Having offered himself throughout the *Furioso* to Agramante, to the fair ladies of Alcina's realm who represent Beauty and Grace, to Alcina herself, to Logistilla, and finally and foolishly to Angelica, Ruggiero stops short of committing his welfare to Bradamante. Throughout the narrative he has been prompt to offer himself to others for the purpose of persuading others to place their faith in him, but when the real test of his faith occurs, when he should trust Bradamante, he falters, even though she has repeatedly proven herself loyal. The price of his failure is the loss of his identity and very nearly the loss of his life. He is forced to fight "under false colors and under another's name" (45.55) for a cause that spells the destruction of all he holds most dear. This is a crystallization of the position he has been in throughout the latter half of the *Furioso* while fighting for Agramante. Now, however, he is stripped of any illusion that time, fortune, or compromise will come to his aid.

What redeems Ruggiero is his allegiance to Leone, whom the narrator justly declares to be a man of lofty and sublime spirit (44.91). Leone, ignorant of Ruggiero's identity, persuades him to assist in a fraudulent scheme to obtain Bradamante, but this misdeed is mitigated by his affection for Ruggiero, despite his being an enemy, and by his rescue of him from certain torment and death. Since Leone is superior to battlefield enmities, he realizes, as he sees Ruggiero marshaling the Bulgars to a victory over his own troops, that although "the warrior may be giving aid to these enemies of his, he is not on that account one of them" (44.90). His first words to Ruggiero in the dungeon express a selfless devotion unsurpassed even by Brandimarte or Ariodante:

> Leon Ruggier con gran pietade abbraccia,
> e dice: "Cavallier, la tua virtute
> indissolubilmente a te m'allaccia
> di voluntaria eterna servitute;
> e vuol che più il tuo ben, che 'l mio, mi piaccia,
> né curi per la tua la mia salute,
> e che la tua amicizia al padre e a quanti
> parenti io m'abbia al mondo, io metta inanti.
>
> Io son Leone, acciò tu intenda, figlio
> di Costantin, che vengo a darti aiuto,
> come vedi, in persona, con periglio
> (se mai dal padre mio sarà saputo)

d'esser cacciato, o con turbato ciglio
perpetuamente esser da lui veduto;
che per la gente la qual rotta e morta
da te gli fu a Belgrado, odio ti porta."

(45.46–47)

Leone embraces Ruggiero with great compassion and says, "Knight, your
prowess binds me to you indissolubly in voluntary eternal servitude and
demands that I rejoice more in your good than in my own, care not for
my own welfare on account of yours, prefer your friendship to that of my
father and all the relatives I have in the world. I am Leone, so you may
understand, the son of Costantino, come in person to aid you, as you see,
under peril (if ever it becomes known to my father) of being exiled or
being perpetually frowned upon by him, for he bears you hatred on
account of his people routed and killed by you at Belgrade."

The narrative sequence makes it clear that Leone can have no ulterior
motive for his generosity, since he is not yet aware of Charlemagne's
edict concerning the single combat desired by Bradamante. Much later
Ruggiero reveals his name and explains how his ire was turned to
reciprocal love by Leone's generous rescue:

Ma perché ordina l'uomo, e Dio dispone,
venne il bisogno ove mi fe' la molta
tua cortesia mutar d'opinione;
e non pur l'odio ch'io t'avea deposi,
ma fe' ch'esser tuo sempre io mi disposi.

Tu mi pregasti, non sapendo ch'io
fossi Ruggier, ch'io ti facessi avere
la donna; ch'altretanto saria il mio
cor fuor del corpo, o l'anima volere.
Se sodisfar più tosto al tuo disio,
ch'al mio, ho voluto, t'ho fatto vedere.
Tua fatta è Bradamante; abbila in pace:
molto più che 'l mio bene, il tuo mi piace.

Piaccia a te ancora, se privo di lei
mi son, ch'insieme io sia di vita privo;
che più tosto senz'anima potrei,
che senza Bradamante restar vivo.
Appresso, per averla tu non sei
mai legitimamente, fin ch'io vivo;
che tra noi sponsalizio è già contratto,
né duo mariti ella può avere a un tratto.

(46.35–37)

But because man proposes and God disposes, there arose that need in which your great generosity caused me to change my mind; not only did I set aside the hatred I bore you, but I brought myself to be yours forever. Not knowing that I was Ruggiero, you asked me to bring you into possession of the lady for whom it would have been as much to ask as to desire the heart out of my body, or my soul. I have made you see whether I wished to satisfy your desire sooner than my own. Bradamante is made yours. Take her in peace. In your good I take far more pleasure than in my own. May it please you also that if I am to be deprived of her, I be deprived of my life at the same time, for I could sooner remain alive without my soul than without Bradamante. Furthermore, while I live you could never possess her legally, for betrothal has already been contracted between us and she cannot have two husbands at once.

In light of such sentiments, it is difficult to fathom how recent criticism has been able to find only "bourgeois" themes in the Leone episode. In this episode, Ruggiero learns the meaning of selfless faith. He turns the consequences of his mistaken mistrust of Bradamante into a vindication of faith by heroically accepting those consequences. He does not try to avoid them by invoking technicalities such as a betrothal agreement (as Marfisa and the others try to do), nor does he try to get around them by invoking, as well he might have done, the fraudulence of Leone's scheme to obtain Bradamante. He merely repays Leone's faith in kind and accepts his overwhelming losses.

When Rodomonte appears at the nuptials and accuses Ruggiero of being a traitor, no reader can deny that there is a certain literal truth in the charge, whether it is taken to apply strictly to Ruggiero's relations with Agramante or whether it is taken in a more general sense. The charge is outrageous only because it comes from Rodomonte and because it is unjust to Ruggiero's intentions. As for his deeds, Ruggiero has been at odds with himself throughout the *Furioso* and more than once has betrayed both himself and those who have trusted him. He is wrong to answer Rodomonte that he has "always" dealt justly with his king and "always" done his duty (46.107), for it is clear that he has not always understood his duty. By having Ruggiero's defeat of Rodomonte be assisted by good fortune when Rodomonte's sword breaks, Ariosto declares that Ruggiero is not fit to make such claims; no man is fit to make them. If any character in the *Furioso* is qualified to declare that he has always been true to his purpose, it is Rodomonte. He has always matched his egotistical outlook with destructive actions. His task has been easy compared to Ruggiero's, for Ruggiero has had to undergo a development through unexpected stages toward integrity. His consistently altruistic intentions have had to be integrated with altruistic behavior. The contrast between Rodomonte and Ruggiero reveals a certain pessimism in Ariosto's outlook. People like Rodomonte have the power to be thoroughly destructive, but no one has the power to be thoroughly good. The burden of the lifetime of even the best of men is a record of moral ambiguity in which actions are ever seen to betray the good intentions behind them, though even this failure can sometimes be for the best. Perhaps the most ominous irony of the Leone episode is that Ruggiero's one avowedly selfish intention in the *Furioso,* his intention to murder Leone, results in his most magnanimous deed. *Pro bono malum.*

5
Orlando

he story of Ruggiero is about the difficulty of learning to trust others, of learning to have faith in them despite their most fearful aspect, their absolute alterity. Asked whether Ariosto depicts any facet of human nature in the *Furioso* as absolute, one might first be inclined to answer no, nothing in that tapestry is without change. Yet the very image of the tapestry, Ariosto's own image, implies unchangingness—the stillness, the finish, and the precision of a picture held together by the mutual pressure of countless threads. The image of the tapestry implies the existence of fixed patterns and a design governing their cohesion. As we have seen, the patterns of the *Orlando Furioso* are its characters. The design that emerges when we study them is Ariosto's outlook. So far, the design suggests that Ariosto was fascinated with the conflict between man's impulse toward faith and the world's instability, between the human need for order and the uncertainty of everything human, and that he saw this conflict as complicated by interlocking paradoxes: the individual's efforts to shape a deity upon which to depend may increase the chaos he detests so much, but the chaos itself may become a salubrious multiplicity, rescuing the individual from suffocation under deities that have proven to be dangerous obsessions. Hence, the moral design of the *Furioso* flows into itself like a Moebius strip, giving the impression of endlessness confined within a single space.[1] The one and the many, multiplicity and unity, are contiguous.

For the patterns in the tapestry, the main tension consists in the absolute otherness of every other pattern, or character, in the design. All instability and disillusionment stem from this otherness, and all hope, as well, for relief from error. Rinaldo may attempt to ease the tension by applying a kind of secularized agnosticism to his relations with others, declaring that since it is impossible to know who is trustworthy, one should avoid situations requiring faith in others; however, his opinions prove to be irrelevant, and his actions cannot ameliorate the worst agonies of human nature to which he is exposed. Whereas Rinaldo lives his life in a moral vacuum, Rodomonte forges a hell for himself by denying the otherness of other people and by attributing godlike qualities to, and investing all of his faith in, himself. Although this makes him the natural adversary of Ruggiero, it does not mean that Ruggiero can espouse the otherness even of Bradamante with as much ease as Rodomonte exhibits in denying all otherness. The central lesson of Ruggiero's *Bildungsroman* is that alterity is a mysterious and fearful, but necessary, god, communion with which demands successive, iconoclastic repudiations of attachments to the self. Ariosto's representation of this discipline exposes all of Ruggiero's weaknesses, at times making him appear the parody of a hero, a Hercules under Omphale's power, but the future itself depends upon the result of this discipline. The narrative assumes from the start that the power to vanquish the world-destroying egotism of Rodomonte must be looked for (but not always found) in natures like Ruggiero's, which are capable of evolving through error after error into genuine altruism. Ruggiero and Rodomonte are exceptional beings. So it should come as no surprise that Orlando, who represents the pattern structurally central to the entire tapestry, stands in a vast moral middle ground where much harm is accomplished and some good, but both by inadvertence. Ironically, Orlando owes his central position in the narrative, not to any moral preeminence, but to moral mediocrity of Herculean proportions.

Ruggiero's painfully slow progress toward selfhood through self-abandonment contrasts sharply with Orlando's lightning speed in abandoning every thought but that of Angelica. Ruggiero hesitates for more than forty cantos before leaving Agramante to join Bradamante, whereas we are no sooner introduced to Orlando in canto 8 than we witness his desertion of Charlemagne and the commencement of his quest for Angelica. The contrast causes us to marvel at the perversity of human nature, which tirelessly manufactures scruples against doing what is right and at the same time passionately pursues a mistaken course of action. "Love" would seem to be the appropriate name for the impulse behind Orlando's action, but the Orlando of Ariosto's poem is "mad," unlike Boiardo's "enamored" Orlando. The title Ariosto chose for his work stresses the difference between his Orlando and Boiardo's, almost as if he were signaling a break with his predecessor and at the same time announcing a continuation. Boiardo's Orlando is in love throughout the *Innamorato,* and Ariosto's Orlando is mad for the duration of the *Furioso.* The berserk rage at the center of the *Furioso* is all of a piece with Orlando's conduct throughout. Little is to be gained by tracing Orlando's behavior back through the *Innamorato* as a preliminary to understanding Ariosto's treatment of his character. Boiardo shows how love can make even the wisest, most valiant of men a "baboon" (2.19.50), while Ariosto's main concern is to study the emergence of a Herculean madness from a man's inability to accept an unalterable condition of life—the otherness of other people. For the Orlando of Ariosto's poem, Angelica is not the eternal feminine, but the eternal other, the focus of the labor that drives him mad. Orlando's quest for Angelica is the most vehement of all the quests in the *Furioso* for a lost Eden. In seeking to possess Angelica in body and spirit, Orlando is seeking to restore the Edenic state in which all souls lie open to one another, in which all otherness dissolves into mutual recognition and multiplicity becomes one. The Orlando of the *Orlando Furioso* does not crave Angelica so much as he craves a prelapsarian world where faith can be replaced by certain knowledge and all instability is eliminated. What he forgets is that hunger for such knowledge lost mankind the first Eden.

The contrast between Sacripante's attitude toward Angelica in canto 1 and Orlando's meditations in canto 8 stresses the degree to which Angelica is a symbol of paradise in Orlando's mind, and it sheds light on a related characteristic of his attitude toward her. This characteristic, which Alfredo Bonadeo describes in an article entitled "Note sulla pazzia di Orlando," is the paladin's firm conviction that Angelica is potentially his to possess, apart from any need to ascertain how she feels about the matter. As far as Orlando is concerned, his possession of Angelica depends exclusively on his own subjective considerations and decisions.[2] At first, this seems to indicate, not a contrast, but a resemblance between Orlando and Sacripante, and a resemblance as well to Rodomonte. However, Orlando is just as far from being the sentimental rapist we see toppled from his horse in canto 1 as he is from considering himself a god and Angelica a mere creature. In the tradition of the troubadours, the *dolce stil novo,* and Petrarca, Orlando regards Angelica as a symbol of salvation. She represents the paradise he seeks to regain. If he fails to consult her feelings about his future possession of her, it is not because he expects his will to dominate her, but quite simply because symbols are not people. They cannot be conversed with. Orlando's communication with Angelica can only consist of the correct propitiation of whatever gods he believes will regain for him his lost paradise. As it turns out, the god he selects to propitiate above all others is the chivalric and courtly role handed down to him by tradition, and in this god he invests all of his faith. He relies on all that tradition has taught him concerning how a mortal must behave in order to be readmitted to paradise. He believes that a traditional mode of behavior, an established role, if adhered to strictly enough, will gain him Angelica's favor. His god will regain paradise for him, and that blissful state will serve as the confirmation of his faith.

The flower of which Orlando speaks in canto 8, stanza 77, is different from Sacripante's rose. It is the flower, in Orlando's opinion, that can place him among the gods in heaven. He would never dream of plucking it against Angelica's will. The thought would never occur to him, as it does to Sacripante, that force might gain him what he desires, because what he desires is not a sexual consummation but a vindication of the god he serves. Hence, the acquiescence of Angelica's chaste spirit is essential to his possession of her. In order for reality to bear witness to his god, Angelica must deliver herself into his hands voluntarily, having been persuaded to do so by the excellence with which he has fulfilled his role. Never again would he have to doubt himself in his relations with others. The simple fulfillment of his role, the adherence to conventions, would eliminate the instability arising from the existence of persons different from himself. Does the world contain any form of madness more common than this?

It is only appropriate that Orlando, the most traditional character in the *Orlando Furioso,* should invest all of his faith in a traditional role. However, his abandonment of himself to this god leads him in the *Furioso* to self-nullification. No tradition is unequivocal, and this is Orlando's first problem. In blending the "Matter of Britain" with the "Matter of France," Boiardo heaped upon Orlando, the *preux* of the *chanson de geste,* the unfamiliar responsibilities of the *courtois* of courtly romance. Ariosto took this volatile mixture, which Boiardo had used for comedy, and adapted it to the study of a type of person who, like most of us, attempts to overcome life's instability by conforming with traditions handed down to him from the past. The very incompatibility of the traditions Boiardo had mixed for comedy's sake provided Ariosto with a convenient means of going one step further and questioning the compatibility of tradition with experience. Ariosto questions, that is, the efficacy of the humanist movement of his age at the same time that he presents us with an everyman figure. Orlando is Ariosto's symbol of the madness of reducing experience to categories suggested by tradition.

We find condensed into Orlando's first appearance in the *Furioso* most of the confusion that will leave him deranged at the work's center. This confusion is introduced against a background of the selfsame classical themes, types, and images that Ariosto's contemporaries hoped would provide models for organizing the chaos of experience. In the introductory stanza (8.71), the classical background is established with an allusion to the eighth book of the *Aeneid,* lines 22–25, in which Aeneas lies awake thinking about the approaching battle against Turnus and his allies:

> La notte Orlando alle noiose piume
> del veloce pensier fa parte assai.
> Or quinci or quindi il volta, or lo rassume
> tutto in un loco, e non l'afferma mai:
> qual d'acqua chiara il tremolante lume,
> dal sol percossa o da' notturni rai,
> per gli ampli tetti va con lungo salto
> a destra et a sinistra, e basso et alto.

> In the night Orlando makes the irksome feathers of his bed take a large share in his swift thought. To one side he turns it and then the other, then gathers it all in one spot, and never holds it still, just as from clear water struck by sunlight or the rays of the moon trembling light leaps with long bounds over wide rooftops, right and left, high and low.

Of this stanza, D. S. Carne-Ross remarks that "when a poet of this period introduces his hero in these Virgilian terms he plainly expects us to pay attention to what he is doing."[3] This is obviously true, and since the two preceding stanzas described the salvation of Paris from the Moors by a rainstorm, we believe that the "swift thought" tormenting Orlando is the same one that once tormented Aeneas, that is, worry over the outcome of the battle to be fought the next day. We believe that Orlando is an Aeneas preoccupied with his responsibility to vanquish the *furor* of Agramante and Rodomonte. However, the next stanza opens abruptly with the phrase "la donna sua," and we find that the "swift thought" is itself a form of *furor.* Instead of an Aeneas, as we expected, we are presented with a burly male Dido. Our expectations are shockingly reversed, but part of the genius of these stanzas is that they do not reduce Orlando to a buffoon, as do so many of Boiardo's descriptions. They even manage, on the contrary, to transfer some of the epic seriousness of Aeneas's circumstances to the plight of the abandoned lover. Narrative strategy contributes largely to this mitigation of Orlando's first show of madness. The narrative between the opening of the *Furioso* and canto 8 so thoroughly distracts our attention from the conflict over Paris that for the moment Paris seems unimportant. We have become so absorbed in the Ginevra and Alcina episodes that we have forgotten about Paris. Furthermore, the image of Angelica tied to the rock on the island of Ebuda, which occupies the stanzas immediately preceding Orlando's introduction, focuses our attention on Orlando's feelings toward her rather than on his duties to Charlemagne. So Ariosto induces us to take an Orlando suffering the pains of Dido as seriously as if he were an Aeneas on the eve of battle.

If we are paying the kind of attention, then, that Carne-Ross believes Ariosto expected of his readers for the Virgilian allusions of canto 8, we must note that canto 8 presents a much more substantial statement of the theme of the *Orlando Furioso,* at least as regards the character of Orlando, than that in the exordium of canto 1, and a much more revolutionary statement, too, as regards the position Ariosto took with respect to previous classical and Renaissance epics and with respect to the very culture in which he lived. As we read Canto 8, we are being told by Ariosto that his culture merits an epic hero more like Dido than like Aeneas. The kind of confusion that leads a person to suicide is more characteristic of that culture, in Ariosto's opinion, than the *pietas* attributed by Virgil to Aeneas. Of epic significance is the question of how one person can so misread another's character, as Dido misread Aeneas's character, that suicide or madness may result. With the figure of Orlando, Ariosto is suggesting that such misreadings occur when the individual looks to others in order to obtain a confirmation of values handed down by tradition. If one takes this approach to others, madness is sure to ensue. Human traditions can never prescribe norms for human experience or even adequately describe experience, nor can they be sufficiently comprehensible to be of use to the individual in the heat of circumstances. They are too often mutually contradictory, and experience too often outpaces them in creating circumstances beyond their purview. Human beings remain mysterious despite them, never wholly categorizable. If regarded as constituting a reality superior to individual experience, they are able to confer only madness on their worshipers. Ariosto introduces the "Matter of Rome the Great," the classical tradition, into the *Furioso* in a manner designed to subvert the moralizing, allegorizing, codifying projects his age devoted to that tradition.

Stanzas 80–83 of canto 8, which consist of Orlando's dream, provide another condensed image of Orlando's destiny, only this time the image is contained within an allusion to the vernacular tradition. The development of the dream is the reverse of the movement that brought Dante to salvation through communion with Beatrice. Orlando's dream opens with a vision of Angelica similar to Dante's vision of that beautiful lady on the riverbank at the entrance to the earthly paradise in the *Pur-*

gatorio, and it ends with a voice proclaiming that Orlando may nevermore hope to enjoy the sight of Angelica in this world. The movement of Dante from the death of Beatrice in the *Vita Nova* to his reunion with her at the close of the *Purgatorio* has been reversed. The dream proclaims that hope of an earthly paradise is illusory and that those who harbor such a hope are doomed to wander through a desert searching in vain for relief (8.81). The brighter the illusion of paradise, the more dessicated will seem the world in which one hopes to plant one's illusion. The dream portrays these illusions as blindingly bright. Orlando will never see Angelica again. Later on, he catches sight of her, but his madness prevents him from recognizing her. The real Angelica is lost to Orlando from the moment we first meet him in the *Furioso,* when he makes her a symbol of paradise. Ironically, the immediate consequence of this dream is the separation of two real lovers. When Orlando awakens and departs in search of Angelica without giving so much as a thought to the meaning of his dream, his loyal companion Brandimarte follows him, leaving Fiordiligi in Paris. Twenty-two cantos elapse before the lovers are reunited only to pursue Orlando to a place where they are separated once and for all by death. The dream simultaneously sets in motion Orlando's doomed quest and a *topos* as ancient as the epic genre itself: the destruction of the loyal companion by the hero's restless longing to surpass the human condition. Thirty-five cantos later, with the delivery of Brandimarte's funeral oration, Orlando fades from the narrative. Far from having gained his paradise, he is left with his humanity severely and permanently diminished. His zealous devotion to his traditional role, his devotion to what seemed to him the avenue to an earthly paradise, has turned out to be the road to benightedness, and he has gone on a journey in the opposite direction from the Dantesque journey to enlightenment.

The Orlando who deserts Charlemagne in canto 8 and sets in motion the train of events leading to the death of his closest friend acts like a mechanical man, taciturn, as Galileo noted, and somber, propelled by conflicting self-conceptions. As a warrior whose services merit a reward from his king, Orlando feels betrayed by Charlemagne, who has not only failed to reward him, but has confiscated Angelica, the one thing dearest to his heart. His outrage leads him even to speculate that Charlemagne entrusted her to the ineffective guardianship of Namo on purpose, to be rid of her. His obedience to his suzerain and his confidence that he could win her back at will caused him to acquiesce in her confiscation, but now that circumstances have upset his expectations he accuses himself of having neglected his responsibility to protect her. As the lover of courtly tradition, he should never have entrusted her to weaker men than himself, and since all of Charlemagne's forces are weaker than he, his acquiescence was inexcusable. The roles of *preux* and *courtois* clash. Obedience to his suzerain and loyalty to his lady are mutually exclusive, but Orlando, mesmerized by his conflicting roles, is oblivious of the dilemma and blinded also to the reality that has brought it into the foreground. While he alternately blames himself and Charlemagne for the loss of Angelica, he ignores the reality that Angelica's flight was occasioned by the defeat in battle of Charlemagne's forces by the Moors. The conflicting traditions in which he invests all his faith can only suggest that his separation from Angelica is to be blamed on himself or Charlemagne, that it was somehow in his or Charlemagne's power to prevent the separation, when in reality evil forces beyond the control of either caused it and threaten to cause more devastation unless they are heeded. Traditional self-conceptions blind Orlando to a real enemy it would be madness not to fear.

Moreover, the contamination of one traditional self-conception by the other causes Orlando to misunderstand the nature of the good he seeks. Insofar as he expects the tangible reward of her virginity from Angelica in return for his protection, he is mistaking Angelica, the courtly lady of one tradition, for the suzerain of the other tradition, and he is mistaking his own role as powerful vassal for his role as lover. Unlike the rewards of the generous suzerain, the courtly lady's rewards are best, according to tradition, when they are intangible and when her lover's services are selfless. Ennoblement of character through self-sacrifice is the reward valued in the courtly and Petrarchan traditions of love. However, Orlando is not content to acquire from his courtship of Angelica a mere standard for the discrimination of all beauty, truth, and goodness in the world. Orlando wants Angelica herself as the just recompense of his labors. She, in body and in spirit, represents to him paradise on earth, and nothing short of physically possessing her is of any value to him. In his confusion, he believes that his service must compel her to grant him her virginity just as surely as his service to Charlemagne has won him titles, treasures, and grants of land. Her free will, in his view, exists to enable her to make a choice vindicating the confused, conventional approach he takes to her. Of course, to Angelica, or to any other woman, the range of possibilities would seem broader.

Having introduced Orlando in these complicated terms as a person blind to good and evil, the narrative propels him into a novella that allows his character to define itself in action—a novella that also links him with Rinaldo and Ruggiero. At its inception, the story of Olimpia bears certain resemblances to the Ginevra episode. Like Rinaldo, Orlando gets blown off course by a storm only to find himself involved in the rescue of a damsel in distress whose story is far more complex than the response he makes to it. One of the ironies, as we shall see, of comparing the Olimpia and Ginevra episodes is that Orlando's chivalric behavior would have been more appropriate if he were rescuing Ginevra and Rinaldo's cynicism more to the point in dealing with Olimpia. At its conclusion, the Olimpia episode forms a diptych with Ruggiero's rescue of Angelica from the sea monster. Orlando's rescue of Olimpia from this monster alludes to Hercules' rescue of Hesione in the *Argonautica* of Valerius Flaccus, just as Ruggiero's deed alludes to the Perseus and Andromeda story in Ovid's *Metamorphoses*. Furthermore, the allusion in Orlando's case also involves ironic treatment of contemporary allegorical interpretation of the mythical story. Ariosto manipulates his classical source in such a way as to restore its liveliness and at the same time ridicule the allegorists. Like Ruggiero, Orlando in this episode creates comedy through the incongruity of his actions with his view of himself, a view agreeing in most essentials with the allegorists' view of Hercules in the classical source. So the Olimpia episode, extending over cantos 9, 10, and 11, begins, like the Ginevra episode, with a hero who is off course in his understanding of the circumstances by which he is confronted, and it ends, like the story of Ruggiero's Ovidian dalliance with Angelica, in an elaborate spoof of Christian humanist meddlings with the classical tradition.

It is fortunate that Olimpia is a lady of abundant words, for she provides thereby everything we need to judge her, and upon our judgment of her depends what we think of Orlando. There are so many words, in fact, that one scarcely knows where to begin an analysis. However, the circumstances in which she finds herself when she tells Orlando her tale of woe are helpful, and so is the reason she gives for telling it. Having exhausted all her resources first in resisting a marriage to Cimosco's son, Arbante, and then in attempting to thwart Cimosco's revenge on her for the murder of that unfortunate son, she finds herself forced to accept Cimosco's terms. Her lover, Bireno, has fallen into the tyrant's hands, and Cimosco has declared that he will liberate him only if she offers up her own person in exchange for Bireno's. She tells Orlando that she would gladly do this but for one overmastering doubt. She fears that Cimosco will break faith and murder both Bireno and herself, denying her the satisfaction of redeeming her lover's life with her own death. Hence, she has been telling her story to every knight who has come her way in the hope of finding one who would pledge himself to force Cimosco to keep his word and free Bireno after she has died. A more moving predicament, it would seem, could scarcely be imagined, and in her telling of it Olimpia has done everything to wring the maximum sympathy from her auditor. It seems as if there is nothing in the world she desires more than to die for her beloved Bireno. However, any knight strong enough to make Cimosco keep his word could also force him to free Bireno regardless of terms or conditions— if, of course, that knight were sufficiently persuaded of the pitiableness and the injustice of Olimpia's plight. As readers, we are forced to ask whether Olimpia's pathetic discourse might not have a thinly concealed purpose quite different from the one she declares. Is she seeking her own martyrdom for love, or someone else's martyrdom to suit her will?

This initial question compels the reader to review some of the details of Olimpia's story with greater care than he might otherwise have exercised. First of all, it is apparent that her love for Bireno has already created a great many martyrs, but neither she nor Bireno has been among them. From the start, as soon as she hears of Cimosco's approaches to her father to arrange a marriage between herself and Arbante, she declares that she would rather be killed than be given thus in marriage (9.26); however, as it turns out, her father and her two brothers are the ones who are killed when they second her refusal. When her father offends Cimosco by breaking off negotiations for the marriage, the war begins, as she puts it, "that drove all my blood into the ground" (9.27)—the figurative use of the expression "my blood" making it seem for a moment as if she shared equally in the suffering occasioned by her course of action.

Stanzas 28–31, describing Cimosco's murder of her father and brothers, are also sophistical. Olimpia's minute description of Cimosco's firearm, which she calls a "hidden snare" [*inganno*], makes it seem as if the weapon and its wielder bore exclusive responsibility for the deaths of her kin. However, the weapon, which Cimosco uses quite openly, can no more be considered a hidden snare than can Cimosco himself be considered solely responsible for the war and its consequences. Only a few lines earlier in her speech, in an effort perhaps to win sympathy for her cause by contrasting her father's amenableness with Cimosco's implacability, she has mentioned that her "good father" could always be counted on to second her likes and dislikes and never to upset her (9.27). At the very opening of her speech, she has made an even stronger statement to the same effect:

Figures in Ariosto's Tapestry

Io voglio che sappiate che figliuola
fui del conte d'Olanda, a lui sì grata
(quantunque prole io non gli fossi sola,
ch'era da dui fratelli accompagnata),
ch'a quanto io gli chiedea, da lui parola
contraria non mi fu mai replicata.

(9.22)

I want you to know that I was the daughter of the Count of Holland, so
pleasing to him (though I was not his only offspring, for I had the
companionship of two brothers) that no matter what I requested of him,
I never had from him a contrary word in answer.

The irony of these statements is that they make the reader—if not
Orlando—suspect that Olimpia has been encouraged from the cradle
to be willful and may therefore be no more pliant than her enemy
Cimosco. One has to wonder if Olimpia's motive for persisting in the
course she describes is really what she declares it to be: loyalty to
Bireno, the person to whom she has pledged her faith. Another possible
motive emerges from her words: a certain ruthless determination to
accomplish her will, ruthless to the extent that she was prepared, after
the demise of her father and brothers, to sacrifice the lives of all her
subjects rather than submit to the marriage with Arbante.

Such rhetorical flourishes in her description of her first meeting with
Bireno as "I used to believe and I still believe, and I believe I believe the
truth, that he loved me and still loves me with a sincere heart" [io credea
e credo, e creder credo il vero, / amassi et ami me con cor sincero]
(9.23) do little to cover up the falseness of her claim that trust and
obligation are the paramount motives for her behavior. Instead, such
rhetoric only shows that words need be nothing but words, empty
sounds arranged in grammatical rows, and need not signify reality at all.
Here the very word for belief is repeated so often that it is reduced to a
mere jingling sound. The unfavorable contrast between Olimpia's description of her relationship with Bireno and what we have already seen
of Ginevra and Ariodante increases our suspicion that Olimpia's words
are hollow. Olimpia has sworn the same oath to Bireno that Ginevra
swore to Ariodante, but Bireno has given no indication that he is a
person in whom one may have confidence. Olimpia is merely taken with
the youth and good looks of someone literally blown ashore in Holland
by an ill wind and delayed there for forty days until the weather improved and he could go about his original business. Ariodante, on the
other hand, gave proofs of his valor before he and Ginevra pledged

their faith, and he followed his intention to stay in Scotland until his services persuaded her father that he was worthy of her hand (5.33–34). Actions bear witness to Ariodante's faith, while Olimpia's words are all that vouch for Bireno's. One cannot help but conclude that a father, two brothers, and a homeland are an exorbitant price to pay for something whose existence can be vouched for only by such words as Olimpia knows how to use. A young woman's "obstinacy" as her people called it (9.34), and not her faith, we suspect, has exacted this price in blood.

When at last her subjects reach a separate accord with Cimosco and deliver her into his hands, she is faced with the choice of softening her "hardened wishes" or else losing her homeland and her life. Her subjects had pleaded with her earlier to surrender voluntarily in order to prevent further carnage, but her answer, according to her own account, had been emphatic:

> Per un mal ch'io patisco, ne vo' cento
> patir . . . e far di tutto il resto;
> esser morta, arsa viva, e che sia al vento
> la cener sparsa, inanzi che far questo.
>
> (9.34)

> For every evil I am enduring I will endure a hundred more . . . and do whatever else is needed, be killed, be burnt alive, and have my ashes scattered in the wind, before I will do this.

However, now that she is provided with the opportunity to make good her melodramatic protestations, now that she is offered that very martyrdom she has all along been declaring is the one thing she desires most, her tune changes slightly. Failure to get revenge on Cimosco before dying would grieve her more, she says, than all of her other injuries. Like a spirit in Dante's *Inferno*, she betrays herself in the effort of self-justification. Revenge is more important to her even than her loss of Bireno. The willfulness to which she sacrificed her homeland and family turns into vindictiveness and leads to the deceitfulness and the ferocity of the murder of Arbante, which Olimpia describes in loving detail:

> Io dietro alle cortine avea nascoso
> quel mio fedele, il qual nulla si mosse
> prima che a me venir vide lo sposo;
> e non l'attese che corcato fosse,
> ch'alzò un'accetta, e con sì valoroso
> braccio dietro nel capo lo percosse,

Figures in Ariosto's Tapestry

che gli levò la vita e la parola:
io saltai presta, e gli segai la gola.

(9.41)

Behind the curtains I had hidden that loyal servant of mine, who
never moved until he saw my spouse come to me, and then did not wait
until he had gone to bed, but raised an ax and struck him in the back of
the head with such a valorous blow that he deprived him of life and
speech. Then I leapt out quickly and cut his throat.

One wonders what could be valorous about that blow in back of the
head besides its sheer force. From Olimpia's shameless description of
this slaughter, it is clear that she herself considers valorous whatever
course of action accomplishes her will. Of course, she had said that this
revenge was to be a preliminary step to her martyrdom. However, the
actual sequel to the murder is her escape through a window and her
abandonment of all her friends to Cimosco's wrath. Olimpia's speech to
Orlando, taken as a whole, is a masterpiece of single-minded selfishness
parading itself as self-sacrifice. Olimpia is so convinced of her right-
eousness that she almost convinces the reader.

Of her success in convincing Orlando there can be no doubt:

Orlando, poi ch'ella la bocca chiuse,
le cui voglie al ben far mai non fur zoppe,
in parole con lei non si diffuse;
che di natura non usava troppe:
ma le promise, e la sua fé le diede,
che faria più di quel ch'ella gli chiede.

(9.57)

Orlando, whose intentions of doing good were never lame, after she
closed her mouth did not pour himself out in words to her, for by nature
he did not use too many, but promised her and gave her his oath that he
would do more than she asked of him.

He gives her exactly what she wanted from the start, not a pledge to
facilitate her martyrdom, but a guarantee of revenge upon Cimosco.
This is the very Orlando in whom Galileo noted a taciturnity and
distractedness verging on madness in all of his appearances in the
Furioso. Although Olimpia's words offer much to think about, Orlando
has nothing to say. The issue looks simple to him. Cimosco and his
firearm are evil and Olimpia is the innocent damsel in distress. The
chivalric code Orlando trusts sweeps away the complexity of his circumstances, and consequently his behavior is mechanical and heavy-

handed. Cimosco may deserve punishment for his cruelty, but his punishment should not redound to Olimpia's advantage, as Orlando will make every effort to make certain it does. The speech against firearms after Cimosco's demise represents a woefully inept response to events, nothing more, in fact, than a gullible acceptance of Olimpia's sophistry. Firearms are no more responsible for a loss of valor in the world or for any special advantage of evil over good than they were for the deaths of Olimpia's father and brothers. Regardless of the means, destruction had to result from the clash of wills between Olimpia and Cimosco. If it symbolizes anything at all, Cimosco's firearm could be said to represent the implacable reality Orlando fails to perceive, the hellish determination of some people to have their own way no matter what the cost. There is something ominous about Orlando's narrow escape from being destroyed himself by this firearm. Possibly his invulnerability is not of the kind that can always protect him from the more virulent realities to which his code-bound sensibility blinds him.

Canto 10 opens with a touch of mordant humor. The narrator builds his extravagant and solemn praise of Olimpia into an argument that young ladies should love only middle-aged men. If the kind of faith that Olimpia demonstrated toward Bireno were not enough to keep him loyal to her, then no young man can be trusted, and of course, it is always to be feared that old men might be unable to bestow the necessary attentions even if they could be trusted. This canto opening parodies Orlando's serious opinion of Olimpia, and through its mock horror, shows that Bireno's desertion of her is no more surprising than Angelica's choice of someone else over Orlando. There is a certain justice in Bireno's leaving her to suffer the death she so insincerely claimed she would gladly accept if it could save him. As the reward of her hypocrisy, Bireno himself forces her to make good her words. By the time we leave Olimpia, with her gaze fixed upon the empty sea, herself no less a stone to all appearances than the stone she is sitting on, we recognize that Orlando's blindness in his dealings with her is the same as that which keeps him from perceiving the harm done by this own infatuation with Angelica. He does not see that his pursuit of Angelica at the cost of the lives of his companions at whose side he should be fighting bears a gruesome resemblance to Olimpia's determination to have Bireno even if it means the destruction of her family and her world. When Orlando sets sail for the island of Ebuda, expecting to find Angelica and instead finding himself face to face with Olimpia again, he is given another chance to see the truth, but he fails this time as surely as he failed before.

There is nothing perplexing about the appearance of the Olimpia episode among those late additions to the 1532 *Furioso*. The episode gives a crucial definition to Orlando's character, just as the Leone episode defines Ruggiero's, so it is difficult to understand why Cesare Segre feels it necessary to find an excuse for the episode's existence in its final scene where Orlando rescues Olimpia from the orca. Segre hypothesizes that the addition of the Leone episode compelled Ariosto to find a means of preventing Orlando from being pushed into the background by Ruggiero. According to Segre, a potential imbalance between the two heroes was corrected by granting Orlando a confrontation both terrible and decisive with the orca. Because of his concupiscence and his use of the magic shield, Ruggiero's rescue of Angelica lacks seriousness, so the argument goes, while Orlando, unassisted by magical contrivances, assumes gigantic stature by battling alone against the orca and the inhabitants of Ebuda. Yet the fact remains inescapable that Orlando ends up in the background anyway at the close of the 1532 *Furioso*, despite the addition of the orca episode. The major trouble with Segre's explanation of the episode is that it does not take into account Ariosto's ironical treatment of Olimpia in cantos 9 and 10. Segre declares that Orlando's rescue of Olimpia is a disinterested, chivalric defense of justice and that the grandeur of Orlando and his deed is proportional to the tragedy of Olimpia, "indomitably faithful to her love, inexorably persecuted by betrayal."[4] However, the ironical treatment of Olimpia turns Orlando's rescue of her into the oxymoron of a chivalric defense of injustice. Trying to explain Ariosto's addition of Olimpia's rescue as an effort to retain for Orlando a prominence in the narrative equal to Ruggiero's, Segre falls into the trap—set perhaps by Ariosto—of arguing that Orlando's deed is morally superior to Ruggiero's and that Olimpia is a paragon of wounded innocence. One curious result of this line of argument is that it leaves the modern critic interpreting Ariosto's scene in much the same way that Renaissance allegorists interpreted the rescue of Hesione by Hercules in the *Argonautica*, the scene upon which Ariosto based Orlando's rescue of Olimpia. That this is a dangerous position for the critic to be in, one can be certain, especially after witnessing Ariosto's burlesque of Ovid's allegorizers in his treatment of Ruggiero's rescue of Angelica.

A more likely explanation of Ariosto's late addition of the scene in question would take into account the obvious—the scene's allusion to one of the exploits of Hercules, the classical hero with whom Orlando is implicitly compared in the title of Ariosto's poem. Ariosto apparently wished to represent more clearly the Herculean madness of his central character, and to do so using the same irony he had already employed successfully in the scene involving Ruggiero. The new scene depends for its effect on a double allusion, both to Valerius Flaccus's account of Hercules' rescue of Hesione and to the body of allegorical interpretation that had attached itself to the account by the time it reached Ariosto. On the one hand, Orlando's mistaken opinion of Olimpia causes him to take a view of his role as her rescuer that agrees with the allegorists' interpretation of Hercules' role as the rescuer of Hesione. On the other hand, the sensuousness, the hyperbole, and the playfulness of Ariosto's scene exaggerate those very qualities of the Latin version that place it outside the field of allegorical interpretation. Ariosto's treatment of the orca as a big fish to be hooked with an anchor outdoes the Latin version in all of these respects. The analogy underlying Ariosto's scene equates Orlando with the allegorists and Orlando's circumstances with the text of the *Argonautica*. Orlando has no more grasp of his circumstances than the allegorists have of the text they presume to interpret. Blindness to the subtleties of literature becomes a metaphor for blindness to the book of life.

We owe the most exhaustive Renaissance attempt to find recondite meanings in the adventures of Hercules to the fifteenth-century humanist Coluccio Salutati, whose *De laboribus Herculis* may have represented for Ariosto a good example of what he regarded as the misguided effort of his age to systematize and render normative for all experience certain traditional texts. According to Salutati, Hesione exposed to the sea monster represents the human intellect exposed to the corruption of material wealth, and Hercules is the virtuous man who liberates the intellect by conquering avarice.[5] Actually, Salutati is inconsistent to the extent that Hesione can represent the intellect or virtue or both according to the requirements of the imagery with which she happens to be juxtaposed at any given moment in the texts he is interpreting. The result, in any case, is that the classical story is reduced, albeit by ingenious means, to moral discourse at a rather low level of cogency and sophistication. The heroic means Orlando uses to vanquish the orca are likewise disproportionate to his feeble understanding of the deed. He himself, like the modern critic and the fifteenth-century allegorizer, regards his deed as a disinterested defense of the right, and he is relieved that Oberto, the king of Ireland, who has become infatuated with Olimpia's physical charms, is available to wreak vengeance on Bireno, for otherwise he would be obliged to do so himself and would thereby lose more time from his search for Angelica. The narrative, which devotes eight stanzas to a blazon of Olimpia's physique, makes it clear that it is not Orlando's tale of wounded innocence that impresses Oberto, and clearer still that it is not necessarily justice that turns Olimpia, who was a countess to begin with, into a queen when she marries Oberto. Instead, in these circumstances lust once again gives a turn to Fortune's wheel. Olimpia's physical beauty wins her a kingdom after her implacable will has contributed to the destruction of her own homeland and her family. Only madness of Herculean proportions could make one think of this as a victory of intellect over passion.

Not only does Orlando misjudge Olimpia's character but he is unconscious of the good he has done. It is ironic that he should expect thanks from the islanders of Ebuda for killing the orca. The orca has determined their way of life for generations, and most people, no matter how evil their customs, would rather keep them than undergo cataclysmic changes. Still, change the islanders must, if justice is to prevail. Orlando, as the agent of change, actually plays the role of mythical Herculean culture hero, but he is so distracted by his concern over the lady tied to the rock (because he has not had time to see if she is Angelica) that he treats the victory of the Irish troops over the islanders, which he has made possible, as if it had nothing to do with him (11.54). His blindness to the good he has accomplished is equal to his blindness to the evil he fosters. The traditional attitudes that Orlando believes will carry him to paradise prohibit scrutiny of the world he lives in. So he goes through life like a sleepwalker, and the people and circumstances surrounding him, as far as he is concerned, are only parts of an orderly dream that has always been and always will be the same. He needs only to play the role dictated for him by the dream in order for his greatest expectations to be fulfilled.

Isabella might well have been better off had she never become involved with Orlando's dream. If she had never met Orlando, she would have been sold by her captors to a merchant and wound up a harem slave, never to lay eyes on her beloved Zerbino again. Having been rescued by Orlando, she is no sooner reunited with Zerbino than she is forced to see her lover cut down by Mandricardo using Orlando's sword. The irony of Orlando's involvement with Isabella comes to light in the contrast between Isabella and Olimpia. Unlike Olimpia, Isabella tells Orlando her story simply for the relief of sharing her sorrow with someone else. Far from having an ulterior motive to persuade Orlando to rescue her, she fears that her words will only render her captivity the more severe when Gabrina reports them to the thieves. As regards her relations with Zerbino, she, unlike Olimpia, has seen proofs of her lover's valor at the tournament called by her father, and Zerbino himself, unlike Bireno, had a good reason for parting with his beloved, a reason that is in itself a reproach to Orlando. He was forced to obey his father's command to lead reinforcements to Paris for the relief of Charlemagne. Moreover, the fact that his father is the king of Scotland reminds us that he has treated Isabella no differently than he has treated his own sister, Ginevra, who might have counted on his aid if the same obedience to duty had not called him too far away to hear the news of her persecution. More importantly, these lovers, unlike Olimpia and Bireno, have brought no suffering and no risks down on anyone but themselves. Isabella's sacrifice of the comforts and security of home in order to elope with Zerbino makes the reader wonder why Olimpia, who never bothered to contact Bireno until a battle was fought and one of her brothers killed, could not have done the same. Finally, Isabella has learned from her experiences to be suspicious of love and to doubt her own judgment. She speaks of "the cruel tyrant Love, who always betrayed his every promise and always watches how he may confuse and dissolve our every rational plan" (13.20). This wisdom gained from experience is a far cry from the cruel vindictiveness that settled into Olimpia's character as obstacles to her desire increased. It is also, of course, the kind of wisdom that might spare Orlando his madness.

The tragic irony of Orlando's encounter with Isabella and Zerbino is that it leaves one of the lovers slaughtered by Mandricardo and the other by Rodomonte, while a similar encounter with the much less deserving Olimpia leaves her better off than she was even before she permitted the destruction of her home and family. Orlando's traditional chivalric behavior leads to the advantage of the undeserving and the destruction of the good.[6] No sooner does Orlando bring about the reunion of Isabella and Zerbino (in canto 23) than he encounters Mandricardo, and, misinterpreting the pagan's arrogance as "great valor" he sets the stage for Zerbino's death. The narrator has suggested that Mandricardo's purpose is to avenge Manilardo and Alzirdo (23.71). However, in the succeeding stanzas Mandricardo himself makes it quite clear that his concern is exclusively egotistical. He wants credit for defeating a knight so powerful that he could leave wounds as large as those Mandricardo measured on the bodies of his dead comrades. When he learns that the person before him is both Orlando and that knight, he is doubly delighted because of the opportunity Fortune has granted him to seize Durindana, the sole object of his journey to the Occident. In fact, it is the oath he swore—the oath not to fight with a sword until he has won Durindana—that elicits Orlando's opinion of his great valor. Although Orlando himself points out that Durindana is "justly" his own (won from Agricane, as the reader may recall, in one of the fiercest battles of the *Innamorato*), he abandons the advantage that is rightfully his and hangs the sword from a tree branch to be the reward of the victor. He does this "per gentilezza," but the ensuing combat has anything but a noble appearance. For lack of swords, the combatants swing at each other with their broken lances like two angry peasants beating each other with poles in a boundary dispute or a quarrel over water rights (23.83). The burlesque battle ends when Mandricardo gets Orlando in a wrestling grip and throws him saddle and all to the ground "with the same sound a sack of armor makes when it falls" (23.88), the noise being such that Mandricardo's horse bolts and runs three miles until it dumps its rider in a ditch.[7] Beneath this comedy lies the tragic irony that Orlando's chivalric gesture nullifies his chance to dispatch Mandricardo before Mandricardo does serious harm.

As in the case of Polinesso, evil has created the conditions necessary for its own misfortune by the time Mandricardo catches up with Orlando in canto 23. Fatuously, Mandricardo considers his meeting with Orlando the apex of good fortune, when in fact his own arrogance has readied him for destruction by causing him to swear to fight without a sword. The reader is primed, at this moment, to witness a just end to Mandricardo's evil. The very object he has sought no matter what the cost to others will now cost him his own life. However, Orlando steps in with his chivalric scruples and frustrates the process of justice, turning the moral drama into meaningless slapstick. Confirmation that Orlando's noble gesture was misguided comes swiftly. In canto 24 Orlando's example has no influence over Mandricardo. It never occurs to Mandricardo to question the fairness of his using Durindana in his duel with Zerbino. His arrogance merely leads him to conclude that Orlando has abandoned his sword out of fear of fighting him for it and has feigned madness to cover up his cowardice. Injustice is never troubled by scruples, false or true, and so Zerbino dies, the victim of Orlando's false scruples and his failure to use one of the rare advantages evil grants its opponents. Zerbino is the first victim of Orlando's madness to bear a name, but certainly not the first victim. The nameless ones, the multitudes who have died on both sides in Rodomonte's attack on Paris, eventually come to be associated with the name of Isabella. By the time she arranges her beheading by Rodomonte, the reader has learned to consider Orlando responsible for the freedom with which Rodomonte commits murder on all sides. While Orlando seeks vindication of his chivalric values in the pursuit of Angelica, he leaves the enemy free to attempt the elimination of the one condition that makes values of any sort plausible, that is, life itself.

The cost to others of Orlando's madness could not be higher, but the cost to himself is also high. His deification of a traditional role blinds him to the characters of other individuals. He is unable to perceive Mandricardo's arrogance and cruelty and Olimpia's incontinence and willfulness. Instead, he sees other people as stereotypical elements of the tradition he worships; hence, other people can do nothing but elude him. Yet the very reason for his worship of tradition was, from the start, to bring him into communion with the one other individual he desires the most. This is the cruel irony of his plight. By excelling as both *preux* and *courtois,* he has hoped to persuade Angelica to shed her otherness. He has hoped to persuade her to make her desires conform with his own, but his behavior has only made her all the more inaccessible. In canto 12, coming upon him and the others in Atlante's palace of illusions, Angelica rejects him as an escort to the Orient for the very reason he thinks should compel her to choose him. The prowess he thinks should persuade Angelica that he alone is worthy of her actually makes him, in her opinion, the quintessence of undesirability. At this point, it is doubtful that she wishes any man to obtain his desire through her means, as her regret over having unintentionally helped Ferraù to get Orlando's helmet suggests (12.64). Her disingenuous excuse for having stolen the helmet, that she only wished to bring a truce to the battle between Orlando and Ferraù, suggests that her regret over having stolen it from Orlando is not half so great as her regret over having become Ferraù's means of possessing it. Angelica's aloofness, her readiness to make a game of the helmet over which the knights are fighting in deadly earnest, is only a natural reaction to the ponderous determination with which Orlando pursues her. His unwavering conviction that she will vindicate his conventional values by conforming with them forces her to make light of them in sheer self-preservation. She senses that the helmet is more real to Orlando than she herself is. In the *Furioso,* Angelica is running for her life in a very real sense, for if she ever allowed herself to be caught by Orlando, her individuality would be suffocated under a monolithic stereotype of femininity. Orlando's approach to Angelica drives her away, forcing her to assert vehemently the otherness he wishes to demolish, and the farther and the faster she flies, the more obsessed he becomes with his traditional gods, disregarding everything else and creating with his disregard conditions ripe for the destruction of lovers who have made each other's alterity their god.

At the opening of canto 24, as a comment on the madness described at the conclusion of the preceding canto, the narrator asks a question that at first seems rhetorical: "And what is a more manifest sign of madness than to lose oneself through wanting someone else?" It is true that Orlando has said in his last coherent utterance prior to the madness,

Non son, non sono io quel che paio in viso:
quel ch'era Orlando è morto et è sotterra;
la sua donna ingratissima l'ha ucciso:
sì, mancando di fé, gli ha fatto guerra.
Io son lo spirto suo da lui diviso,
ch'in questo inferno tormentandosi erra,
acciò con l'ombra sia, che sola avanza,
esempio a chi in Amor pone speranza.

(23.128)

I am not, no, I am not what I seem to the eye. That which was Orlando is dead and buried. His most ungrateful lady has killed him, so much war has she waged against him by breaking her faith. I am his spirit divided from him which wanders through this inferno tormenting itself, so that I may be with this shade, which is all that remains, an example to him who places his hope in love.

So he has lost himself on account of his desire for another person and has proven thereby that there could be no more obvious sign of madness than such a loss. However, what then is one to say of the long discipline to which Ruggiero is subjected, which culminates in the sacrifice of himself to Leone as punishment for his failure to trust Bradamante? Clearly, one can lose oneself as Orlando does and go mad, or one can, like Ruggiero, achieve sanity with the same loss. So the narrator's question must be answered both yes and no depending on the circumstances, and the most important of these involves the voluntariness with which the loss of self is incurred. We are back once again to the scriptural injunction: "He that findeth his life shall lose it: and he that loseth his life for my sake shall find it." Ruggiero gains sanity at last by willing the loss of himself to another. Orlando loses his sanity because he is so certain of having found it. In his traditional role, he believes that he has found his life, his identity, and his sanity and that all that remains is for the world to conform. When the world—in the shape of Angelica—fails to do so, and worse, gives evidence that there was never a foundation in reality for any of his hopes, he loses everything. We say that he goes mad, but we must admit that there is nowhere for him to go. Since he was never in possession of himself in the first place, his overt madness can amount to nothing more than an intensification of the state he has been in all along.

In canto 23, at the point of his crisis, Orlando is struggling to stay afloat in a whirlpool of words and signs; if these were all he had to contend with, he would probably be able to save himself. In directing his energies toward the assertion of a traditional role as his god, Orlando becomes a master of words despite his taciturnity, a speaker of many languages including Arabic, in which he converses so expertly that he is able to deceive his enemies. He can do with words as he pleases, because traditions are made of words. Neither the ode written by Medoro on the wall of the cave nor the names on the trees are enough to overwhelm him. Words can be forgeries, he reasons. They can convey malicious lies, or they can be signs pointing to occult realities, to anything but the obvious. He was able earlier to construe Olimpia's words so as to render her an innocent damsel in distress and himself a chivalric defender of the right, but now that the words touch him more closely, his power over them grows even greater. It is particularly ironical that Medoro's ode, written in Arabic and translated for us into Italian from Turpin's version in French, should be modeled on a Latin poem praying for a special dispensation against the intrusion of reality upon a place perfect for its beauty. For it is also Orlando's fervent wish to cover the words he sees with more words until his god and his paradise are safe from desecration by the real.

Experience, however, is Orlando's downfall, just as experience is the downfall of tradition and the undoer of words. Orlando is invulnerable to words, but not entirely to experience, which can leave him disillusioned even if it fails to enlighten him. The sight of smoke rising from rooftops and the sounds of dogs barking and herds lowing draw him into the town and into the cottage and then into the very bed where Angelica first gave herself to Medoro. The image of Orlando writhing in that bed, surrounded by walls, windowsills, and door frames inscribed with the intertwined initials of Angelica and Medoro, is one of the most powerful in the *Furioso*. It is the image of someone who has crossed over to the other side of words and who is viewing them from the inside, from the perspective of the experience that produced them, and not with the detached omnipotence of the interpreter. Experience, as ineffable as the sight of the bracelet he recognizes as his former gift to Angelica, seizes him and transfixes him with the one obvious meaning of the signs that surround him. One wonders if the result, the ensuing frenzy, would not have been the same for the allegorizer of the Hercules

Figures in Ariosto's Tapestry

myth if the texts on which he exercised his powers had been able to open up and plunge him into the presence of the truth that produced them. If one's entire value system, and hence one's mental stability, depends on practicing "fraud on oneself" (23.118), then one must do everything possible, in life as in reading, to avoid confinement to that small room where the truth is inescapable.

Since Orlando has nowhere to go when he leaves that room, his madness turns him into a caricature of his former self. He directs his Herculean energies to uprooting the trees that bear the lovers' initials, much as he had formerly struggled to keep his vision distorted enough to exclude the possibility that such a love could occur. He may proclaim that he is no longer himself, and he may tear off his armor, the outward symbol of his former self, but his madness at this stage represents nothing more than an intensification, stripped of all sane appearances, of his behavior since his introduction in canto 8. When Rodomonte and the others lift Charlemagne's siege of Agramante's camp in canto 27, it makes no difference that Orlando has gone mad, for he would not have been present anyway. However, his frenzy does provide him with an excuse for his absence that Rinaldo lacks. In deserting Charlemagne at this critical moment in order to pursue Angelica, Rinaldo proves that despite his prudent demeanor he is scarcely more valuable than a madman to the cause he supports. The ugliest reflections of the madness, though, are reserved for Orlando himself. In canto 29, he finally meets Rodomonte, the enemy he should have prevented from setting fire to Paris and slaughtering so many people, the enemy who, if dispatched at that time, would not have been able to drive Isabella to suicide. Here, at the bridge built to commemorate Isabella, Orlando has the opportunity, despite his madness, at least to punish Rodomonte for the crimes he had neglected to prevent him from committing earlier, and the reader is primed by the cruelty of Isabella's death to see this late piece of justice enacted. However, the count in his madness is the same as he has ever been—too distracted by his great concern (29.42) even to notice the evildoer. Earlier, devotion to his traditional role had blinded him to reality and caused his actions to be good or ill only as chance dictated; now his frenzy over life's failure to vindicate that role produces the same effect. Disillusionment is no better than delusion.

The pity of this is not so much that Orlando must suffer, but that his disillusionment leaves the field open to the ruthless egotism of Rodomonte. The evil that commemorates its victims by going in search of more victims gets off with impunity, with a mere dunking in the river where it seeks to drown its prey, while Orlando dashes off to wreak destruction on two innocent peasants. Orlando meets these two coming toward him along a narrow path similar to Rodomonte's bridge, where there is room for only one person at a time to pass. They yell at him to step aside, just as Rodomonte did, but now, by sheer chance, Orlando hears their cries and attempts to do to both of them what he should have done to Rodomonte. This encounter with the peasants, "grave and suitable to be narrated in song," as the narrator declares, and "right for the story" (29.50), condenses into a single image the sheer absurdity of Orlando's behavior throughout the narrative, and with the cruelty of his murder of one of the peasants, calls attention to the painful consequences of that behavior. Olimpia is exalted and Isabella is driven to suicide; Zerbino dies and Mandricardo lives to obtain the object of his desire, Durindana; Rodomonte is spared retribution for his murders and an innocent peasant is torn in two. All of this results from the fraud Orlando has practiced on himself. Ariosto's irony is never more acerbic than when he has the narrator report that one of the peasants survived to tell the story, though he had to throw himself off a cliff to escape the madman:

> Quanto è bene accaduto che non muora
> quel che fu a risco di fiaccarsi il collo!
> ch'ad altri poi questo miracol disse,
> sì che l'udì Turpino, e a noi lo scrisse.
>
> (29.56)

> How well it fell out that the one who was in danger of breaking his neck did not die! For he reported this miracle to others until Turpin came to hear of it and could write it down for us.

This joyful exclamation must contain the ultimate in disrespect for human life. However, the narrator's infatuation with his story mirrors only too well Orlando's obsession with a role that has had about as much relevance to the real world as one of Turpin's tall tales.

After the skirmish with the peasants, Orlando has his only encounter with Angelica in the entire narrative, and he fails to recognize her. He sees her as a desirable object, but he does not recognize her as Angelica, and as it turns out, he is just as content with her horse, which he seizes when she puts the ring in her mouth and disappears, as he would have been with her. What becomes of this horse—ridden for miles without rest or sustenance, injured when it is forced to leap a ditch and falls in, hauled for more miles on the paladin's back, and finally, when Orlando can no longer support it or it support itself, dragged along by the reins tied to its right rear leg—is precisely the kind of treatment Angelica would have received had she fallen into Orlando's clutches:

Avrebbe così fatto, o poco manco
alla sua donna, se non s'ascondea;
perché non discernea il nero dal bianco,
e di giovar nocendo si credea.

(29.73)

He would have done as much, or little less, to his lady if she had not concealed herself, because he could not tell black from white, and he thought he was helping when he did harm.

We must ask, though, what difference it would have made if Angelica had fallen into Orlando's clutches before the onset of his frenzy. Would she have fared much better? Granted that she would not have received physical abuse, would she not, however, have been unrecognizable to him then too, except as an object of desire to be treated in certain conventional ways, and would not this conventional treatment of her be just as absurd as tying a horse's reins to its right rear leg and dragging it backward instead of riding it forward? Did Orlando ever have a clear enough conception of Angelica as another person to be able to take any different satisfaction from her than he could from a horse? To this last question, the narrative replies (with its sexual innuendo), yes, he did, but it was not a very sophisticated conception. The whole narrative up to and including Orlando's crisis has demonstrated that he was never able to tell black from white and as a consequence could not avoid doing harm when he thought to do good. A wounded horse has been riding him right from the start.

That Orlando's madness is all of a piece from beginning to end contributes much to the pathos of his character, as does the nature of the madness, rendering inaccessible that which he desires most. Other elements may also attract our sympathy, but the scenes of overt madness are ruthlessly comic. They expose and define Orlando's character in a way that stamps it for all time with absurdity. In those personal notes of his to the text of the *Furioso,* Galileo registers disturbance with the comedy at the opening of canto 30, in which Orlando bargains with a shepherd, trying to persuade him to trade his healthy mount for Angelica's dead mare: "It seems to me that for a madman he is too full of words, and sooner those of a buffoon than of an insane person."[8] If we become caught up in the details of Orlando's behavior throughout the narrative, as Galileo did, we cannot help but notice potentially tragic paradoxes in his character and be tempted to regard the madness, when it finally becomes overt, as the realization of these tragic potentialities. However, the narration of the mad scenes forbids us to take such a view. Instead, it forces us to ask whether Orlando at any time undergoes the self-recognition and reversal of fortune essential to tragedy. We could say that Ruggiero's dagger brought Rodomonte the tragic recognition that he is only mortal, and not the god he insisted he was, but can we say that Angelica's loss of maidenhead brought Orlando a similar enlightenment? Putting the question this way makes it clear that it would have been preposterous for Ariosto to treat Orlando's crisis as anything but comic. In fact, the overt madness as an intensification of Orlando's previous benightedness is the opposite of tragic self-recognition. Orlando's madness may produce tragic consequences for those who have the misfortune to become involved with him, but it produces no such consequences for him. Later his wits return, he fights the battle of Lipadusa, and he delivers Brandimarte's funeral oration, but even then he does not recognize his direct responsibility for Brandimarte's death. Wisdom through suffering never comes to Orlando; hence, despite certain spectacular appearances to the contrary, his character never changes in the *Furioso*.

The encounter with the shepherd follows the pattern of the other mad scenes in caricaturing Orlando's earlier behavior. The apparent reasonableness with which Orlando offers a dead horse for a live one is very humorous, as are the familiar horse-trading expressions he uses. In fact, the familiar expressions are precisely what lend the madman's approach to the shepherd its comical appearance of reason, and herein lies the analogy with Orlando's approach to Angelica all along. The familiar, conventional sentiments he expresses toward her in canto 8 appear reasonable by virtue of their very familiarity and conventionality, even though there is no rational basis for them in his relationship with her. He does not know Angelica's personality when he utters those sentiments, nor does he begin to understand it at any other time during the narrative, so at no point can it be said that he actually loves Angelica. Orlando worships a conventional conception of love, not Angelica. It is Angelica's misfortune that her appearance happens to fit the conception perfectly and so triggers expectations having nothing to do with what she is. From her point of view, Orlando's love is a dead abstraction that he is offering her in exchange for her lively self. He is offering her a dead horse for a live one, and woe to anyone, including herself, who presents an obstacle to the exchange. For failure to conform with Orlando's expectations, mad as they are, the shepherd pays the penalty of a shat-

Figures in Ariosto's Tapestry

tered skull. The fact that Orlando persists in his madness, riding his horses to death and exchanging them for live ones at the cost of the lives of the owners who resist, suggests that the madness is endless and incurable. The dead abstraction with which Orlando hopes to unlock the bounty of life has a sinister and a lasting grip.

What then are we to think of Astolfo's fabulous intervention, and what credence should we lend Saint John the Evangelist's revelation that Orlando's madness was sent from heaven as temporary punishment for his desertion of the Christian cause? Astolfo's journey to the moon and his colloquy with Saint John will be discussed in full in the next chapter, where Astolfo's adventures, taken as a whole, will be the focus. For the moment, it is enough to examine the impact on Orlando of the restoration of his wits. Apparently he undergoes an astonishing change, from raving lunatic to sober wise man. The narrator declares that upon regaining his wits Orlando becomes not only wiser and manlier than before but also is liberated from his infatuation with Angelica, whom he now regards as nothing more than a base object. From this point on, "he addressed his every study, his every desire, to getting back everything that love had once taken from him" (39.61). Such a radical and abrupt change, all by itself, would be enough to create suspicion, but the comical circumstances in which it is effected, with the wits administered like snuff or smelling salts, demand a skeptical reading. What can it mean, we wonder, that Orlando has returned to an improved version of his former self? Would it not be better if, like Ruggiero, he were able to discard that former self, exchanging it for a new one more receptive to reality? How much more clear-sighted is it of him now to regard Angelica as a "cosa vile" than it was of him before to regard her as an earthly paradise? Orlando's sudden return to sobriety can not have brought with it a clearer understanding of Angelica or of himself than he had before. The change is too facile. We doubt that it has enabled him to tell black from white or to avoid doing harm when he means to do good.

Significantly, his first impulse upon regaining his wits is to round up the accoutrements of his old self—the horse Brigliadoro, the sword Durindana, the horn of Almonte—lost during his overt madness. It is a nice narrative touch that he will never be able to regain the helmet that fell into Ferraù's hands after Angelica stole it. Ferraù's unexplained disappearance from the narrative as of canto 35 ensures that Orlando's madness will cost him one loss he is able to feel. If the trappings of his traditional role are all that concern him on his return to consciousness, we may be certain that vindication of that role was always Orlando's primary concern. During his overt madness, he became disillusioned because life failed to conform to expectations inspired by the tradition. Life—Angelica—was *ingratissima* and disloyal for failing to conform, so in a fit of grief-stricken rage Orlando set out to get revenge on reality, tearing up trees by their roots and stripping himself of the accoutrements of the role that life betrayed. Yet, in his madness, he merely showed himself nakedly for what he had always been. Now that his delusion has returned, his first and only thought is to reassemble all of its imposing paraphernalia. The sanity Orlando regains at Astolfo's hands amounts to nothing more than the return of his old delusion, along with all of its dreadful costliness to those involved with him. Now that he regards Angelica as a "vile thing" one wonders what the next object of his desire will be and how that object will elude the approaches prescribed by his conventional outlook. What will his next bout of madness be like?

It is ironical on two counts that Ruggiero's horse, sword, and armor should wash up on the beach near Biserta, where they are found by Orlando and used by him in the battle of Lipadusa. Agramante's treachery in breaking the truce during Ruggiero's single combat with Rinaldo made conditions ripe for the weapons of his strongest supporter to fall into the hands of his mortal enemies—another case of evil creating its own misfortune. But it is ironical, in light of Orlando's sole motive for fighting at Lipadusa, that arms lost by someone in a hazardous effort to come to the aid of his sovereign should happen to come to Orlando at all. Orlando's motive for accepting the challenge of Lipadusa could not be more clearly spelled out:

Lo 'nvito di Gradasso e d'Agramante
e di Sobrino in publico fu espresso,
tanto giocondo al principe d'Anglante,
che d'ampli doni onorar fece il messo.
Avea dai suoi compagni udito inante
che Durindana al fianco s'avea messo
il re Gradasso: onde egli per desire
di racquistarla in India volea gire,

stimando non aver Gradasso altrove,
poi ch'udì che di Francia era partito.
Or più vicin gli è offerto luogo, dove
spera che 'l suo gli fia restituito.
Il bel corno d'Almonte anco lo muove
ad accettar sì volentier lo 'nvito,

Figures in Ariosto's Tapestry

e Brigliador non men; che sapea in mano
esser venuti al figlio di Troiano.

(40.56–57)

The invitation of Gradasso, Agramante, and Sobrino was proclaimed in
public, and was so welcome to the prince of Anglante that he ordered the
messenger to be honored with ample gifts. He had heard from his
companions earlier that Gradasso had buckled Durindana to his side,
whereupon he formed the intention of journeying to India out of the
desire to get it back, thinking to find Gradasso nowhere else when he
heard that he had departed from France. Now there is offered him the
place nearer by, where he expects restitution of his belongings. The
handsome horn of Almonte as well moves him to accept so gladly the
invitation, and Brigliadoro no less, which he knew to have come into the
hands of the son of Troiano.

Far from accepting the challenge in order to protect Charlemagne's
realm, Orlando was on the verge of departing for India to regain Durindana. Now he is delighted to be spared the trouble. It might be objected
that with the destruction of Biserta and the imminent baptism of Ruggiero, Charlemagne is no longer in danger and Orlando is free to do as
he pleases. However, the narrative sequence does not permit this objec-
tion. In canto 40, Orlando is not even aware of Ruggiero's existence,
much less the fact that he is to be baptized and to become a bulwark of
the Faith. As for the destruction of Biserta, how could it deliver Charlemagne from peril while Rodomonte is still alive? If Orlando cared to
make amends for the losses incurred by his madness, he could make an
obvious beginning by seeking out Rodomonte. That this course of
action never crosses his mind confirms that he is still just as mad as ever.
His absorption with his role and its trappings blinds him, as it always
has, to the human needs the role was originally designed to serve. At the
end of his career in the narrative, he is the epitome of tradition gone
bankrupt by replacing substance with outward show. His distribution
of Ruggiero's arms—when he gives Oliviero the armor that might have
saved Brandimarte's life and Brandimarte the horse that might have
spared Oliviero his crushed foot—symbolizes his inability once again to
take advantage of both the misfortunes evil brings down on itself and
his own good fortune in having regained consciousness in time at least
to be of genuine use against Rodomonte.

It is pitiful enough that Orlando attaches more significance to the
loss, incurred by his madness, of certain objects associated with his role
than to the loss of many lives, and that his first intention is to reassemble

the objects rather than to make amends for the lives; but Ariosto insists
on intensifying the sense of waste. In canto 43, Orlando delivers Brandimarte's funeral oration, which begins thus:

O forte, o caro, o mio fedel compagno,
che qui sei morto, e so che vivi in cielo,
e d'una vita v'hai fatto guadagno,
che non ti può mai tor caldo né gielo,
perdonami, se ben vedi ch'io piagno;
perché d'esser rimaso mi querelo,
e ch'a tanta letizia io non son teco;
non già perché qua giù tu non sia meco.

Solo senza te son; né cosa in terra
senza te posso aver più, che mi piaccia.
Se teco era in tempesta e teco in guerra,
perché non anco in ozio et in bonaccia?
Ben grande è il mio fallir, poi che mi serra
di questo fango uscir per la tua traccia.
Se negli affanni teco fui, perch'ora
non sono a parte del guadagno ancora?

(170–71, italics mine)

Oh my strong, oh my dear, oh my faithful companion, lying here dead,
but living, I know, in heaven where you have earned a life that heat and
frost can never take from you, *forgive me* if you see me weeping, for I
grieve, not that you are not with me here below, but that I am left here
and am not with you in so much joy. Without you I am alone, nor is there
anything I can obtain on earth anymore that will please me without you.
If I were with you in tempest and with you in war, why not also in ease
and fair weather? *Great indeed is my failure,* since it bars me from leaving
this mire to follow in your path. If I were with you in your toil, why am I
not now the partner also of your reward?

At the center of both stanzas, Orlando begs forgiveness, and we expect
that he is about to acknowledge his responsibility for Brandimarte's
death. We are disappointed both times, however. Both stanzas trail off
into the commonplace sentiments of a survivor's lament. How much
more human is the grief of Fiordiligi! She avows that she would rather
have Brandimarte here below than see him gone away to any paradise in
the sky. She feels the cruelty of his having been killed just when he might
have experienced the real joy and leisure of his homeland, to which he
fell heir the moment before he departed for Lipadusa. Orlando ends his
speech with a statement that no one could have given his life away with
more profit to others and with more honor than Brandimarte did, and

Figures in Ariosto's Tapestry

though this statement contains some truth, it sounds hollow coming from Orlando. Foremost in the reader's mind is that Brandimarte died from a blow to the head which resembled a hatchet wound and was delivered by Gradasso with the sword Durindana. Brandimarte died, we know, not out of loyalty to any public cause, but because he was loyal to the man whose madness delivered a deadly weapon into the enemy's hands and whose continued madness prevents him from understanding the kind of loyalty that died on his account. We doubt that a public dominated by the likes of Orlando and Rinaldo is worth such a death, and we know, in any case, that the threat posed by Agramante had ceased long before the battle of Lipadusa. From a public standpoint, that battle was anticlimactic.

After the funeral oration, Orlando fades from the narrative. In first begging Ruggiero's hermit to cure Oliviero, who was "fighting for the Faith of Christ, reduced to perilous terms" (43.19), and then in rewarding the hermit for his miraculous cure with a picnic of prosciutto and cheese, Orlando contributes to the mildly farcical atmosphere of that island episode. However, not much more can be said of him. For the rest of the narrative, he stands by while life goes on around him. Ruggiero develops into another Brandimarte and slays the adversary whom Orlando should have destroyed many years and many cantos earlier. Ruggiero and Bradamante form a union that Orlando will never attain. We may wonder what will become of Orlando the next time his god is put on trial. Will he go mad again, or will the role he worships accidentally be vindicated? We never wonder, though, whether he will change his outlook. His fabled invulnerability symbolizes the stolidity of a character that cannot be changed, no matter what is done to it. It symbolizes, not power, but sinister impotence. It leads, not to communion with others, but to deepening isolation. Orlando is never to live a life of individual freedom. Instead, he will always live life according to someone else's account of it.

6
Il Lucido Intervallo (24.3)

ike Rinaldo, Astolfo is a relatively minor character whose involvement in crucial episodes wins him special attention. He has been as successful as Rinaldo in leading critics to make sweeping claims concerning his significance for the *Orlando Furioso* as a whole. The main lines of interpretation were established in the sixteenth century and have come down to us with remarkably little change despite some elaboration. In the 1584 edition of the *Furioso* published in Venice, there appeared Giuseppe Bononome's allegory, in which Astolfo becomes a symbol of literature: "In Astolfo, there is an encomium of letters. With the resounding horn of eloquence and with the book of his wisdom, both of which things he had from Logistilla, he is made the tamer of monsters, and he obtains more by himself than all the others with arms."[1] In 1966, we find that Astolfo is still a symbol of literature, but that he also represents the genius of the poet:

> With his horn, book, horse, and lance, Astolfo is the complete yet unassuming master of magic. He is often foolish, to be sure, but never a fool. He is the still eye in a storm of absurdity; the grotesque and silly and pathetic, and even deadly, transpire around him, but never touch him. Astolfo is the master of his environment: the knight who comments warily on chivalry, the lover who knows better than to expect too much of love, the magician who is unawed by magic, he is like the poet, who comments, or is the filter for comment, on the poem and the nature of art. Like Ariosto, Astolfo is the supreme and superb ironist, more so because he does not seem so, unobtrusive yet ubiquitous, soaring above all creation, a figure from outside the world of the poem . . . yet intimately related to the main characters, and action, of the poem. Like the poet, Astolfo knows everything (or can find everything out: the poet "reads" Turpin; Astolfo uses his magic book) but never seems to *do* much. And like the poet, Astolfo is the benign master of illusion without illusions himself, the constant antithesis of all that is viewed seriously, the comic, the clownish, superficial-seeming man who knows pro-

found, even deadly truths. Astolfo is the genius of the *Orlando Furioso,* the poet looking at himself with irony.[2]

One lesson of the history of literary criticism is that once a metaphor, however tenuous, for the process of literary creation can be seen in a literary image, the door flies open with a gust of wind, and every idea on the critic's shelf gets rattled at least once. In fact, the *Furioso* reveals that Astolfo is the master of practically nothing (not even of his book, which he would be unable to read without its index and table of contents), that he loves no woman at all except Alcina, of whom he has ridiculously high expectations, and that he has nothing whatsoever to say about chivalry and very little to say about anything else. On the other hand, he is almost always *doing* something. The main problem readers have with him is that, unlike Rinaldo, he has practically nothing to say about his exploits, yet his fabulous deeds beg for interpretation. One would like to believe that Astolfo symbolizes literature or the poet, but even Bononome's modest allegory is unconvincing, for if Astolfo's horn is supposed to represent the resounding eloquence of literature, why does everyone, good and bad, run away from its blast? It is doubtful that Bononome could have been pondering the question that troubles so many twentieth-century humanities teachers when they survey their semester enrollments. If there is a connection between Ariosto's characterization of Astolfo and the process or the effects of literary creation, it is not as apparent as Bononome or his modern colleague wish it to be.

The other major line of Astolfo criticism began eleven years earlier than that of Bononome. In his *Bellezze del Furioso,* published in Venice in 1573, Orazio Toscanella declares that the name *Astolfo*

> is used for the contemplative man who penetrates heaven and hell with his wit, and not the earth alone. In this work, he explores not only all parts of the world, but he goes also into the infernal regions and to the earthly paradise. The name is also used for the fortunate and happy man, since he accidentally acquires the golden lance, the hippogryph, the horn, and the other lucky things Ariosto assigns him.[3]

Toscanella shows no concern over the curious contradiction between the two parts of his statement, but then the orthodoxy of his time might have made him feel comfortable with the idea that Astolfo, as a contemplative man, could also be considered a fortunate man. However, if we look to the 1960s again, our problems with the sixteenth-century critic's pronouncement are resolved for us by Mario Santoro's essay "L'Astolfo Ariostesco: *Homo Fortunatus,*" which remains unsurpassed as a systematic effort to demonstrate that Ariosto's characterization of Astolfo is a detailed representation of reality, an act of psychological analysis leading to an understanding of a familiar human type.[4]

Santoro's essay, like his perceptions concerning the characterization of Rinaldo, requires careful consideration. Santoro discards Toscanella's formulation about the contemplative man, but he revives the other half of Toscanella's statement in a thought-provoking way. He provides an exhaustive and illuminating argument that Astolfo's behavior conforms with a pattern of behavior described by the humanist Giovanni Pontano in one of his treatises as that of the "typically fortunate man." According to Pontano, this person always acts impulsively and suddenly, driven by a natural impetus to confront, without reflection or counsel, without doubt or hesitation, the most perilous adventures, and contrary to all rational expectation, this *homo fortunatus* always succeeds, despite his apparent foolishness. He comes by all of his qualities naturally, just as some people are born with blue eyes and others with brown, so he can never be said to be responsible for his successes. His nature impels him to do what time, place, and circumstances require, and if he were to pause to use his judgment or seek advice, he would only nullify or diminish his luck. Ordinary people can never make the best of their luck because they always allow their reason or judgment to interfere. Santoro argues convincingly enough, up to a point, that Ariosto modeled Astolfo's behavior on this pattern. In fact, if one refrains from asking any questions about the larger contextual implications of this argument, Ariosto seems to be the Renaissance's most avid disciple of Pontano. However, we have already seen what is likely to be a parody of Pontano's *De prudentia* in Ariosto's characterization of Rinaldo, so it would be well to reserve judgment in the case of Astolfo as to just how much credit Ariosto gave the moral-philosophical observations of any particular humanist author.

In the case of Astolfo and Pontano's *homo fortunatus,* it could be argued that Ariosto regarded this character-type as a charming but preposterous fiction. In order for such a person to survive, Ariosto might be implying, he would need more than a book that shows how to overcome the commonest illusions of mankind; he would also need a magic horn, a magic lance, and a flying horse. And if he had all of these props and were able to survive in the world of ordinary men, he would almost certainly wage war with giants, extend the boundaries of the known world, discover the realm of Prester John, and learn the secrets of trapping the south wind in a wineskin and of turning rocks into horses and leaves into ships. The degree, then, to which the behavior of

Ariosto's Astolfo conforms with that of Pontano's *homo fortunatus* may well be the degree to which Ariosto considered Pontano's observations ridiculous. The difficulty of any attempt (including Santoro's essay) to see Astolfo as a mimetic representation of reality or as a study of ordinary human behavior is due to the consistency of Ariosto's portrayal of Astolfo as a supernatural figure. The result is that as soon as the reader observes qualities in Astolfo's behavior which seem appropriate for average people, he must, by dint of the outlandish context in which the character operates, regard these qualities as outlandish too. Interestingly, the only time Astolfo becomes involved in a wholly realistic set of circumstances occurs not in the *Furioso,* but in the *Cinque Canti* (4.54–74), when Astolfo himself narrates the story of his adulterous passion for Cinzia. However, the fabulous context is present here too, since Astolfo and his interlocutor, Ruggiero, have become trapped in the belly of a whale. That the story of Astolfo's mundane passion for a married woman should be in the *Cinque Canti,* a fragment left out of the *Orlando Furioso,* only suggests that Ariosto insisted that Astolfo always be associated in the reader's mind with the supernatural.

Another problem with Santoro's analysis has to do with its implications for those larger questions involving Astolfo's effect on the total narrative. If being the *homo fortunatus* is the essence of Astolfo's character, then Ariosto seems to be saying that the only hope—not of relief, to be sure, but of temporary mitigation—for Orlando's madness is good luck, or at least association with a lucky friend. Tempting though this conclusion may be, it must be rejected, because it would render the lunar voyage meaningless. If Astolfo is merely the fortunate man, the lunar voyage is reduced to a lucky discovery, and the reader is discouraged from seeking profound thematic connections between it and Orlando's condition. So Santoro's thesis proves unfortunate in that it inhibits thought concerning Astolfo's impact on the larger narrative. However, the detail and the accuracy of Santoro's observations demand a certain measure of consent. Possibly Ariosto was familiar with Pontano's ideas and adapted some of them to his characterization of Astolfo, but it would be preposterous to believe that Ariosto's sole purpose was to create a copy of Pontano's model. His purpose may have been satiric, or more interestingly, it may have been to suggest that a person would be fortunate indeed to possess whatever qualities Astolfo possesses other than those of the *homo fortunatus.* Perhaps such a person would be more fortunate than any natural person could consistently be, but then all of us, in brief lucid moments, are fortunate enough, like Astolfo, to experience the exhilaration of release from the selves we have laboriously boxed ourselves into. If one irrefutable statement can be made about Astolfo, it is that his progress from incarceration in the myrtle tree to moon flight astride the hippogryph represents release.

In a sense, Astolfo is a hypothetical character—an examination, on Ariosto's part, of the proposition that it would be fortunate if humanity could embody the traits of such a character more often than is the case in this world. Astolfo's association with the supernatural then becomes Ariosto's way of saying that Astolfo is the product of his creator's wishful thinking. While Ariosto was probably all too familiar with cynical men like Rinaldo, it is unlikely that he was acquainted with anyone who could sustain the avidity and the adventurousness of Astolfo for longer than a brief interlude. *Avventuroso* and *volonteroso* are Ariosto's adjectives for Astolfo, and while they do not, at first glance, offer a key to understanding the character as a whole, they do at least signal the traditional aspects of Astolfo that interested Ariosto the most. In the *Furioso,* gone is the braggart of the *Innamorato* lording it over Charlemagne and his court for having rescued them from Gradasso—though through no merit of his own—and gone is the jester of earlier tradition making fun of his knightly colleagues and of Orlando in particular.[5] Instead, it is the adventurous, the willing, the avid, the audacious Astolfo who asserts himself in the *Orlando Furioso.* He is the only character who consistently expects the unexpected and revels in unforeseen outcomes. Hence, he is the only character to whom the dictum of the opening canto, "Ecco il giudizio uman come spesso erra," ceases to apply at a certain point, and this alone is enough to make him seem supernatural.

From the start of the *Furioso,* with his release from imprisonment in the myrtle tree and his visit to Logistilla, Astolfo leads an existence different from any that he had led before in literature and different from that of all the *Furioso*'s other characters—so different, in fact, that it seems that Ariosto designed his characterization to focus attention on contrasting elements of those more ordinary characters' behavior. Like Rinaldo, Astolfo serves as a frame-character, but his exploits stand at the opposite end of the picture from Rinaldo's. If Rinaldo represents an extreme of cautious pessimism, Astolfo symbolizes a kind of optimism that must be treated humorously despite its attractiveness, because the world gives only the faintest glimmers of evidence that there is any foundation in reason for it.

The reader's experience of Astolfo is similar to Astolfo's experience of the world. The reader enjoys Astolfo's exploits without expecting to

Figures in Ariosto's Tapestry

find verisimilitude in their depiction, just as Astolfo manages to enjoy the world without imposing on it the expectations we see Ruggiero, Orlando, and Rodomonte struggling to accommodate. He accepts the multiplicity, the variety, and the shape-shifting nature of his universe without trying to subdue it by dedicating himself to an ideal. Unlike Ruggiero, Orlando, and Rodomonte, and therefore unlike the rest of humanity, he does not seek to superimpose deities, or ideals, of his own making upon an intransigent world and then wage a private crusade against circumstances. Consequently, his sense of time differs sharply from theirs. For them, time is *chronos,* and for him, time is *kairos.* For Astolfo, time is a series of occasions to be enjoyed or made use of, while for the others, time is duration, a devourer, to be vanquished and bent into the service of bringing an ideal to fruition. In his meeting with Senapo in cantos 33 and 38, Astolfo becomes the image of *kairos,* the handsome winged youth healing the blindness and relieving the starvation of old father time. He is able to chase the Harpies, that "infernal troop of avengers" (33.108), back to hell because he is the antidote to the condition that gives rise to them. The Harpies of the *Furioso* are like those of the *Aeneid.* With their fair faces and foul posteriors, and with their desecration of life's banquet, they symbolize waste of the delights of the moment by men who starve themselves in the present in order to pursue an alluring and uncertain goal. With his assault on the Earthly Paradise, Senapo epitomizes these men and becomes Ariosto's symbol of the pathos of deluded humanity. When Senapo learns of the winged youth's arrival, he mistakes him for an angel of God or a new Messiah, but Astolfo corrects him:

Rispose Astolfo: "Né l'angel di Dio,
né son Messia novel, né dal ciel vegno;
ma son mortale e peccatore anch'io,
di tanta grazia a me concessa indegno.
Io farò ogn'opra acciò che 'l mostro rio,
per morte o fuga, io ti levi del regno.
S'io il fo, me non, ma Dio ne loda solo,
che per tuo aiuto qui mi drizzò il volo."

(33.117)

Astolfo answered, "I am not an angel of God, nor am I a new Messiah, nor do I come from heaven. I too am a mortal and a sinner, unworthy of so much grace conceded me. I will do everything possible to rid your kingdom of this evil monster, by death or by rout. If I succeed, praise God, not me, for here to your aid He directed my flight."

This is not the Astolfo of earlier tradition, never one to be humble or pious. Astolfo's insistence on his humanity in this most mythic of scenes is vital to an understanding of his role in the *Furioso*. For he represents a form of release from delusion within the reach of ordinary sinners, if only for the space of an interval. Creation is rich enough, he is saying, for people to find in it a brief respite from the human condition.

To understand Astolfo's significance in the *Furioso,* one must trace his relationships with Senapo's counterparts throughout the epic. At first, this would seem a daunting task because almost all of the *Furioso*'s characters share Senapo's affliction. However, certain juxtapositions and connections stand out. Astolfo shares Ruggiero's experiences with Alcina and Logistilla, he restores Orlando's wits, and he has significant connections with Rodomonte in the earlier and later cantos of the epic. A careful examination of these connections is necessary if we are to understand the characterization of Astolfo and the reason that Ariosto selected him to make that voyage to the moon which "has generally been regarded as an interpretative key to the larger epic, a summation of Ariosto's thematic concerns," as one of the shrewdest readers of the lunar allegory has recently put it.[6]

In the case of Rodomonte, Astolfo makes his appearance at the time of the assault on Paris as the principal figure in a long digression that takes the narrative away from the carnage and into the exotic realms of the East. In an earlier chapter, we observed that Astolfo's adventures there diminished Rodomonte's stature. Rodomonte's scheme to subject the entire world to his own demands comes to appear as deluded as Senapo's effort to conquer the Earthly Paradise. Like Senapo, Rodomonte is blind and destined to starve, for, as Astolfo reminds us, the world is to large to be conquered by Rodomonte. Astolfo's victories over Caligorante and Orrilo, introduced just when Rodomonte seems invincible, foreshadow Rodomonte's downfall. Caligorante provides an image of the monstrous uses to which human ingenuity can be put, as he deploys his mythical net "made of thin threads of steel, but with so much skill that every effort to unravel the weakest part would have been in vain" (15.56). What proves to be indestructible about Rodomonte and inextricable from his character is his own conviction, formed and fostered by all of the art and human ingenuity at his disposal, that it is his prerogative to subject all other selves to his will. Throughout the *Furioso,* his every effort is devoted to the reinforcement of this conviction, and the immediate result is the carnage in Paris, carnage iconographically epitomized by Caligorante's cannibalism.

On the other hand, Orrilo represents the charmed life people with such ugly convictions often lead. No amount of attrition is enough to destroy them. Doralice, Isabella, and Bradamante deal Rodomonte's ego one decapitating blow after another, but like Orrilo, he merely picks up his severed part and reappears a little later the same person he was before. When Astolfo brings horn and book to his comical confrontations with Orrilo and Caligorante, he symbolizes a world too large to be compressed into conformity with obsessions as narrow and destructive as Rodomonte's. It is the uncertain world, to which Astolfo gives himself instead of trying to reduce it is his own dimensions, that holds the likes of Rodomonte by the nose; Rodomonte is not in control. Astolfo's destruction of Orrilo symbolizes Rodomonte's helplessness.

> E tenendo quel capo per lo naso,
> dietro e dinanzi lo dischioma tutto.
> Trovò fra gli altri quel fatale a caso:
> si fece il viso allor pallido e brutto,
> travolse gli occhi, e dimostrò all'occaso
> per manifesti segni esser condutto;
> e'l busto che sequia troncato al collo,
> di sella cadde, e diè l'ultimo crollo.

(15.87)

And holding that head by the nose, he shaves it all front and back. Among the other hairs he found by chance that fatal one. Then the face turned wan and ugly, rolled its eyes, and showed itself by manifest signs to have been brought to its decline, and the trunk, which was following after, amputated at the neck, fell from the saddle and gave its final shudder.

Death, with all of its sure signs, is the limit posted by reality to all human illusions, no matter how durable they seem to have become, and death is the only limit for those, like Rodomonte, who worship a golden calf, an inflexible vision of reality that will never admit the unforeseen and hence the need to change.

Twenty-three cantos later, Astolfo's other connection with Rodomonte also involves the unforeseen, and it involves Agramante as well. Back from his voyage to the moon, Astolfo invades Agramante's kingdom in Africa with an army of Nubians placed at his disposal by Senapo. When Agramante receives the news, he disclaims responsibility for the disaster:

> Quantunque io sappia come mal convegna
> a un capitano dir: non mel pensai,
> pur lo dirò; che quando un danno vegna

da ogni discorso uman lontano assai,
a quel fallir par che sia escusa degna:
e qui si versa il caso mio; ch'errai
a lasciar d'arme l'Africa sfornita,
se da li Nubi esser dovea assalita.

Ma chi pensato avria, fuor che Dio solo,
a cui non è cosa futura ignota,
che dovesse venir con sì gran stuolo
a farne danno gente sì remota?
tra i quali e noi giace l'instabil suolo
di quella arena ognior da' venti mota.
Pur è venuta ad assediar Biserta,
et ha in gran parte l'Africa deserta.

(38.38–39)

No matter that I know how ill it suits a captain to say, "I did not think of it," I shall say it anyway, for when a hurt far beyond all human consideration occurs, there seems to be excuse good enough for that failing. And this is precisely where my case lies, for I erred in leaving Africa unprovided with arms if it was to be assaulted by Nubians. However, who would have thought, besides God alone, to whom no future thing is unknown, that a people so remote should come in such a great horde to do the place injury—between whom and us there lies the unstable floor of that sand shifted every hour by the winds? Still they have come to lay siege to Biserta, and they have laid Africa waste in great part.

The glaring irony of Agramante's words is that he speaks them in France, a land remote from his own and where he has led a great host on an expedition of conquest. If he were able to cross a sea of water, why should not the Nubians cross a sea of sand for the same purpose? Responding to his request for counsel, Sobrino begins by expressing the wish that Agramante had never listened to Rodomonte, who had urged him to invade France, among others

li quali ora vorrei qui avere a fronte:
ma vorrei più degli altri Rodomonte,

per rinfacciargli che volea di Francia
far quel che si faria d'un fragil vetro,
e in cielo e ne lo 'nferno la tua lancia
seguire, anzi lasciarsela di dietro;
poi nel bisogno si gratta la pancia
ne l'ozio immerso abominoso e tetro.

(38.49–50)

Figures in Ariosto's Tapestry

whom I would like to have here now face to face, but more than the others Rodomonte, in order to cast it in his teeth that he intended to do with France that which could be done with a fragile piece of glass, and follow your lance into heaven and hell, or rather leave it behind, and then in time of need sits by scratching his belly and wallowing in black, abominable idleness.

Rodomonte, upon whom Agramante had pinned his hopes, has unexpectedly deserted him in his hour of need, France is unexpectedly strong, and now the unexpected, personified by Astolfo, has occurred again with the Nubian invasion of Africa. By reminding him of Rodomonte's desertion, Sobrino is tacitly reproaching Agramante for having followed advice at the start of his campaign that showed an utter disregard of the unforeseen. Soon after, when Agramante has his spurious vision of Rodomonte and, as a consequence, breaks his solemn oath not to interfere with the single combat between Ruggiero and Rinaldo, he suffers his final attack of deluded confidence that he can master adverse circumstances for which he never prepared his army. Moreover, Ariosto chooses this moment to stress the counterpoint between Rodomonte and Astolfo by bringing the prisoners Rodomonte had taken at the tower erected in Isabella's honor to shores occupied by Astolfo's Nubian troops, who promptly liberate the prisoners so they can join in the siege of Biserta. The uncertain universe conspires against those who overrate their capacity to dominate it; hence, the reader accepts without difficulty the miraculous destruction of Agramante's fleet, as it seeks to escape France, by Astolfo's armada made of leaves cast upon the water.

If the juxtaposition of Astolfo with Rodomonte always seems ominous for Rodomonte and his allies, it would be reasonable to suppose that interaction between Astolfo and the character who finally vanquishes Rodomonte might be auspicious, and it is, up to a point. Ruggiero looks good when he enables Astolfo and the rest of Alcina's jilted lovers to escape the paralysis of their old infatuation. Ruggiero may be fortunate in finding Alcina as infatuated with him as Astolfo once was with her, but it speaks well of his nature that he can grow tired of the sybaritic existence he has led in her company. Astolfo, we suspect, would never have been able to get enough of Alcina. He himself declares that she represented to him the epitome of all the world's goodness (6.47). So we find Ruggiero, much to his credit, playing the same role for Astolfo that Astolfo later plays for Senapo. Astolfo begins his career in the *Furioso* blind and starving, because he believes that he has been ejected from an earthly paradise. It takes a person like Ruggiero, capable of emotional growth, to release him from his wooden obsession.

What then happens is most interesting, for Astolfo benefits more than Ruggiero from Logistilla's instruction. In fact, Astolfo, always depicted as irresistible to women in Italy's pre-Ariostan romances of chivalry, benefits so much from this instruction that he becomes celibate. He is the only character in the *Furioso* to overcome passion—not even Rinaldo accomplishes this. Conversely, Ruggiero has scarcely left Logistilla's classroom when he becomes consumed with lust for Angelica—understandably, some would say, since the woman is naked when he meets her. Ariosto's point could only be that Logistilla's instruction, if it could take hold in a human being, would produce the very thing that Astolfo becomes for the rest of the narrative—a human being in theory only. The serene detachment of the contemplative man from the passionate confusion of this world is not possible, in Ariosto's opinion, except insofar as some people, in their lucid moments, are able to see that reality is vaster and more complex than they thought it was. Human beings at their best are typically like Ruggiero, prone to error, prone to passion, intensely involved in the world's activities, and always developing their capacity for attachment to others. To the extent that this development depends on detachment from oneself, albeit momentary, Astolfo represents something to which Ruggiero must aspire.

Even in the grip of Alcina's spell, Astolfo is able to provide Ruggiero with useful advice. Appropriately, considering the role he will play after his release from the myrtle tree as one who professes that the world's multiformity is more than one person's vision can comprehend, Astolfo warns Ruggiero of Alcina's "fickle disposition accustomed to love and unlove in the same instant" (6.50) and concludes ominously:

Io te n'ho dato volentieri aviso:
non ch'io mi creda che debbia giovarte;
pur meglio fia che non vadi improviso,
e de' costumi suoi tu sappia parte;
che forse, come è differente il viso,
è differente ancor l'ingegno e l'arte.
Tu saprai forse riparare al danno,
quel che saputo mill'altri non hanno.

(6.53)

I have been glad to warn you of her, not that I think it will help you. Still, it may be better that you go not unforewarned and that you know her habits in part, for perhaps, just as your face is different, your wit and your ways are different also. Perhaps you will know that which a thousand others have not known—how to fend off the injury.

Most critics have wisely stopped short of declaring this scene a parody of Dante or Virgil. The Polydorus episode of the *Aeneid* and the Pier delle Vigne episode of the *Inferno* have a certain serious relevance to Ruggiero's condition at this stage of his development. The talking tree of the *Aeneid* warn Aeneas that he has come to an inauspicious place, because the king of the land has sold to the enemy a child entrusted to his protection. Although the significance of this warning for Aeneas's mission, which involves Ascanius and later Evander's son, Pallas, is obvious, it is also clear that captivation by Alcina would represent for Ruggiero the abandonment of commitments to his king and his beloved in exchange for gross material luxuries. However, Dante's talking tree in the wood of suicides has an even more profound significance for Ruggiero.

In Chapter 4 we observed that the delusion governing Ruggiero's dealings with Alcina represents a suicidal paralysis of the mind. However, the allusion to Dante in this scene with Astolfo suggests a more specific interpretation of Ruggiero's psyche, one that is relevant to his behavior long after he leaves Alcina. According to Dante, Pier delle Vigne committed suicide because he valued the appearance of rectitude more than the knowledge of doing right. An early sign that Ruggiero must struggle with this evil appears at the boundary of Alcina's realm in his battle with that group of monstrosities representing various types of vicious and degrading behavior. When the battle begins to overwhelm Ruggiero, the narrator notes:

Se di scoprire avesse avuto aviso
lo scudo che già fu del negromante
(io dico quel ch'abbarbagliava il viso,
quel ch'all'arcione avea lasciato Atlante),
subito avria quel brutto stuol conquiso
e fattosel cader cieco davante;
e forse ben, che disprezzò quel modo,
perché virtude usar volse e non frodo.

(6.67)

If he had decided to expose the shield that once belonged to the necromancer (I speak of the one that dazzled the sight, the one that Atlante left tied to the saddle), he would have defeated that ugly horde in an instant and made it fall down blind before him. Yet perhaps it is just as well that he scorned that method, because he wished to use his own prowess and not fraud.

According to Caretti, in the notes to his edition of the 1532 *Furioso,* "se . . . avesse avuto aviso" cannot mean "se avesse pensato" or "se avesse avuto in mente," because the seventh line of the stanza suggests that Ruggiero already held in scorn the kind of fighting that makes use of external aids like the magic shield. So the phrase must mean "se avesse deciso." Ruggiero decides not to use the shield, even though he can see that he is being overwhelmed by an army of evil creatures, and even though, as the opening lines of the next stanza state, he would rather die than be taken prisoner by them. Furthermore, he has just learned from a talking myrtle tree that the powers ranged against him are greater than anyone can vanquish unassisted. Ruggiero may suffer a necessary defeat in this battle, as we observed in Chapter 4 (necessary if he is to learn his limitations), but what will happen to him if he ever forgets the lesson he learns here? In the future, when death may be the loser's share instead of embarrassment over a temporary bout of self-indulgence, would it not be suicidal for Ruggiero to insist on confronting evil alone and unaided?

However, sixteen cantos later, this is precisely the kind of suicide we fear Ruggiero will commit when he tosses the magic shield down a well. With its assistance, he has just won a bloodless battle against a band of foolish knights and their criminal instigators, but he rides off "with a red face that he dares not lift up for shame" (22.90), wondering if he will ever be able to live down the opprobrium of having won a victory not due entirely to his own prowess. The lesson of Alcina has been forgotten, that a victory over evil is worth more than a demonstration of prowess. Instead, the appearance of rectitude is more important now to Ruggiero than a victory over evil, more important than virtue itself. By this time, Astolfo's many victories—over Caligorante and Orrilo, over the killer women of Alessandretta, and over Atlante's illusionism—all with the aid of magic weapons, remind the reader that the better part of wisdom may be to gain the victory and not to worry too much about to whom or to what it is due. Astolfo's ready use of his magic paraphernalia throws into high relief the fatal flaw that has entered Ruggiero's character at this stage of his development. When the vastness of the world can produce more varieties of evil than one man can cope with, Astolfo's shameless rejoicing over his victories contains a kind of wisdom Ruggiero would do well to acquire if he wishes to avoid committing suicide.

In canto 22, it is Astolfo's turn to release Ruggiero from incarceration. The manner in which he does so contrasts ominously with Ruggiero's repudiation of the shield in the same canto. One of Atlante's spirits, disguised as a peasant, steals Rabicano and lures Astolfo into the palace of illusions, where Ruggiero, Bradamante, and many other prisoners are chasing phantasms. After searching for the steed high and low, inside the palace and out, "without fruit at all that whole day" (22.15), he decides not to spend another day struggling in vain. Instead, "perplexed and fatigued from going around in circles, he realized that the place was enchanted" (22.16), and he avails himself of the external aid—in this case the magic book—required to release him and everyone else from the unusual circumstances into which they have fallen. He recognizes that the unstable universe can confront a man with more challenges than his own resources, however great, can overcome, and consequently he avails himself of whatever aids the same unstable universe casts his way. As we have already observed, Ruggiero's combat with Rodomonte in the closing stanzas of the *Furioso* reveals that he has acquired by then the lucidity to follow Astolfo's example. When Rodomonte breaks his sword, Ruggiero accepts the advantage this gives him. He does not lay down his own sword, no matter how noble the gesture might appear in the eyes of Charlemagne or Bradamante or the rest of the courtiers gathered to witness the combat. Here the victory over evil is more important than the performance of a role, despite the many spectators. Although Ruggiero is not given a chance to slay Rodomonte with his sword and must slay him with a dagger instead, his retention of the sword for as long as he is able represents a major victory over himself.

To follow Astolfo's example in this climactic last battle of the *Furioso,* Ruggiero has had to acquire the ability to step out of character when circumstances demand it of him. Astolfo's relationship with Ruggiero in the *Furioso* is surprisingly similar to his relationship with Rodomonte insofar as his task in both cases is to warn that the process of self-fashioning can be self-destructive and that sometimes an abatement of the effort is called for. Whether the self in question directs its energies toward the subjugation of other selves or revels in placing itself at the disposal of others, its endeavors can turn out to be suicidal. Circumstances are too many and too varied to be met with a single course of action or a single set of values; yet it is precisely the multiformity of circumstance that drives men to create gods and then dogmatically to stake their integrity on single-minded dedication to these deities. Astolfo represents a way out of the dilemma. Ariosto designed Astolfo as an apparent *deus ex machina,* as a representation of a kind of relief which appears to come out of nowhere but which is in fact only the lucidity required of every human being who grows "perplexed and fatigued from going around in circles." This is the lucidity that calls for an abatement of the struggle when it ceases to be effective and that enables one to see, if only for an interval, that the created self is no more than the product of one's own artifice and not an eternal, indestructible ideal to be defended at the cost of one's life and sanity. This is also the lucidity that calls, at certain critical moments, for a passive receptiveness to a world which, though it may be unstable, is also a repository of a stunning variety of forms and circumstances, and which therefore may proffer more effective assistance than all one's own efforts can produce. There is no earthly paradise, Astolfo keeps reminding us, but there is the unforeseen, which can be an ally if only it is recognized and used to advantage.

One of Astolfo's first experiences upon arrival in the Earthly Paradise is to eat a hearty meal with a dessert of fruits so delicious that he has to admit that Adam and Eve were not without excuse for their disobedience (34.60). If there were an Earthly Paradise, it would be full of comical revelations about the world. At the center of Ariosto's imagined paradise is the ironic revelation that things were never the way poets depict them. Appropriately, it is Saint John the Evangelist, the author of Revelations, who delivers this revelation. The corrosive comedy of the text implies that since he is a writer, he should know what he is talking about, and the readers can trust his words as if they were gospel. However, when Saint John reduces his own gospel to the level of the literature he has just been debunking, the reader is left wondering whom he can trust:

> Non sì pietoso Enea, né forte Achille
> fu, come è fama, né sì fiero Ettore;
> e ne son stati e mille e mille e mille
> che lor si puon con verità anteporre:
> ma i donati palazzi e le gran ville
> dai descendenti lor, gli ha fatto porre
> in questi senza fin sublimi onori
> da l'onorate man degli scrittori.

> Non fu sì santo né benigno Augusto
> come la tuba di Virgilio suona.
> L'aver avuto in poesia buon gusto
> la proscrizion iniqua gli perdona.
> Nessun sapria se Neron fosse ingiusto,
> né sua fama saria forse men buona,
> avesse avuto e terra e ciel nimici,
> se gli scrittor sapea tenersi amici.

Figures in Ariosto's Tapestry

Omero, Agamennòn vittorioso
e fe' i Troian parer vili et inerti;
e che Penelopea fida al suo sposo
dai Prochi mille oltraggi avea sofferti.
E se tu vuoi che 'l ver non ti sia ascoso,
tutta al contrario l'istoria converti:
che i Greci rotti, e che Troia vittrice,
e che Penelopea fu meretrice.

Da l'altra parte odi che fama lascia
Elissa, ch'ebbe il cor tanto pudico;
che riputata viene una bagascia,
solo perché Maron non le fu amico.
Non ti maravigliar ch'io n'abbia ambascia,
e se di ciò diffusamente io dico.
Gli scrittori amo, e fo il debito mio;
ch'al vostro mondo fui scrittore anch'io.

E sopra tutti gli altri io feci acquisto
che non mi può levar tempo né morte:
e ben convenne al mio lodato Cristo
rendermi guidardon di sì gran sorte.
Duolmi di quei che sono al tempo tristo,
quando la cortesia chiuso ha le porte;
che con pallido viso e macro e asciutto
la notte e 'l dì vi picchian senza frutto.

Sì che continuando il primo detto,
sono i poeti e gli studiosi pochi;
che dove non han pasco né ricetto,
insin le fere abbandonano i lochi.

(35.25–30)

Neither was Aeneas so pious, nor Achilles so strong, nor Hector so fierce
as it is famed. There are thousands upon thousands upon thousands who
can in truth be ranked before them. The gift, however, of palaces and
great villas by their descendants has caused them to be placed in these
honors sublime without end by the honored hands of the writers. /
Augustus was neither so saintly nor so mild as the trumpet of Virgil
proclaims him. Having had good taste in poetry pardons him his evil
proscriptions. No one would know if Nero were unjust, nor would his
fame perhaps be any the worse even had he had heaven and earth for his
enemies, if only he had known how to keep the writers his friends. /
Homer made it appear that Agamemnon was victorious, that the Trojans
were cowardly and sluggish, and that Penelope, faithful to her spouse,

had suffered a thousand insults from the suitors. But if you wish the truth not to be hidden from you, turn the whole story to the contrary: the Greeks were routed, Troy was victorious, and Penelope was a whore. / You hear, on the other hand, what fame Elissa, whose heart was so pure, left behind; she came to be reputed a harlot for the sole reason that Maro was no friend of hers. Do not wonder that I am pained by this matter and speak so fully about it. I love writers, and I am doing my duty by them, since in your world I was a writer, too. / And above all others, I made an acquisition that neither time nor death can take away, and it was right indeed of my Christ, whom I praised, to repay me with a reward of such moment. I sorrow for those who live in these hard times when courtesy has barred the door. With wan countenance, lean and desiccated, they knock there fruitlessly day and night. / Whence it is, to take up where I started, that poets and scholars are few, for even beasts desert those places where they have no food and shelter.

Modern Ariosto criticism no longer dwells on the notion that this is a cynical jab at stingy patrons; instead it focuses on the relevance of these stanzas to Ariosto's concern throughout the *Furioso* with the relation of literature to reality. As one recent critic discussing this passage puts it, "the poem teaches us to mistrust literature because it is fiction and because it has a relationship with reality difficult to define."[7] However, now that we have observed Astolfo in action, we can also say that the *Orlando Furioso* teaches us to mistrust the selves that are created by us in much the same way that poems are created by poets. To the degree that we consciously fashion ourselves, our identities are fictions, albeit necessary fictions, and will always, like poems, bear an uncertain relation to reality. Ruggiero and Rodomonte, as authors of themselves, and for that matter everyman as the author of himself, must remember this lesson or risk insanity. As Rodomonte learns, it can be a fatal error to mistake the product of one's artifice for reality, and Ruggiero learns in Alcina's realm that such a mistake is likely to end in the oblivion of stagnant self-indulgence. Saint John's revelation is that things are never quite what we wish them to be when our purpose is self-justification. Instead, at such times, the world is filled with false evidence.

When, at the conclusion of his lament for the starving poets, Saint John turns back to Astolfo with that knowing smile that so abruptly replaces the blazing anger that had made his eyes look like two fires, the reader has to suspect that all of the foregoing was only an act, and the bathos into which the saint's lament lapses in its last line only confirms the suspicion. It is precisely this knowing smile that the reader has encountered time and time again in the *Furioso,* only not from Saint

John, but from Ariosto himself, whenever he has caused his narrator to cast doubt on the story by swearing that it conforms in every detail to Turpin's account. The laughter the reader has shared with Ariosto all along, and often engaged in at the narrator's expense, has always come about because reality is far more complicated than any story can ever reliably portray; hence, all stories are potentially comical if seen in the light of the incidents upon which they are based, and all story-tellers are poseurs. Ariosto himself poses as Boiardo's continuator, and his narrator as Turpin's scribe. By declaring that everything was just the opposite of what Homer and Virgil depicted it as being, Saint John intentionally sheds doubt on his statements. We are prepared to believe that things were different from the way Homer and Virgil depicted them, but to insist, as Saint John does, that they were exactly the opposite only calls attention to the haze of uncertainty that will always surround them. So the saint's smile is really an acknowledgment that no one, including himself, has ever been, or ever will be, able to represent reality just as it is, especially since everyone is biased. Of course, the patron who sought to immortalize himself in the verses of the poets he subsidized would be a fool, because the immortal poem, though it might contain his name, could never be anything but a fiction, and as such, a kind of lightning rod to draw down on itself the doubts of all posterity. All human creations are fictions, the saint insists, and one's only saving grace lies in awareness of this truth. That it should be Astolfo with whom Saint John shares this revelation is only logical, since Astolfo's function throughout the narrative has been to remind the reader that the human self is only a fiction subject to the errors of all fictions.

The meeting of Saint John and Astolfo establishes an analogy between the creation of literary fictions and the creation of selves, and it does so at the significant point in the text where the reader learns that Orlando's wits are to be restored. The analogy between literature and life, though certainly relevant to the cases of Rodomonte and Ruggiero, is particularly germane with regard to Orlando. As characters, Rodomonte and Ruggiero, by the time of their appearance in the *Orlando Furioso*, are only one generation old, having appeared for the first time in literature in the *Orlando Innamorato*. On the other hand, Orlando is practically timeless. Almost half a millenium's worth of stories precede his appearance in the *Furioso*. When the narrator of the *Furioso* announces that he will say something about Orlando that has never been said before in prose or rhyme, he is making a promise that Ariosto's contemporaries would have considered impossible to fulfill. However, Ariosto's ingenuity managed to produce the miracle by making the character's problem with life similar to the problem of the person who would tell a story about him. If the story-teller has to cope with a massive tradition, the same is true of the character.

The Orlando of the *Orlando Furioso* suffers the difficulties of a person who enters a world in which his story is already written for him. One is reminded of Don Quixote at the opening of book 2 of his adventures. Orlando's task is to live the story, and the story is a complex one, blending traditions that never accommodated each other very well in the past. Ariosto's genius was to see in this confusion a poignancy that has been acknowledged even by critics who otherwise deny that the *Furioso*'s characters have a complex and consistent human psychology.[8] Orlando's madness results, not so much from unawareness of the limitations of his own artifice in the process of self fashioning, as from his failure to place in perspective an imposing, though confused, artifact— a self handed down to him by tradition in much the same way that those great poems of Homer and Virgil, to which Saint John refers, are handed down to all of us. His position is poignant because he has inherited his maddening burden from ages preceding him. In attempting to lift this burden from his shoulders, if only temporarily, Astolfo is again attempting to cure the blindness resulting from forgetfulness of the fallibility of human artifacts. However, this time the artifact, a self formed by generations of human industry, proves to be too much for Astolfo. His intervention serves only to restore an illusion too powerful to be destroyed.

The relevance to Orlando's madness of Astolfo's journey to the moon is clear. The lesson Astolfo learns there—that even the human artifacts that are the finest and the most hallowed by tradition have at best an uncertain relation to reality—is crucial in Orlando's case. Not even the *Iliad,* the *Odyssey,* and the *Aeneid* can be taken for granted as reliable depictions of the way things were; instead, Ariosto implies, their major value resides in the questions and the doubts they stimulate in the minds of critical readers. Orlando's madness results from his having been an insufficiently critical reader of the self he inherited from a tradition not nearly so ancient or revered as that of Homer or Virgil. He asks none of the questions of that self that would help to clarify its relation to his circumstances. Conversely, Astolfo on the moon is full of questions, not only about the meaning of various articles on that lunar junk heap no one could understand without help, but also about the pageant of the Parcae, Old Father Time, and the river Lethe, whose iconography would have seemed to Ariosto's contemporaries too obvious to require a second thought. At first, Astolfo may seem foolish for asking questions about the meanings of things long taken for granted, but when his questions give rise to startling and unexpected revelations, his foolishness begins to look like wisdom. The text implies that if Orlando had not taken for granted the validity of the roles handed down to him of *preux* and *courtois,* much waste and human suffering might have been avoided. As it is, he can be brought back to himself with Astolfo's assistance, but despite his remorse there is every likelihood that the imposing and contradictory demands of that self will produce the same effects again and again.

Astolfo differs from all of the *Furioso*'s characters except for Rinaldo, because he does not hunger as persistently as they do for the absolute. Having once suffered at the hands of Alcina on account of his role as the handsome ladies' man, he discards this feature of himself, along with the wisecracking and the boastfulness of his former self, in order to embrace the unexpected and to explore the unstable world from all the vantage points fortune provides him. The very ease with which he does this makes him too fabulous to be considered fully and consistently human, but not so fabulous that he is unable to represent what humans can accomplish in moments of clarity. There can be no stability without integrity, and no integrity unless humans consciously fashion themselves and guard against betraying their created selves; however, the self, as the product of human artifice, is only as near to being invulnerable to the onslaught of circumstance as human beings themselves have ever been, and hence, at critical moments must be discarded briefly or else become the cause of its creator's destruction. The self is not an indestructible ideal, no matter how much faith it requires for its conservation.

Rinaldo's prudent response to this perilous condition is to try to find a loophole. For him, the story of the magic dog of canto 43, who pays the price of everyone's faith, is an accurate representation of the human condition. In this dog's world, he reasons, where the instability of everything, and especially of human desires, can subvert the best intentions and the strongest pledges, it is best to conduct oneself in such a way as never to trust in the principles, the absolutes, and the pledges of faith that people claim determine their behavior. However, it is precisely where Rinaldo, from his earthbound vantage point, sees only cause for pessimism that Astolfo, from his aerial perch, sees and symbolizes hope. Rodomonte, Ruggiero, and Orlando are many things, but they are not hypocrites. Their hunger for the absolute is sincere, and so is their fashioning of selves that correspond to their ideal. Moreover, such endeavor is as essential to civilization as is the fashioning of great poems. It is only when art is mistaken for nature and a role is mistaken for a reality that paralyzing dreams of an earthly paradise ensue. Astolfo represents the freedom of some human actors to correct their mistakes by stepping out of character and surpassing themselves once they recognize that their creative energies have become destructive.

7
Fables of Gender

It is very true that nature intends always to bring forth the most perfect things, and therefore it intends to bring forth man as a species, and not the masculine more than the feminine. Indeed, if it always brought forth the masculine, it would create a manifest imperfection, for just as from the body and the spirit there results a compound nobler than its parts, which is man, there also results from the companionship of masculine and feminine a compound preservative of the human race, without which the parts would be destroyed. And therefore masculine and feminine are always together, nor can the one exist without the other. Hence, that which does not possess the feminine cannot be called masculine (according to the definition of the one and the other), nor feminine that which does not possess the masculine. And because one sex by itself exhibits imperfection, the ancient theologians attribute both one and the other to God. That is why Orpheus declared Jove to be masculine and feminine, why it is to be read in Holy Scripture that God created man masculine and feminine in His likeness, and why poets speaking of the gods often confuse the gender.[1]

n discussing Ariosto's treatment of his female characters, one needs a chart to steer through treacherous waters, hence the placement at the head of this chapter of a sober statement about women (and men) by a contemporary whom we know Ariosto respected. Castiglione may have created in the persona of Giuliano de' Medici, to whom these words are attributed in book 3 of *Il cortegiano,* a more trustworthy guide to understanding the women of the *Furioso* than Ariosto's own narrator, who sheds doubt on his reliability the moment he announces that a woman is grinding away his wits just as Angelica is grinding away Orlando's. Ariosto's narrator disqualifies himself at the outset as a judge of women, and we soon see proof of his incompetence. In one place, losing his wits altogether, he laments Angelica's escape from Orlando's mad assault, as if she and a thousand other women deserved the revenge

Orlando would inflict on her. In another place, he warns his female readers to skip the story he is about to tell, for it might give them offense, as if the story were anything but a satirical thrust at male egotism. Where women are concerned, Ariosto's narrator misses the point of Turpin's narrative with comic regularity. His own self-confessed infatuation with a certain woman causes him to worship or revile, approve or disapprove of, the various women in his story according (we suspect) to the treatment he is receiving from her at the moment of his judgment. One even senses that a certain pervasive misogyny on his part, present regardless of his *amour,* stems from a conviction that love means thralldom to the opposite sex. On the subject of women, Ariosto carries the unreliability of his narrator to extremes, giving us, as readers, a powerful inducement to impose sanity where it seems to be absent.

So it seems well to start from the obvious premise, provided by Castiglione and shared, we sense, by Ariosto, that women are human beings no less than men, and to proceed with the hypothesis that the *Furioso*'s female characters deserve the same detached analysis Ariosto invited for his male characters. Ariosto seems, moreover, to have designed his narrator's injustices toward women as a special stimulant to such analysis, encouraging the reader to supply the unbiased point of view and showing that in that point of view and in those female characters resides much of the true subject of the *Furioso.* Ariosto's frequent use of the *querelle des femmes* as a means to expose the foolishness of men, whether in his fifth satire or in Rinaldo's pontifications or in the Innkeeper's Tale, strongly suggests that he considered women the equals of men.

His fifth satire—an unavoidable point of departure for a discussion of the *Furioso*'s women—poses as a diatribe against women, but its true satirical bite is directed at male claims to superiority. The humor of this satire depends on the satirist's sly pretense of benightedness when he advises his newly married cousin (who offended him by not informing him of the marriage) on the proper treatment of wives, using as the major premise of his arguments the assumption that women constitute a species quite apart from men and slightly lower on the evolutionary scale. With that premise, everything that follows naturally centers on keeping these dangerously clever animals chaste and steadfast, and the conclusion, of course, is that the offending part must be sealed just as one muzzles a dog. Since moral arguments are wasted on subhuman creatures, the mechanical solution is all that remains. Of course, a man who takes such a view of women would be a terrible fool for marrying one of them, but that is precisely the point of the satire: men are terrible

Figures in Ariosto's Tapestry

fools if they consider their wives less human than themselves. So the satirist is telling his negligent cousin something like this: "If you think so little of me that you would neglect to inform me of your marriage, I think you deserve advice such as this. Like a lot of men, you are a fool."

Ariosto always plays cat and mouse with his reader, but because of the peculiar intensity of the play when women are concerned, we should be aware that the female characters of the *Orlando Furioso* raise issues of exceptional importance. Living under the influence of Isabella d'Este, and having won her admiration for his poem long before it was published in its first version, Ariosto was understandably inclined to make some startling claims for women, or at least to make his female characters the vehicles of some of his more important thoughts. There is literary evidence, moreover, that at the dawn of the sixteenth century, long before the appearance of *Il cortigiano*, and just at the time of Ariosto's earliest labors on the *Furioso*, the courts of Ferrara and Mantua were particularly receptive to sane ideas on the subject of womanhood. In 1500 or 1501, Mario Equicola wrote *De mulieribus* at the request of Margherita Cantelma, a resident of Ferrara and a friend of Isabella d'Este. In this brief treatise, he argues that God created man the rational animal with both sexes *in potentia*, and not man the male of the species, and that in any case, when we join the angels after death, distinctions of gender will make no difference. He deplores contemporary mores that place women in a state of bondage, and he advocates education as a means of certain progress toward equality in fact as well as theory.[2] Ariosto was unquestionably well enough acquainted with Equicola and his circle during the early years of the *Furioso*'s composition to have been familiar with the contents of this treatise.[3] Also, the existence of other treatises written at about the same time and within the Ferrarese orbit, echoing Equicola's ideas or else going beyond them, proves that the young Ariosto was exposed to an intellectual climate particularly favorable to serious consideration of female equality. He knew thinkers who could see that women exist to do more than provide inspiration to men and ornament to courtly functions.

It is not at all surprising to find a recent feminist critique of the *Furioso*'s ladies in armor, Bradamante and Marfisa, in which the author, Lillian Robinson, argues that the two women are allowed "a greater degree of moral innovation" than the men and that the "chivalric guise" of Bradamante and Marfisa

enables them to exemplify new ideas entering an old system, just as they are, in their own persons, new "forms" wearing traditional armor. By similar extension of the bodily symbolism, their knightly role makes it possible to bring a principle that was understood to be female into the strictly masculine realm of politics.[4]

The principle in question is that of flexibility, and Robinson rightly believes that Ariosto endeavored to raise flexibility "from a habit of mind to a moral principle." While Astolfo, more than the other male characters, exhibits flexibility in the face of human nature's worship of illusions, his association with the marvelous precludes his being regarded as a fully human innovator in society. Furthermore, the lucidity he represents gives individuals like Orlando only the most limited benefits: Astolfo merely restores their old illusions. Hence, Robinson's claim that in the *Furioso* "the progressive spirit, in fact, is identified as feminine and it is the female warriors who introduce it into the military and political organization of society" is especially provocative. If we are looking (though possibly we should not) for a character to whom Ariosto gives his unconditional approval, we are left with the *Furioso*'s female characters to choose among by process of elimination. Ruggiero may finally overcome his absolutist adherence to the chivalric code of honor, but it takes him so long to do so that we are often forced to wonder if the happy outcome of his story would be possible without the intervention of fortune. Could Ariosto have designed the *Furioso* so as to present an implicit revaluation of qualities traditionally regarded as feminine? Did he himself regard these qualities as more important for the continuance of civilization than those traditionally regarded as masculine?

For a proper response to these questions, proper in the sense that it would do violence neither to the text of the *Furioso* nor to our understanding of its larger cultural context, reference to the quotation from *Il cortigiano* at the head of this chapter helps. It reminds us that the shrewder moralists of Ariosto's time, including Equicola, refused to be drawn into partisanship with one sex or the other. In their opinion, the qualities of one sex unalloyed by those of the other amounted to manifest imperfection, or to put it differently, neither the man who cultivated his masculine qualities to the exclusion of his feminine ones nor his ultrafeminine counterpart could be regarded as approaching the human ideal. The concept Castiglione appears to be shaping in the third book of *Il cortigiano* is especially intriguing since he assumes it will be acceptable to the majority of his cultivated readers. The attainment of humanity, he suggests, depends on transcendence of stereotypes based on gender. The most fully human of human beings, regardless of their

Figures in Ariosto's Tapestry

sex, will have learned to strike a balance within themselves between qualities considered to be typical of one sex or the other, and these people will be the true conservators of civilization. In this light, it is easy to see how Ariosto, if he agreed with Castiglione, might have wished to attempt a revaluation of qualities assigned to the sex more subject to disparagement in his day. Every author of note questions what it means to be human, and if he happens to be a Renaissance author with a strong belief in equality of the sexes, he will consider it his duty to correct the imbalances he perceives in his readers' thinking about gender. Ariosto undertook this endeavor by means of his characterization of the woman warrior, and he did so without resorting to any claim that women are inherently superior to men or more "progressive." That a certain female character of the *Orlando Furioso* (who could be none other than Brada-mante, since Marfisa's portrayal partakes of the grotesque) succeeds in transcending her gender and striking the human balance more effective-ly than the other characters, male or female, only indicates Ariosto's concern with placing a higher valuation than they were receiving on special qualities his age attributed to women. The narrator of the *Furioso* may fail in various comic ways to praise women as he often proclaims he wants to praise them, but Ariosto himself succeeds well enough.

Ariosto concentrates most of what he has to say about womanhood in his characterization of Angelica, Bradamante, and Marfisa. When An-gelica and Marfisa take center stage, womanhood is Ariosto's main theme, and when Bradamante is at the center, the subject is not only womanhood but its potential to become something more. The stories of Angelica and Marfisa deal with obstacles to female transcendence of gender in a society dominated by males. Ariosto assumes the role of pathologist in telling them. The armor worn by Bradamante and Mar-fisa, along with their martial deeds, symbolizes their incursion into masculine territory. Since armor is used for protection in battle, women who wear armor have assumed responsibility for their own protection, have decided to achieve their ends by their own means, and have declared themselves challengers to all adversaries who would deny them the freedom to determine their own destinies. The armor, then, is a manifesto, an open declaration of intent. It contrasts with the devious means that even the best of the women who do not wear it are reduced to using if they wish to govern their own lives. The women in the *Furioso* have a proclivity to use fraud, just as the men have a proclivity to use force, and examples of the use of the one against the other in rela-tionships between women and men pervade the work. The story of

Grifone and Orrigille could be interpreted exclusively in these terms. The human balance Ariosto sought to represent would require men to yield some of their autonomy and women to learn to fight openly for theirs; it would require men to learn the value of passivity and women to practice open self-assertiveness. Ruggiero's story bears out this hypothesis as far as men are concerned. Let us look at the strictly female side of the question.

ANGELICA

An early sixteenth-century treatise on women dedicated to Margherita Cantelma and written in Ferrara provides a useful caveat for criticism of Angelica's character:

> The law and government of reason is given to men by God that they may fear God and observe his commandments above all other things dear to them . . . if our enemy the devil uses from time to time the beauty of a woman and her delightful appearance to throw a man to the ground and drag him into sin, what fault, what blame for that, can be in her, who works not toward that end, nor thinks to do the man injury?[5]

We must resist the temptation to hold Angelica responsible for the ills that befall her pursuers; and yet the temptation is strong. Perhaps we fail to distinguish between Ariosto's Angelica and Boiardo's. The Angelica of the *Innamorato* is a cold-blooded, detached manipulator of men. She resembles that Lidia with whom Astolfo converses in the hell to which he has driven back the Harpies in canto 34 of the *Furioso*. A pawn herself in her father's quest for dominion, Boiardo's Angelica delights in using her beauty to make pawns of the men who fight over her. "Use or be used" seems to be her philosophy. Her unrequited passion for Rinaldo impresses us as being a just punishment for her self-centered treatment of everyone else. By the moral criteria of the *Furioso*, this earlier Angelica would be damned for having abused the faith she has encouraged others to place in her. This, however, is not quite the same Angelica we find in the *Orlando Furioso*. Ariosto's Angelica has lost much of her power to manipulate men because the men themselves have become more sinister and less gullible in their relations with her. She still has the power to attract, but Ariosto regards this power as her nemesis. That which attracts men to her—her physical beauty—also blinds them to her humanity. In the estimation of her pursuers, Orlando being the chief among them, she is reduced to whatever her beauty happens to represent to each of them. She becomes a symbol, and since a symbol is literally an object, she is reduced to an object to be fought over by men who have no consideration for her feelings. At the opening of the *Orlando Furioso,* she is defined as "the damsel who was to be the reward of the victor" (1.10).

Having observed this much about the new Angelica of Ariosto's poem, can we still agree with the opinion of her delivered by the ingenious gentleman of La Mancha?

> That same Angelica, Mr. Curate (said the knight), was an unsettled rambling young woman, that longed after novelties and left the world as full of her impertinent actions as of the fame of her beauty. She undervalued a thousand noblemen, a thousand valiant and discreet admirers, and contented herself with a yellow-haired page, who had neither fortune nor reputation, but that of being grateful to his friend.[6]

Allowing for Cervantes's irony, we can condemn Angelica for her choice of Medoro over all of the famous knights of her day only if Ariosto provides evidence that he himself disapproves of the choice. The behavior of Orlando and Rinaldo, the main contenders for Angelica, and Medoro's apparent loyalty to Dardinello, the kind of loyalty so conspicuously missing in Orlando and Rinaldo, suggest that Ariosto applauds Angelica's choice. The narrator may exclaim,

> O conte Orlando, o re di Circassia,
> vostra inclita virtù, dite, che giova?
> Vostro alto onor, dite, in che prezzo sia,
> o che mercé vostro servir ritruova?
> Mostratemi una sola cortesia
> che mai costei v'usasse, o vecchia o nuova,
> per ricompensa e guidardone e merto
> di quanto avete già per lei sofferto.
>
> Oh se potessi ritornar mai vivo,
> quanto ti parria duro, o re Agricane!
> che già mostrò costei sì averti a schivo
> con repulse crudeli et inumane.
> O Ferraù, o mille altri ch'io non scrivo,
> ch'avete fatto mille pruove vane
> per questa ingrata, quanto aspro vi fora,
> s'a costu' in braccio voi la vedeste ora!

(19.31–32)

O Count Orlando, O King of Circassia, your renowned prowess, say, what good is it now? Your lofty honor, say, in what price is it held, or your service, what reward does it find? Show me one single courtesy she ever used toward you, either past or present, in compensation, in reward, in recognition of all that you once suffered for her. O King Agricane, if ever you could return to life, how harsh it would seem to you that in the past she showed you so much aversion with cruel, inhuman repulses. O Ferraù, O a thousand others I record not, who have passed through a thousand trials in vain for this ungrateful one, how bitter it would be for you to see her now in the arms of this man!

However, his vehemence only betrays the erroneousness of his opinion. Medoro is in no respect less worthy of Angelica than any of her aristocratic pursuers, even though, as we shall see, it may be difficult to consider him more worthy. If there is a genuine reason to disapprove of Angelica's behavior in the *Furioso*, it is not to be singled out in her choice of Medoro, nor in any act of hers in the narrative, and yet the sum of her deeds, along with the contrast she makes with Bradamante, strongly suggests that Ariosto ranks her low on the moral scale occupied by his female characters. There is even a certain ludicrousness about her story, which one critic has recently described as "une épopée burlesque sur les dépucelages manqués."[7]

Angelica is undoubtedly a complex character who has had a history of polarizing readers' responses. In one instant, she has us commiserating with her over the ills brought down on her by her beauty, and in the next, we are laughing at her foolishness. Upon analysis of Angelica's character, D. S. Carne-Ross, who strenuously denies that Ariosto entrusted his larger meanings to his characters, builds the argument that oxymoron is a major organizing principle of the *Furioso*:

> Ariosto did not simply accept the principle of variety and treat it more artistically [than did Boiardo]: he intensified it to the point where it sets up a kind of modal discord. This is a feature of the *Furioso* as a whole, but nowhere is the poetic tone so consistently mutable, nowhere does it modulate so rapidly from one viewpoint to another and provide such juxtaposition of contrasting images as in the scenes which have to do with Angelica.[8]

Another extended passage from the same essay eloquently defines the main problem in analyzing Angelica's character:

> If we attend the way this poem is written and mark its constant variation of style and mode, we come to recognize that it moves not only on different but often irreconcilable levels; that in shifting from one viewpoint to another it offers not merely different but irreconcilable images. Auden somewhere tells the story of Henry James, in the days when he frequented Maupassant's salon, putting on his top hat which a young woman had just filled with champagne. I do not believe this story, Mr. Auden comments, *because I am*

unable to contemplate James in such a situation. The *Furioso* would in effect be prepared to contemplate both visions: James in his patrician dignity; James dripping absurdly with champagne. Both how unlike each other, both how true. It contemplates the Angelica of the Verginella stanza, a half divine presence before whom the elements bow down in homage; and the tumbled girl who lies unconscious in the hermit's arms. The strayed lamb of Orlando's pastoral fancy; and the calculating young woman who uses her charms on Sacripante.

Are the sublime and ridiculous postures in which Angelica is portrayed truly irreconcilable? Despite his insistence that they are, Carne-Ross suggests that the combination of disparate images has a certain verisimilitude. If this is the case, perhaps there is also a consistency underlying their inconsistency. Actually, the discord is not half so intense as Carne-Ross imagines; to see this, one need only separate the visions Orlando and Sacripante have of Angelica from what we actually witness her doing and saying. Carne-Ross's example of Henry James, dignified patrician and drawing room clown, would serve well to describe Proust's fiction, not Ariosto's. Still, there remains the problem of explaining the ambivalent response Angelica herself provokes, and of doing so without falling into the trap set by Ariosto of blaming her for the abuses committed by her pursuers.

The Socratic dictum that ill treatment of people makes them worse than they would otherwise be might help us here. The ill treatment Angelica suffers takes its toll on her character. Her very struggle against those who regard her as "a half divine presence," as a symbol and an object, may at times entice her to deal with these enemies on their own terms, and thereby to acquire some of the taint of their behavior. The world, as represented in the *Furioso,* may be awed by Angelica's sublime beauty, but it also does its best to reduce that beauty to a baser, more current metal, and half succeeds, despite Angelica's resistance. Canto 1 demonstrates the process. Angelica no sooner takes flight, rejecting her status as prize of the victor in battle, than she runs into Rinaldo, whom she loathes. The double allusion in stanza 11 to the *Inferno* (15.122–23) and the *Aeneid* (2.379 ff.) creates sympathy for Angelica and ridicules Rinaldo, who is tacitly compared with a sodomite racing over the burning sand of Dante's hell. Rinaldo's passion seems even baser when it causes Angelica the kind of fear experienced by a person who suddenly realizes that he has been betrayed by enemies he thought were friends, the second allusion being to the episode of the *Aeneid* in which a Greek, during the fall of Troy, finds himself at the mercy of Aeneas and his band because he thought they were Greeks. Angelica experiences a sudden revulsion against a love that might be just as dangerous as virulent hatred. The same emotional realism inheres in that allusion to Horace (*Carmina* 1.23) in stanza 34, where Angelica is described in the terms Horace used to depict the fear of a young girl becoming aware of sexual passion for the first time. The imagery is especially effective in its new context because the behavior of Rinaldo and Ferraù suggests that all else besides lust is hypocrisy. This is the great goodness of the knights of old! In various ways, some of which are not so subtle, Ariosto depicts Angelica in canto 1 as inhabiting a dark wood of sin and error. Lovers are enemies disguised as friends, and love is only a name for unscrupulous lust trampling all civilized values underfoot. Here the act of love is no more than a violation of integrity and a reduction of the beloved to an object worth no more than other objects. Ferraù is as absorbed in searching for a helmet as in pursuing Angelica. What are Angelica's alternatives in such a world?

The alternatives which Angelica perceives and which thereby define her character are presented in her encounter with Sacripante. Having escaped from Rinaldo and Ferraù, she comes upon a pleasant grove and a thicket of roses and flowering hawthorne. Ariosto's description of this bower metamorphoses conventional poetic images into a portrait of the young woman's psyche:

> Ecco non lungi un bel cespuglio vede
> di prun fioriti e di vermiglie rose,
> che de le liquidi onde al specchio siede,
> chiuso dal sol fra l'alte quercie ombrose;
> così vòto nel mezzo, che concede
> fresca stanza fra l'ombre più nascose:
> e la foglia coi rami in modo è mista,
> che 'l sol non v'entra, non che minor vista.

(1.37)

> Lo, she sees not far away a pretty thicket of flowering hawthorne and vermilion roses seated by the mirror of the limpid stream, sheltered from the sun among the lofty shadowing oaks, and so empty at the center that it affords a cool retreat among the deepest shadows. The branches and leaves are intertwined so that the sun does not enter there, much less a feebler vision.

The pink and white blossoms establish a symbolic relation between the young woman and the thicket in a manner so conventional as to seem stale; however, the images that follow are puzzling and even troubling. They unfold in darkness. Some flowers, to be sure, bloom best in the shade, but not where they are shut off from the sun, as these seem to be.

These flowers appear to derive their light from their own image reflected in the flowing brook, but this can be only the faintest of images. When Angelica withdraws into the hollow within the thicket, she completes her identification with the floral imagery and recedes into ever deepening shadows. Taking cover within shadows that are already in the shade, she becomes a figure of self-contemplation carried on in the dimness of utter solitude. Here, not only the eye of the sun, but all eyes, are barred from penetration. The eyesight and sunlight analogy implies that being in the light and being visible may be life-giving for most creatures, but not for Angelica, at least in her own opinion. Being seen regularly imperils her integrity, which Angelica believes her virginity represents. From her point of view, she can be herself only in her own company, and the only safe regard to have fixed upon her is her own. All others seek to exact a fatal compromise. The more delightful one is to the eyes of others, the better it is to be invisible.

Angelica's outlook is understandable considering the repeated assaults she has suffered from suitors so arrogant they cannot conceive of themselves as unwanted. However, the self can be in as much danger of dissolution in radical retirement as in immersion in the world. What meaning can the face in the mirror have if we have no other faces with which to compare it? How can one know oneself without being known to others and knowing them? There is considerable pathos in Angelica's situation. The pathos might even have contributed to a tragic effect if Ariosto had allowed her to fall into the clutches of a certain madman. As it is, Ariosto gives her a brush with tragedy when all of her evasions throughout the narrative succeed only in leading her to a barren seashore in the escort of a person unable to defend her against an onslaught of the madness she has been fleeing all along. The image of Angelica hidden in the thicket represents the plight of a person trying to do the impossible—to conserve her integrity where she herself would be unable to discern it. Where there is no light no flowers can grow, and where there is no reception for other selves there can be no separate identity, only at best an engulfing narcissism.

When Sacripante enters reciting some Italianized verses of Catullus, Angelica's state of mind reveals itself in action. The fatuousness of Sacripante's Verginella speech (an adaptation of the speech recited by some coy virgins to their suitors in Catullus's original) is consistent with a certain ineffectualness that had clung to his character throughout the *Orlando Innamorato*. He was always the knight who seemed the least likely to succeed, and for this very reason Angelica is attracted to him, if not as a lover, at least as a companion. She needs an escort home to

Cathay, and she reasons absurdly, though understandably, that she would be safest in the company of a weak man. Her decision to reveal herself to Sacripante in this scene has the same motivation as her choice of him over Orlando at the palace of illusions later on, the choice that drew a comment from Galileo about the proclivity of attractive women to take weak men for their companions. The Verginella speech falls upon Angelica's ears as a confirmation of the outlook that has driven her into hiding. She is of no value, she hears, except as a prize, and once she is won she will be of no concern to anyone but the victor. However, the contestant in this scene has given considerable evidence of malleability, so why not use him and then discard him, why not use him as an instrument just as he would her? Deceit would seem justifiable in the circumstances. When Angelica emerges from the thicket crying, Peace be with you, my maidenhead is still where it has always been, she is described as a Diana or a Venus making an entrance on the stage. It is not the real Angelica, presumably, who decides to meet Sacripante on his own terms and make use of him. This is only an act. The real Angelica still lies concealed backstage in her thicket of hawthorne and roses. However, the dilemma here for Angelica is that her integrity is forfeit whether she tries to preserve it by concealment or deceit. Acting in one sense involves acting in another. Her actions, if deceitful, may amount to stage acting, but they are her own actions. One cannot play along with another's base or foolish behavior without being infected with baseness and foolishness.

Angelica's use of concealment and deceit is doomed to cause her failure. In isolation, integrity has no meaning; in the world, there is no security except in corruption. Angelica never becomes aware of the turn taken by Sacripante's thoughts because he is unhorsed and humiliated by Bradamante before he has a chance to act. With Sacripante's decision to pluck the morning rose before the opportunity eludes him, Ariosto makes a crucial adjustment of Angelica's image away from Boiardo's portrait of the sovereign manipulator and more toward reality. Angelica's attempt to manipulate Sacripante renders her vulnerable to abuse. When she herself plays along with his delusion, ostensibly approving of the exaggerated significance he attaches to her virginity, she encourages him to conclude that she will be his if he takes it. Angelica's willingness to let herself be thought of as something less than a human being, to let herself be thought of in strictly sexual terms like that graphically symbolic rose, exposes her to danger. Ariosto's treatment of the rose imagery throughout this episode reminds one of Georgia O'Keeffe's large canvasses filled with anatomically explicit flowers.

The point of this treatment, though, is to stress Angelica's error, albeit provoked by Sacripante, of letting herself become identified with the lowest common denominator of her femininity—a sexual organ. In doing so, she weakens what protection she could hope for from moral strictures applying to human beings. She abdicates her humanity. Restoration of the human balance comes swiftly, though, in the form of Bradamante, whose armor here represents the open determination to be regarded as human, to be regarded as something more than a sexual creature. The toppling of Sacripante from his horse then symbolizes nothing more than the fact that human beings cannot be acquired like objects by taking them. If Angelica were able to follow Bradamante's example, she could probably find her way home to Cathay by herself. Angelica's rescue by a woman implies just as much reproach for her as for Sacripante; it is Angelica's fatal flaw that the reproach is wasted on her.

A dreamlike logic governs Angelica's story up to her rescue from the orca. Having consented to be regarded as nothing more than an extension of her sexual parts, she enters a nightmare world populated with runaway horses, lascivious magicians, and marriages to devouring monsters. Her story takes on the surrealistic quality we have already noted in Ariosto's representation of Ruggiero in Alcina's paradise. Ariosto enables us to see the world from Angelica's distorted point of view. Her encounter with the hermit presents a condensed image of her adventures earlier with Rinaldo, Ferraù, and Sacripante. She meets someone who cultivates an appearance of trustworthiness, but no sooner has she confided in him than he shows himself to be a lecher. Moreover, his lechery succeeds so well in making the world unmanageable for her that she is forced to give over her very consciousness while he tries to do as he pleases with her. This, in her view, is what her pursuers' jousting and fighting is all about, so it is only appropriate that the hermit's attempts to penetrate her are described in a jousting metaphor. The hermit's impotence is a necessary feature of the nightmare, for how can something be said to be experienced by a person who is anesthetized while it is happening to her? As far as Angelica is concerned, her pursuers might as well be impotent, for what they would do could only happen to a part of her while the rest of her slept—while her humanity slept or remained buried in that thicket of hawthorne and roses. Ironically, after Angelica acquiesces in being regarded as a sexual toy, the world not only denies her any right of self-determination but also denies her the very sexual gratification others seek in her.

Ariosto revolutionizes the characterization of Angelica, turning

Boiardo's cold-blooded egotist into a study of frigid self-abdication. Relinquishing one's humanity, no matter how strong the provocation, places one beyond the pale. The comforts of intercourse (in every sense) vanish and the world seems a dangerous wilderness. Whether in flight, concealment, or deceit, Angelica's every deed suggests that she regards herself, not as someone who does things, but as something to which things are done. The pressure of being regarded as such by others proves too much for her. Although she struggles against these others, she is unable to discover an alternative to their view. Passivity is the theme of her only speech in the *Furioso*:

> Stupida e fissa nella incerta sabbia,
> coi capelli disciolti e rabuffati,
> con le man giunte e con l'immote labbia,
> i languidi occhi al ciel tenea levati,
> come accusando il gran Motor che l'abbia
> tutti inclinati nel suo danno i fati.
> Immota e come attonita stè alquanto;
> poi sciolse al duol la lingua, e gli occhi al pianto.
>
> Dicea: "Fortuna, che più a far ti resta
> acciò di me ti sazii e ti disfami?
> che dar ti posso omai più, se non questa
> misera vita? ma tu non la brami;
> ch'ora a trarla del mar sei stata presta,
> quando potea finir suoi giorni grami:
> perchè ti parve di voler più ancora
> vedermi tormentar prima ch'io muora.
>
> Ma che mi possi nuocere non veggio,
> più di quel che sin qui nociuto m'hai.
> Per te cacciata son del real seggio,
> dove più ritornar non spero mai:
> ho perduto l'onor, ch'è stato peggio;
> che se ben con effetto io non peccai,
> io do però materia ch'ognun dica
> ch'essendo vagabonda io sia impudica.
>
> Ch'aver può donna al mondo più di buono,
> a cui la castità levata sia?
> Mi nuoce, ahimè! ch'io son giovane, e sono
> tenuta bella, o sia vero o bugia.
> Già non ringrazio il ciel di questo dono;
> che di qui nasce ogni ruina mia:
> morto per questo fu Argalia mio frate,
> che poco gli giovàr l'arme incantate:

per questo il re di Tartaria Agricane
disfece il genitor mio Galafrone,
ch'in India del Cataio era gran Cane;
onde io son giunta a tal condizione,
che muto albergo da sera a dimane.
Se l'aver, se l'onor, se le persone
m'hai tolto, e fatto il mal che far mi puoi,
a che più doglia anco serbar mi vuoi?

Se l'affogarmi in mar morte non era
a tuo senno crudel, pur ch'io ti sazii,
non recuso che mandi alcuna fera
che mi divori, e non mi tenga in strazii.
D'ogni martìr che sia, pur ch'io ne pèra,
esser non può ch'assai non ti ringrazii."
Così dicea la donna con gran pianto,
quando le apparve l'eremita accanto.

(8.39–44)

Dazed and immobile on the unsteady sand, with her hair loose and
disheveled, with her hands clasped and her lips motionless, she kept her
weary eyes raised to heaven as if accusing the Great Mover of having bent
the fates all to her destruction. Motionless, as if stunned, she remained
awhile, and then she let go her tongue to grief and her eyes to tears. / She
said, "Fortune, what more is left for you to do that you may quench your
hunger and have enough of me? What more can I give you henceforth, if
not this wretched life? But you do not crave it, for you were swift just
now to pull it from the sea when it might have ended its miserable days,
and only because it pleased you to see me suffer still more before I
die. / Yet I cannot see how you can harm me more than you have already.
Because of you, I am driven from the royal city to which I expect to
return nevermore. I have lost my honor, which is worse, for even if in
reality I did not sin, still, by being a vagabond, I provide the means for
everyone to say that I am unchaste. / What in the world is left of good
for a woman whose chastity has been stolen? Alas, it harms me that I am
young and rightly or wrongly considered beautiful. In no way do I thank
heaven for this gift, for all my ruin is born of it. Because of it, my brother
Argalia died. Of little use to him were the enchanted arms. / Because of
it, Agricane the king of Tartary undid my father, Galafrone, who in India
was the great khan of Cathay, whence I have arrived at such a pass that I
change my lodgings from one day to the next. If my belongings, if my
honor, if you have taken my people from me, and done the worst you can
do to me, for what further sorrow do you wish to preserve me? / If
drowning me in the sea was not a cruel enough death in your opinion, I
repine not, provided that I may sate you, at your sending some beast to

devour me, just so that you keep me no longer in these torments. For every torture that may befall, provided that I perish of it, it cannot be that I will not thank you enough." Thus spoke the lady with great weeping, when there appeared to her the hermit by her side.

As Angelica sees it, God, Fortune, and her beauty are responsible for her plight. This would be sophistry were Angelica not totally sincere. She believes she is the tragic victim of her beauty, which one senses she would like to spell with a capital letter. However, the coyness with which she introduces the subject, not claiming forthrightly that she is beautiful, but merely averring that she is rightly or wrongly considered so, deflates her tragic pose. It reminds us that it was not so much Angelica's beauty that wrought the destruction of her father and brother as it was the devious use to which that beauty was put. In the *Innamorato,* Galafrone unleashed forces beyond his control when he prostituted his daughter's beauty to his ambitious purposes, and now, in the *Furioso,* we find Angelica herself unconsciously behaving in a similar way. If one believes, as she does, that one is unable to take command of one's life, it follows that most of one's actions will be devious. The helpless must enlist the help of others, and what better way to do this than to convince them that they will receive something they want in return for their services? Of course, this is precisely what Angelica has done with Sacripante, dangling herself before his eyes as the sexual prize to be won if he does her bidding, and when this abject behavior fails, it results in a further confirmation of her helplessness. She is caught in a vicious cycle, but she is not the tragic victim she would like to think herself. Instead, she makes herself (as events at the conclusion of her speech suggest) a magnet to attract lecherous hermits.

The progression of images in the development of Angelica's character—from the melee of canto 1 with Rinaldo and Sacripante at its center, to the hermit who bridges cantos 1 and 8, and finally to Proteus and the orca—moves from the real to the increasingly surrealistic. Ariosto first looks at the young woman from the detached perspective of an outsider and then gradually moves in until he ends by representing the world as it appears to her. The first part of canto 8 portrays the nightmare of an abject spirit for whom the protean world is reduced to a threatening syndrome. Women are raped and abandoned and then punished for the crimes committed against them. Nothing makes sense. The creatures of the sea lay siege to the land, and virgins are offered to a beast in expiation of a crime committed, not by them, but against one of their number. Reduced to its essentials, the story of Proteus and the

Ebudans may represent the *Furioso's* ghastliest moment of black comedy. A rapist abandons his victim, the victim's father executes her as punishment for having been raped, then the rapist returns to avenge himself on the murderer, and finally the murderer's subjects appease the rapist by handing over to him one young woman after another as human sacrifice. A nightmare could not exist without roots in reality, and even Castiglione reminds us that the men of his time had far more power to destroy a woman's life than women had to destroy a man's, but the utter helplessness of women in this story, the utter absence of any shred of self-determination on their part, rings untrue to life, whether in the sixteenth century or at anytime. It is easy to see how Angelica could be provoked to take such a view of her plight by the behavior toward her of an Orlando or a Rinaldo, but the determination of other beautiful women in the *Furioso* suggests that Angelica's view is dangerously distorted. Ariosto enables us to understand Angelica and to sympathize with her, but he is too shrewd not to see and comment on the defects of a character as prone as hers to regard itself as powerless.

We have already observed, from the standpoint of a study of Ruggiero's character, how ironic his rescue of Angelica is, and now we are in a position to observe a further irony. From the standpoint of a study of Angelica, this rescue completes the scene begun with Sacripante in canto 1, but interrupted by Bradamante. It brings Angelica's story full circle, as such a story could only be brought. There is no room in Angelica's character for escape from the vicious cycle in which she is caught. Considering herself powerless, Angelica can only hope that rescue from her nightmare will come from without. She believes that it must fall out of the sky and that the rescuer must be a man, since all women, in Angelica's view, are helpless. Bradamante's lightning appearance in canto 1 left no impression. So Angelica has no recourse but to hope for rescue at the hands of her persecutors themselves, for men are her persecutors. It follows, then, that her only means of procuring the help she believes she requires will be her physical beauty, the very thing she blames for having rendered her helpless to begin with. The image of Angelica chained naked to the rock embodies this paradox, her nakedness serving simultaneously as a symbol of her powerlessness and as a powerful enticement to Ruggiero to rescue and then violate her. In canto 1 Angelica exposed herself in a figurative manner to Sacripante in order to obtain his assistance, and now she finds herself exposed again.

Here Angelica's exposure draws to her both the orca and Ruggiero, the persecutor and the savior at the same time, and the savior, Ruggiero, soon becomes as bad as the persecutor. This scene symbolizes Angelica's malaise. She presents herself to the world in precisely such a way as to evoke the response she fears the most, and yet it is difficult to blame her for this, because the world has provided her with little evidence, besides Bradamante's rapid appearance and disappearance, to suggest that there is a better way to accomplish her purposes. Still, Bradamante's appearance, however brief, makes us resent the hypocrisy in Angelica's eagerness to use her beauty to achieve her ends while she demands sympathy as a victim of that beauty. She treats her beauty both as a means of gaining help and as the excuse for her inevitable failure. Meanwhile, she herself is as good as invisible. She takes no responsibility for her actions since she believes they can always be rationalized as reactions to a world that will not permit her to be otherwise than she is. The ring she recovers from Ruggiero symbolizes the negativeness of her character, which will never emerge from hiding and assert itself in the open. That the ring might symbolize reason in this episode is the most unlikely of unlikelihoods.

Perhaps Angelica's worst deed in the *Furioso* was her acceptance of the bracelet that becomes the engine that moves Orlando into overt madness. Orlando is headed unavoidably for a collision with reality, and his very pursuit of Angelica forces her to make light of the objects to which he attaches importance. However, it is impossible fully to exonerate Angelica for having accepted the bracelet in the first place, because she understood that Orlando regarded it as a tangible expression of his faith. It does not mitigate her wrongdoing that Orlando's faith was not in her, but in a false illusion, and that as a consequence he deserves his suffering. If anything, this increases Angelica's culpability, for she understood that acceptance of the bracelet could only mean, as far as the giver was concerned, acceptance of what it symbolized to him. The shepherd and his wife to whom Angelica gives it may be a deserving couple, but there must be a better way, we conclude, to preserve one's integrity than to practice deceit. After witnessing Angelica's treatment at the hands of Rinaldo, Orlando, Sacripante, and Ferraù, we may perceive a certain poetic justice in her treatment of the bracelet as a prize to be done with as she sees fit, but this is nonetheless a form of justice to be expected of thieves who are insensitive to the feelings of others. The bracelet is possibly Ariosto's most effective symbol of the taint Angelica acquires from dealing with her pursuers on their own terms. Angelica's cruel disregard for what the bracelet means to Orlando is an evil sprung up in response to the evil of Orlando's own overbearing, if unconscious, arrogance. However, the episode that concludes with the giving away of the bracelet is one of the most equivocal episodes in the *Orlando Furioso,* one that must certainly be examined in any analysis of Angelica's character. At its center is Medoro, our opinion of whom does much to influence our final judgment of Angelica.

Just as this episode ends in canto 19 with the ethical murkiness of Angelica's disregard for the bracelet, it begins in darkness in canto 18 after a day of defeat for the Moors at the hands of Rinaldo's British reinforcements. Medoro declares his desire to bury his leader, Dardinello:

> Volto al compagno, disse: "O Cloridano,
> io non ti posso dir quanto m'incresca
> del mio signor, che sia rimaso al piano,
> per lupi e corbi, ohimè! troppo degna esca.
> Pensando come sempre mi fu umano,
> mi par che quando ancor questa anima esca
> in onor di sua fama, io non compensi
> né sciolga verso lui gli oblighi immensi.
>
> Io voglio andar, perché non stia insepulto
> in mezzo alla campagna, a ritrovarlo:
> e forse Dio vorrà ch'io vada occulto
> là dove tace il campo del re Carlo.
> Tu rimarrai; che quando in ciel sia sculto
> ch'io vi debba morir, potrai narrarlo:
> che se Fortuna vieta sì bell'opra,
> par fama almeno il mio buon cor si scuopra."
>
> (18.168–69)

Turning to his comrade, he said, "O Cloridano, I cannot tell you how much it hurts me that my lord remains on the field, alas, too noble a food for wolves and ravens. Remembering how kind he always was to me, I feel that even if this spirit of mine were to depart in honoring his fame, I would not be repaying or dissolving my immense obligations toward him. So that he will not remain unburied in the midst of the countryside, I intend to set forth and find him, and perhaps God will wish me to go thither unseen where the camp of King Charles reposes. You will stay behind, for if it is carved out in heaven that I must die, you will be able to tell the story. If Fortune forbids so handsome a work, my good heart will at least stand revealed by fame."

Ariosto critics have too often succumbed to the temptation to disregard the latter half of Medoro's utterance. Medoro begins so well, with a declaration of selfless loyalty beyond death, that one wishes to shut one's eyes to his conclusion, a callow expression of vainglory. However, the temptation to put on blinders must be resisted or else the Virgilian allusion will be lost. Virgil's episode of Nisus and Euryalus begins in book 9 of the *Aeneid* with a question concerning the ambiguity of human motivation, a question that cuts to the center of Virgil's concern throughout the epic: "Dine hunc ardorem mentibus addunt, / Euryale, an sua cuique deus fit dira cupido?" Are we responding to principles greater than ourselves when we take action, or are we merely deifying our own ill-considered impulses? One wonders if there could have been a question of greater significance to Ariosto when he was composing the *Orlando Furioso* and developing its major characters, all of them in the throes of the dilemma posed by the Latin poet.

It is no wonder, then that Ariosto seized on the ambiguity of his model and intensified it. Comparing Ariosto's imitation with its Latin model emphasizes the darker side of Medoro's motivation. In the Virgilian episode, Nisus, the older man and the instigator of the action, tells his companion to remain behind so that the younger life may be preserved in case of failure [Te superesse velim; tua vita dignior aetas]. But Medoro, to whom Ariosto gives the role of instigator, shows only his juvenile desire to win fame and his disregard of his friend's life. He sees no fame to be won in such private and plebian concerns. In the midnight butchery of the Christian troops, Ariosto continues to stress Medoro's darker side. Medoro's butchery contrasts unfavorably enough with Orlando's disdain of such cowardice when Orlando leaves Paris and passes through the sleeping Moorish encampment to begin his quest for Angelica; however, when the narrator notes that Medoro disdains to strike any members of the "ignoble plebian class," preferring instead to slaughter nobles, we have to gasp at the perversity of Medoro's mind. He becomes a parody of chivalrous valor. Hence, when, during Medoro's prayer, the moon breaks through the clouds to reveal the corpse of Dardinello, the narrator's ironic parenthesis, "whether it were by chance or yet his abundance of faith," seems appropriately skeptical. The rest of the scene, up to the wounding of Medoro and the death of Cloridano, may go on to vindicate Medoro, depicting him as genuinely grief-stricken over the death of Dardinello; but we are unable to forget the baser side of Medoro's behavior and the selfish motive that accompanies his noble sentiments. We never learn whether Dardinello receives a decent burial, but the cost would be high even if we could be sure that he did.

Despite his own taste for bloodshed, Cloridano emerges as the more sympathetic figure in this episode (just as his counterparts do in their stories—Nisus in the *Aeneid,* and Dymas in book 10 of Statius's

Thebaid). Cloridano performs a much greater deed than that of Medoro when he lays down his life for his young friend. He has no hope of fame to issue from his deed. His only motive is *fede* pure and simple, and he has already demonstrated that he has no illusions that cause him to undervalue life. When Zerbino's troops approach, Cloridano is the one who advises that they drop Dardinello's body and run, " 'for it would be not too shrewd an idea to lose two living men to save one dead one' " (18. 189). Cloridano is the wiser of the two, so his sacrifice is worth more than Medoro's. To the extent that Medoro let a baser motive enter into his decision to seek Dardinello's corpse, he must assume responsibility for his sacrifice of a man better than himself to his own hunger for glory. The outcome of Medoro's adventure suggests that he attaches too high a value to *fama* and misunderstands the meaning of *fede,* which is to value the life of one's friend more than one's own. Dardinello being dead and Cloridano being alive, Medoro's choice was simple, if only his mind had been freer of delusion.

Who, then, is the person to whom Angelica gives herself? Is he morally superior to Orlando and therefore more deserving of reward? The text forces us to conclude that he is no better than Orlando. That midnight butchery, so graphically described, lingers in memory. To be sure, *if* Medoro's loyalty to Dardinello were unclouded by a baser motive, it might serve as a reproach to Orlando for his abandonment of Charlemagne, but then Medoro would be a different person, and the outcome of his adventure might well be so different as not to leave him where he can be found and pitied by Angelica. As it is, we suspect that if Medoro had Orlando's power he would be just as dangerous as Orlando, not only to his enemies, but also to his friends. The text implies that Angelica pays (though not heavily, of course) for her cruelty in disregarding the symbolic meaning of Orlando's bracelet by giving herself away at last to a man no better than Orlando. Medoro prospers beyond his wildest dreams, but the text shows no more deservingness on his part than on that of a person who holds a winning lottery ticket. Ariosto is more deceptive and elusive in his treatment of the union of Angelica and Medoro than usual. He leads the reader who is overly sympathetic toward Angelica to draw conclusions about Medoro that will not stand up under scrutiny. If we fail to recognize Angelica's faults, we will be inclined to enlist Medoro into the company of Ariodante, Brandimarte, and Zerbino, where he does not belong. Medoro's faith is defective by comparison with theirs, and his union with Angelica is resoundingly inconsequential. Faith is not rewarded with beauty and limitless riches in this union, nor is persecuted femininity rescued from male rapaciousness. The best that can be said is that one rather supine person gathers enough energy to throw herself into the arms of another person whom she perceives to be as helpless as herself, and she thoroughly enjoys the experience.

The entire Medoro episode bridging cantos 18 and 19 comprises, a lovingly contrived Ariostan red herring. If it contains any poetic justice at all, this justice applies exclusively to Angelica. The episode does not provide punishment for her, but at least it defines her once and for all and renders superfluous any further participation on her part in the narrative. Having abdicated any responsibility for her future, she falls in love with the carcass of a handsome boy. It seems right that things should turn out to be so. Medoro's prostrate, unconscious form is as far from posing the kind of threat embodied in Orlando or Rinaldo as could be imagined. If one's self-conception renders one powerless against such threats, as Angelica's does, there is no alternative but to seek a nonentity as a mate. Is this not the justice that self-abdication calls down on itself? It would be pointless to require that Angelica should suffer punishment beyond this, or even to begrudge her the enjoyment of Medoro's humble company. Even our mercurial, unreliable narrator, after a moment of hotheadedness, is able to see this. It might be more fairly said of Ariosto's Angelica what has been said of Boiardo's Angelica, that she has very little autonomy and scarcely any life whatsoever, apart from that conferred on her by her pursuers, Orlando being the chief among them.[9] This is her great failure. She is the woman who breaks under the pressure of the chase, who supinely adopts her pursuers' opinion that she is powerless to assist herself or to deny anyone the right to treat her as he pleases. Flight is her only recourse, invisibility her only hope.

MARFISA

If the character of Angelica represents a meditation on the role gender can play in the suppression of humanity, the same is certainly true of Marfisa. It is difficult to conclude that great talents are wasted when Angelica rides out of the world with her humble spouse at her side; however, Marfisa gives evidence time and again of exceptional potentialities marred by a fatal narrowness of purpose which, we must recognize, has been thrust upon her because she is a woman. No woman in the *Furioso* suffers more on account of her sex than does Marfisa. Ariosto gives us the essence of her character in canto 26, when Mandricardo, intending to give her to Rodomonte in compensation for

Figures in Ariosto's Tapestry

Doralice, claims her as the prize of his victory over Viviano, Malagigi, Aldigiero, and Ricciardetto:

Marfisa, alzando con un viso altiero
la faccia, disse: "Il tuo parer molto erra.
Io ti concedo che diresti il vero,
ch'io sarei tua per la ragion di guerra,
quando mio signor fosse o cavalliero
alcun di questi c'hai gittato in terra.
Io sua non son, né d'altri son che mia:
dunque me tolga a me chi mi desia."

(26.79)

Marfisa, lifting her face with a haughty expression, said, "Your opinion is quite mistaken. I concede that you would be speaking the truth, that I would be yours by right of war, if my lord happened to be one of these knights you have thrown to the ground. I do not belong to one of them, nor am I anyone's but my own. Therefore, let him who desires me take me from myself."

This is the only scene in the whole of Marfisa's life in the *Innamorato* and the *Furioso* in which she condescends to put on female attire, and no sooner does she do so than she is treated in exactly the same way we have seen Angelica treated. The men assume she has neither the right nor the power of self-determination. Her open defiance of Mandricardo is far nobler than Angelica's flight and furtive acquiescence, since open assertion of autonomy is always better than self-abdication. However, Marfisa carries her defiance to an extreme. Rebellion becomes her style of life—she wears her armor constantly, and not only is she always prepared to fight, but she actively seeks combat, preferring to fight even when there is no reason to do so and when other solutions are available. We suspect that her acceptance of the "right of war" means that she considers life a state of constant warfare in which it is unsafe to depend upon anyone other than herself.

Ariosto depicts Marfisa as a driven being. In the *Innamorato,* she wore her armor because she had vowed not to take it off until she had defeated the three greatest kings of the earth. *Superbia* was her dominant trait, and the most memorable image of her in the *Innamorato* depicts her pride being brought low by Brunello as he rides before her with her stolen sword, baring his rear end to her view. In the *Furioso,* there is scarcely any reference to Marfisa's vow; instead, we are left wondering why she always wears armor, why she is constantly on her guard and anxious for a fight, and why she so frequently gives notice that she is prepared for a struggle of wills. *Superbia* ceases to be the motivating force of her character, and with it vanishes the shrill and vulgar tinge lent by Boiardo to her belligerent nature. We come to believe she is reacting against circumstances that are not her fault, and in this she resembles Angelica to a certain extent, like the obverse side of the coin on which Angelica's image is stamped. Marfisa's reaction to the circumstances that shape Angelica's life, a life plain in every respect except for its physical beauty, may be that of an extraordinary woman who is nonetheless unable, like Angelica, to make of her life something more than a reaction.

Like Angelica, Marfisa is a virgin upon her first appearance in the *Furioso,* but unlike Angelica, she remains one to the end of her days beyond the *Furioso*'s narrative when, we are told, her destiny is to aid Bradamante in avenging the death of Ruggiero. Ariosto's narrator even suggests that the phoenix emblem she wears on her helmet may denote, not pride, but an intention to remain a virgin:

> Marfisa se ne vien fuor de la porta,
> e sopra l'elmo una fenice porta;
>
> o sia per sua superbia, dinotando
> se stessa unica al mondo in esser forte,
> o pur sua casta intenzion lodando
> di viver sempremai senza consorte.

> (36.17–18)

> Marfisa issued from the gate, and on her helmet she bore a phoenix, either, on account of her arrogance, to denote herself unique in the world for strength, or else to celebrate her chaste purpose of living forevermore without a consort.

We know, at this juncture, that Marfisa no longer considers herself the strongest fighter in the world. She has been won to admiration of Ruggiero's prowess and also aided by him in the battle in canto 26 with Mandricardo and Rodomonte. Hence, these lines may be regarded as Ariosto's explicit rejection of Boiardo's characterization of Marfisa. In the *Furioso,* militant self-sufficiency, not pride, characterizes Marfisa, ennobling her and at the same time diminishing her human potential. It is significant that these lines describe her as she issues from the city of Arles to fight Bradamante, who has had no greater purpose throughout the *Furioso* than to achieve a union with the consort of her choice. The repeated pummelings Marfisa takes from Bradamante's magic lance, which knocks off her helmet, plunging the phoenix emblem in the mud, denote the fatal impotence of Marfisa, who is bent on defining her character primarily through rebellion and determined to remain self-sufficient at the cost of forming attachments to others. The element of slapstick in this combat stresses the futility of Marfisa's resolve when confronted with a more fully human determination, even if that determination is expressed only in the form of Bradamante's mistaken jealousy. The phoenix here is not a symbol of human potentiality, but literally a mythical, unnatural creature.

Despite her failings, Ariosto does Marfisa considerable justice. Bradamante, in a jealous rage, may deny Marfisa any courtesy, "as to one whom I hear to be endowed with every kind of rudeness and arrogance" (36.21); however, Ariosto has been very careful to distinguish between Marfisa's self-sufficiency and Rodomonte's egotism. Driven to take refuge in Arles, Agramante was unable to persuade Rodomonte to leave his narrow bridge long enough to come to his aid even after he had offered him a kingdom and a royal bride. The case with Marfisa is very different:

> Già non volse Marfisa imitar l'atto
> di Rodomonte: anzi com'ella intese
> ch'Agramante da Carlo era disfatto,
> sue genti morte, saccheggiate e prese,
> e che con pochi in Arli era ritratto,
> senza aspettare invito, il camin prese:
> venne in aiuto de la sua corona,
> e l'aver gli proferse e la persona.

(32.6)

> Marfisa in no way wished to imitate the behavior of Rodomonte. Instead, as soon as she heard that Agramante had been undone by Charles, his people killed, despoiled, and taken captive, and that he had withdrawn with a few followers into Arles, she set out on the road without awaiting an invitation. She came to the aid of his crown, offering her person and her substance.

This generosity is characteristic of her behavior throughout the *Furioso*. She tends most often to take sides with the disadvantaged, and while in the *Innamorato* she would have done this only to make a proud display of her strength, the same cannot be said of her motive in Ariosto's work. We learn enough about her past from Ariosto—a past predating her earliest appearance in the *Innamorato*—to conclude that she may have deep sympathies with the weak and the disadvantaged and that these may arise from her experiences as a woman.

When Marfisa presents herself to Charlemagne in canto 38, she delivers herself of an account of the years of her life from the time that she was stolen from Atlante as a child until she set forth as a knight errant to foreign parts:

Nutrimmi un mago infin al settimo anno,
a cui gli Arabi poi rubata m'hanno.

E mi vendero in Persia per ischiava
a un re che poi cresciuta io posi a morte;
che mia virginità tor mi cercava.
Uccisi lui con tutta la sua corte;
tutta cacciai la sua progenie prava,
e presi il regno; e tal fu la mia sorte,
che diciotto anni d'uno o di duo mesi
io non passai, che sette regni presi.

(38.14–15)

I was nurtured until my seventh year by a magician from whom the Arabs stole me then. They sold me as a slave in Persia to a king whom I put to death when I grew up, because he sought to take my virginity. I killed him and all his court, drove out all his wicked progeny, and seized the kingdom. Such was my destiny that I seized seven kingdoms before I was one or two months past my eighteenth year.

Having been kidnapped and sold into slavery and then nearly having been raped, Marfisa has learned one lesson well: survival depends on constant vigilance, on constant, strenuous assertion of one's autonomy. It is no wonder that she feels ill at ease with the knowledge that there may be a man in the world with enough strength to overpower her. The wonder is that she has managed, through open competition with men and success against them, to avoid the hatred of the male sex she encounters and scorns in the city of Alessandretta. The pity of her early experiences as a woman is that they have permanently armored her against that crucial abandonment of autonomy required by trust and hence necessary to any meaningful intercourse with other human beings. In the *Furioso* she is a loner, an isolated being, whose outrage remains unmitigated to the last. The best that can be said for her rage is that it becomes focused when she learns of her membership by birth in Charlemagne's community.

Marfisa's armor ennobles her when the outrage she has imbibed as a woman is directed against injustice. However, the same armor diminishes her when it serves as a manifesto of rebellion against nature by denying and concealing her sexual being. Marfisa's career in the *Furioso* proves that gender cannot be transcended through a refusal to acknowl-

Figures in Ariosto's Tapestry

edge its existence. The relatively minor episode of Marfisa's involvement with Gabrina reveals the delicate balance of her characterization. In canto 20, she parts company with her comrades in the adventure of the city of Alessandretta,

> dicendo che lodevole non era
> ch'andasser tanti cavallieri insieme:
> che gli storni e i colombi vanno in schiera,
> i daini e i cervi e ogn'animal che teme;
> ma l'audace falcon, l'aquila altiera,
> che ne l'aiuto altrui non metton speme,
> orsi, tigri, leon, soli ne vanno;
> che di più forza alcun timor non hanno.
>
> (20.103)

> saying that it was not praiseworthy for so many knights to travel together. For starlings and doves go in a troop, deer and the fallow-deer, and every other animal that feels fright, but the bold falcon and the proud eagle, who do not place their hope in help from others—bears, tigers, lions— go their way alone, having no fear of any greater force than their own.

That the others do not, as the narrator notes, share her opinion suggests that they value the intercourse of other human beings—society, such as it is—more than the stark self-sufficiency Marfisa strives for. The life of bears, tigers, and lions does not hold the same attraction for them that it holds for Marfisa, but then they have never suffered abuse resulting from men's misconceptions of womanhood. When Marfisa meets Gabrina in her solitary path, she happens upon a means of revenging herself on the holders of these misconceptions. Her encounters with Pinabello and Zerbino measure the justice and the injustice of her revenge. How far beyond reason does Marfisa's rebellion against erroneous custom carry her? How far can a rebellion against society's errors go before it becomes a rebellion against nature, against the very condition itself of sexual differentiation?

Marfisa's natural generosity and compassion cause her to give the aged Gabrina a ride over the rough country in which she finds her. One cannot be faulted for acting generously in such circumstances or for not inquiring too closely into the worthiness of the person one assists. Nor can one be faulted for feeling outraged at such insolent treatment of an elder as Gabrina receives from Pinabello's lady. However, the arrogance of this lady is especially annoying to Marfisa, for it is founded on the very misconception of female worth against which Marfisa revolts most vehemently. Pinabello's lady firmly believes that a woman's worth depends on her physical appearance. In her opinion, all aged and homely women and all women whose first concern is not their physical beauty may be regarded to varying degrees as objects of derision. When Marfisa unhorses Pinabello, who has undertaken to champion this view, and strips the arrogant lady of her finery, we cannot help but regard her as having justice on her side. She is asserting the claim that women are human beings, not pretty ornaments, and as such deserve to be treated with respect no matter what their age or physical appearance. If society fosters such views as that taken by Pinabello and his lady, then society is wrong, and Marfisa is right to carry on her solitary rebellion. If the adventure with Gabrina had ended here, and if we knew nothing of its consequences, we would have no reason to consider Marfisa's heroism equivocal. But the adventure continues, as always in Ariosto, and the reader is required to discriminate the good from the bad in Marfisa's behavior. Dressing the aged and ugly Gabrina in the youthful finery of Pinabello's lady may serve as a reproach to that lady, but the reproach does not restore Gabrina's dignity. Being turned into a memento mori makes Gabrina look like a monkey dressed in human attire. To disparage society's vain concern with physical appearances is well and good in moderation, but Marfisa's vehemence renders the disparagement itself ridiculous. How much right does Marfisa have, we must ask, to take offense when Zerbino, in his turn, finds the aged Gabrina laughable?

Moral principles, no matter how noble and true, have always suffered at the hands of vehement advocates who dogmatically apply them to cases that do not accommodate them. Marfisa's use of Gabrina to test the principle that women are human beings, not pretty objects, ends up doing the principle more harm than it does its detractors. Pinabello and his lady learn nothing from their encounter with Marfisa, unless it be the lesson of force, which will let them go on to inflict on others the same humiliation that Marfisa has inflicted on them. Wounded vanity seeks to heal itself by wounding others. While Marfisa can be forgiven her outrage with this pair, it is difficult to absolve her of blindness toward Gabrina. Marfisa may not know much about Gabrina's past, but surely she should see the vanity in Gabrina's unawareness of her absurd appearance. When Gabrina grows livid with rage over Zerbino's amusement at the spectacle she makes, she shows herself to be even vainer than Pinabello's lady. Marfisa is blinded by her passionate advocacy of a principle, so she fails to see its perversion in the case she has undertaken to defend.

When Marfisa first met Gabrina her intention was simply to perform a humane act by helping an elderly person on her way, but Pinabello and his lady came along and caused Marfisa to see Gabrina as a symbol to be borne aloft on horseback like a banner. When Zerbino pokes fun at this grotesque emblem of feminine liberation from thralldom to fair appearances, he is laughing at the ludicrous want of decorum in the old woman's youthful garb. Doubtless, he would have laughed just the same at an old man in boys' attire. However, the expression he lends his amusement is tinged with the same sexual bias exhibited by Pinabello and his lady. "Warrior," he says, "you are full of good sense for guiding a damsel of such a kind that you need not fear finding anyone who will envy you on her account" (20.119). The grotesque sight coming upon him unawares elicits an unconscious, spontaneous expression of just those prejudices against which Marfisa is constantly on guard. She has created a circumstance designed to elicit the response that antagonizes her the most; but Zerbino is guilty, too, for playing Marfisa's game. His words imply, whether he intends them to or not, that only youthful and physically attractive women are worth fighting for, that nothing else but appearance matters in a woman. So it is not surprising that he lets himself be drawn into a fight rather too easily when Marfisa assails his own male vanity. That he should be left in thralldom to the old hag seems fair at first, but of course it is not; Gabrina as an individual, and not as a symbol, has already shown herself to be infected far worse than Zerbino with those prejudices Marfisa detests. Furthermore, by honoring his promise to serve Gabrina, Zerbino demonstrates a quality that more than compensates for his mild, unconscious disparagement of the female sex. Were it not for Zerbino's possession of "the faith that girds a beautiful soul" (21.1), Marfisa's game would be for naught.[10]

The destruction of such men as Zerbino, men of conscience and loyalty, can do nothing in the long run to advance Marfisa's crusade, and yet her encounter with him enlists his best quality—his faith—in the process of his destruction and subdues his goodness to the service of evil. Would Marfisa have been so free in the first place to make an issue of Gabrina if she had not cut herself off from the human companionship of her comrades in the adventure of Alessandretta? The isolation to which Marfisa subjects herself in her assertion of self-sufficiency cuts her off from mitigating influences and plunges her into a state of self-absorption from which there is no escape. With Gabrina she creates a self-fulfilling prophesy. The world's response to the grotesque emblem of the old woman in youthful attire cannot help but confirm Marfisa in her conviction that she must always be on her guard against those who would reduce her human worth to a fair female appearance. She need only interpret the laughter Gabrina occasions as an assertion that physical beauty is a woman's chief means of distinction, and then the world becomes a jungle where only bears, tigers and lions can survive with dignity. Marfisa needs to keep the enemy constantly in sight, because her identity is founded on rebellion. She requires the existence of the evil she detests so much, to the point where she will seek it out and find it even in people who, like Zerbino, are more than ordinarily inclined to recognize the rights of other people, male or female.

Moreover, by insisting that Zerbino keep a straight face at the spectacle of Gabrina, Marfisa is demanding that nature itself, in the form of sexual attraction and repulsion, be repressed sufficiently for there to be no laughter at the sight of a parody of physical beauty. Her militant virginity demands an annulment of the senses. Physical beauty should not even be considered a noteworthy womanly attribute. Marfisa's rebellion becomes a struggle, not against social mores alone, but against nature itself, and she herself takes on the air of a human anomaly. Even in her most sympathetic moment, in canto 26, when she defies Mandricardo, the glimpse we are given of her body suggests a grotesque disfigurement. Her face retains its feminine beauty, but her masculine body resembles that of Mars. In her struggle against a world permeated by male misconceptions of female worth, Marfisa fails to become more human than strict definition by gender allows. Instead of transcending gender, she turns herself into a creature mocked and diminished by sex. Since nature will not be vanquished or denied, the violence of her struggle ends only in her own deformity.

Violence, outrage, constant vigilance, stark aloofness from other human beings—these characteristics distinguish and disfigure Marfisa in every adventure. The extreme ambivalence of her character—its nobility and its absurdity—is never more apparent than in the city of Alessandretta. A more vivid image of the sexual warfare waged by women against men than that depicted by the society of Alessandretta would be difficult to imagine. The entire episode is drenched in sexual hostility. Having been betrayed and abandoned by their lovers, the original settlers institutionalized their revenge, turning courtship and sexual love into combat. Their aim was to get even with the male sex for its greater freedom and power by converting marriage into bondage and sexual intercourse into a grinding competition. Alessandretta is Ariosto's image of the female hatred of men that inevitably arises in any society that denies women control over their destinies; however, this hatred is also depicted as a self-defeating syndrome, not only because of the sexual frustration it causes the women themselves but also because

Figures in Ariosto's Tapestry

it denies them the humanity of living in harmony with the other half of their species. It takes only a lucid interval, represented by Astolfo's blowing of the magic horn, for everyone, male and female, to run in horror from their self-imposed suffering. We are never told whether the women of Alessandretta regroup after their salubrious fright, but presumably they do, and always will do, as long as women are compelled by social mores to regard themselves as powerless in relation to men. The syndrome will return to its old virulence until it breaks apart under internal stresses, only to rise, phoenixlike, over and over again, except in its sufferers' lucid moments. Marfisa scorns the women of Alessandretta because their hatred is only a by-product of submission to the norms against which she openly rebels. If only she were content to scorn them and rise above their vindictiveness toward men, all would be well; however, Marfisa believes that she can overcome the women of Alessandretta, and hence the syndrome they represent, by sheer force of will and the denial of her sexuality. In this, she becomes ludicrous, brandishing her sword as the solution when it is only too obvious that enlightenment is called for to correct an imbalance between the sexes. The phallic image of the sword mocks Marfisa's irrelevant outlook. To the extent that life is sexual and sexual problems call for sexual solutions, Marfisa's benightedness is absolute. Where nature is of no help to her, she is confident that she can use her sword to compensate (19.69).

Ariosto is emphatic, throughout the *Furioso,* in demonstrating that the worst ills of human nature will not yield to force and that the enemy is never quite so easily discernible as Marfisa believes, especially when the enemy has made incursions into one's own character. Marfisa's relations with Ruggiero and Bradamante expose, with greater clarity and poignancy than elsewhere, the damage suffered by her character. After the comic pummeling she takes from Bradamante, Marfisa learns of her parentage and rebukes Ruggiero, in canto 36, for continuing to support Agramante despite his knowledge that Agramante's father and uncle joined in the destruction of the parents she shares with him. Ruggiero's continued allegiance to Agramante at this point is misguided, but it would be difficult to admire him if he turned against Agramante for the reason Marfisa now does. There are better reasons for Agramante to lose the allegiance of his best warriors than any accident of lineage or history. He deserves punishment in his own right for his own deeds. Marfisa might have offered as a better reason for her disaffection with Agramante his execution of Brunello, intended to ingratiate himself with her, when she herself, though severely provoked, would not condescend to so mean a deed. However, her judgment is so clouded that she would continue to serve a king capable of currying favor with her in so pusillanimous a way. It is a blot on the generosity of her character that she requires the pretext of her parentage to bring her to a repudiation of Agramante. We suspect, however, that this pretext works better than clear-sighted judgment because it taps that reservoir of rage Marfisa carries within her wherever she goes.

Equally as benighted as her rebuke of Ruggiero for serving Agramante are her repeated assurances to Bradamante that she will force Ruggiero to keep faith with her, as if private agreements between individuals were subject to enforcement. Faith being voluntary, Marfisa's assurances are preposterous, and when they end in her taking up the sword to defend a false claim—that Ruggiero and Bradamante are already legally married and no union between Bradamante and anyone but Ruggiero can be licit—we feel compelled, despite our longstanding sympathy with the lovers, to take sides with the opposition. Marfisa makes a good cause look bad, and Bradamante's father, Amone, does not hesitate to hammer home the falseness of Marfisa's position. At this point, no one but Leone can make right the deplorable circumstances created by Ruggiero's failure to trust Bradamante to bring about their union. Ruggiero's selfless loyalty to the man who has saved his life has to influence that man to give him his life again. That Ruggiero's loyalty succeeds also in effecting the moral regeneration of Leone himself, who had used Ruggiero in a fraudulent scheme to obtain Bradamante, confirms us in our conviction that the faith of one person in another can be the only justification of a union between Ruggiero and Bradamante. To give Marfisa her due, we must admit that her resolution to fight for Bradamante creates the circumstances that force Leone to seek Ruggiero and discover the truth. Marfisa's forceful action changes events for the better. However, her failure to understand these events is decisive for her character. It means that she will use the very armor that symbolizes her forthright and independent character as a means of sealing herself off from any loss of autonomy whatsoever. It means that she will be unable to prevent herself from carrying her repudiation of the vulnerability of her sex over into a denial of the experience of trust itself. Anger will always be her substitute for love.

BRADAMANTE

The same student of the *Orlando Furioso* who describes Angelica's story as a burlesque epic of failed deflorations speaks of "la voie spécifique de l'héroïsme féminin, qui est celle de la fidélité en amour."[11] The truth of

Figures in Ariosto's Tapestry

this observation is borne out time and again in the narrative as one female character after another, from Ginevra and Olimpia to Isabella and Fiordiligi, parades herself before us asking to be judged according to her fidelity to the man she loves. Even when the claim to judgment by this criterion is spurious, as in the case of Olimpia, critics will grasp at appearances in order to apply it, and in doing so will overlook in fair women evils bordering on the satanic. Angelica and Marfisa are defective because this unique avenue to heroism has been closed to them, partly by their own doing, and partly by a world that has been rendered frightening and outrageous by its male inhabitants. Ariosto makes it clear in episode after episode that there is only one way for his female characters to achieve heroism. So, at first glance, it seems that Ariosto regarded women as leading narrower, more restricted, more disadvantaged lives than those of the men of his day. However, the question must be asked, Did Ariosto ever affirm, in any passage of the *Furioso*, the existence of other routes to heroism for his male characters than this one to which his female characters appear to be confined? Does the story of Rinaldo, or that of Orlando or Rodomonte, suggest any clear alternative? Does Ruggiero's long evolution bring him to any nobler capacity than that of exhibiting the same fidelity to Bradamante that she has exhibited toward him ever since the work's opening pages? Does he not end where she began?

Brandimarte, reborn in the Ruggiero who emerges from the storm to be converted on the hermit's island, stands alone in the *Furioso* as the one male character to whom Ariosto gives his unqualified approval, yet Brandimarte's loyalty to Orlando, which is the reason for this approval, differs in no significant respect from Bradamante's loyalty to Ruggiero. Apart from the motive of sexual love, which only lends itself to comic treatment in the scenes depicting Bradamante's jealousy of Marfisa, there is even less difference between Bradamante's faith and Brandimarte's than exists between their names on the printed page. The transposition of letters required to make one name into the other is so slight, and the blending of *lover* and *warrior* effected by the transposition so suggestive, that one cannot help but wonder if Boiardo, who invented the names, did not intend to depict Bradamante in his unfinished third book of the *Innamorato* as another Brandimarte. Ariosto apparently sensed an intention of this sort and went on to realize it in the *Furioso*, shifting the sexual balance, though, by granting Bradamante the prominence that Brandimarte had enjoyed in the *Innamorato*. In the *Furioso*, the selfless loyalty of the two characters comes to be identified as a quality more specifically feminine than masculine;

hence, the male characters of Ariosto's poem find themselves ranked on a moral scale according to their capacity to exhibit a feminine trait of fidelity to a single other person, regardless of pressing public commitments. It is significant that Ruggiero's allegiance to Agramante becomes defensible for the first time, after almost forty cantos, only when this allegiance is motivated by personal love for the private man, rather than by punctilious concern with the honor of serving the public official, the king and suzerain.

Faith in another human being—private, intimate, unconditioned by public scrutiny—is the highest value Ariosto aspires to represent in the *Orlando Furioso*. No other allegiance transcends or embellishes it, not even, as we shall see, the commitment to dynasty that clings to the character of Bradamante like a cumbersome appendage. It comes as a surprise at the end of the 1532 *Furioso* that the sole purpose of Ruggiero's many adventures has been to school him in this value and that the sole reason for the many delays of his union with Bradamante has been the need to bring him into harmony with her as an exponent of this value. The altruistic intentions, as opposed to deeds, with which Ruggiero enters the narrative tend to obfuscate, for the reader as well as for Ruggiero, his need to become the thing he professes in words to be. Moreover, Ariosto's relegation of the quality of *fede* to his female characters and to male characters occupying only small portions of the narrative acts as a trap for the unwary or the sexually biased reader, who soon finds his search for truth misdirected toward the more flamboyant male characters and the lengthier episodes involving them, as if the truth were to be discovered in mere quantities of action and in glamorous appearances. It is never immediately apparent, though the fact is always present, that the quest of the principal male character of the *Furioso* will never end in success until he becomes spiritually identical with the principal female character. It is no accident that "le donne" is the first word of the *Orlando Furioso*.

The trait that served, almost without our thinking about it, as the standard by which we judged one female character after another is the trait that determines the worth of all of the male characters. The love relationship has all along been the one area allotted to those female characters for their heroism, and this turns out to be, not a limitation, but an advantage, because the love relationship calls into play that faith in another person by which men and women become something more than mere sexual entities. Women, who are destined by social convention to live for love, are in a better position than men to understand the importance of trust. It is precisely this *fede*—this trust and fidelity at the personal level—that Bradamante, in donning her armor, brings into the military and political organization of society. To the extent that the reader is more concerned with Bradamante's success than with Charlemagne's, Ariosto is successful in asserting the primacy of faith over the more public virtues of honor and courage in battle or of commitment to a cause. Instead, these public virtues are subordinated to the dispositions of private individuals.

The major peril Bradamante faces in her mission is the same one that destroys Brandimarte. One's very life depends upon the disposition of the person in whom one places one's confidence. Because of Ruggiero's benightedness at the opening of the *Furioso,* Bradamante finds herself in canto 2 in the dangerous company of Pinabello. Her anxiety over Ruggiero's well-being—misplaced, ironically, since he and Atlante's other captives are delighted with their perpetual carousing—only serves to relax her guard, cloud her judgment, and marshal her sympathies on the side of the cowardly Pinabello, whose story might otherwise have alerted her to his unworthiness. The conjunction of Bradamante with Pinabello makes a neat contrast between impotent self-pity and active compassion. Pinabello weeps and places his hope in the help others can provide, while Bradamante determines to rescue her beloved or else take the consequences of failure, which could only be grimmer for her than for the others, since the whole purpose of Atlante's magical contraption is to prevent her from joining Ruggiero. When she decides to abandon the public cause and pursue her allegiance to Ruggiero despite the messenger's arrival with news of the peril in which the territories entrusted to her by Charlemagne stand, she endangers herself, not because she is derelict in a higher duty, but because the object of her faith is engaged for the time in ignoble dissipation and can only draw her into company that will use her ingenuous loyalty against her.

Bradamante's image is not tarnished in the reader's eyes when she abandons Charlemagne for Ruggiero. Instead, Ruggiero's self-indulgence and self-absorption, depicted as inevitable in his development throughout the first twenty cantos of his story in the *Furioso,* lend a certain pathos to Bradamante's decision. Until and unless Ruggiero ceases of his own accord to be the callow youth, Bradamante's faith is doomed to failure. While she might have won considerable honor in the service of Charlemagne, there is nothing she can do to dispel the miasma of illusion in Ruggiero's brain. No sooner does she advance against one illusion than another replaces it. The enchanted castle gives way, only to be replaced by Alcina's isle, which is replaced in its turn by Logistilla's paradise, until all ends again in a palace of illusions. Bradamante is entirely at the mercy of processes that must work themselves out within Ruggiero, and to the extent that she deludes herself into thinking that there is something she can do, she risks her life to no end but the pure satisfaction she can take in having risked it for her beloved's sake. Still, this is the proof of faith, that it continues to believe despite a preponderance of discouraging evidence.

It is significant that the one instance in the *Furioso* in which Bradamante, instead of Ruggiero, can be held responsible for delaying their union occurs when she leaves Ruggiero's side in order to revenge herself on Pinabello. This is her only bloodthirsty act in the *Furioso,* and she pays dearly for it, not only in the present, with separation, but also in the future beyond the narrative, when, we are told, her murder of Pinabello adds fuel to the Maganza clan's hatred and contributes to their motive for murdering Ruggiero (46.67). Even sooner, within the narrative itself, Pinabello's corpse provides Gabrina with a means of placing Zerbino's life in jeopardy. Bradamante narrowly escapes sharing the responsibility for Zerbino's death, which later falls entirely on Orlando's shoulders. It hardly seems blameworthy that Bradamante should revenge herself on a person who attempted to take her life, and it also seems excusable that her one act of bloodthirsty violence should be directed against a person who attempted to thwart her in her devotion to Ruggiero by taking advantage of her loyalty. Pinabello is evil, and yet the fury of Bradamante's revenge betrays her blindness to the processes in which she is caught up on account of her loyalty. Pinabello was only the immediate cause of her peril when he let go of the branch and plunged her into Merlin's tomb; she was brought into companionship with Pinabello in the first place by Ruggiero's genial captivity in a palace of voluptuous pleasures. Ruggiero's inability to respond to her faith in him made her vulnerable. To take violent revenge on an exploiter of this vulnerability, as if he alone were the cause of grief, represents a blindness that must lead to dire consequences. Perhaps Ariosto is suggesting that the tragedy of the best of human beings lies in their blindness to the inadequacies of those other frail human creatures in whom they trust. Bradamante's excessive fury with Pinabello separates her yet again from Ruggiero. It delays his baptism by leaving him more susceptible to Agramante's appeals than he might have been if still in her presence, and it exacerbates evil tempers that will finally destroy all the good she has sought. Human frailty, Ariosto appears to be saying, is such that it cannot help but limit the duration of its noblest joys.

Of course, the dynastic theme, which has awaited its entrance until Bradamante's weakest moment, the moment she falls both literally at

Pinabello's hands and figuratively owing to her companionship with him, appears to offer the promise of duration. The prophesy that a noble race will spring from her union with Ruggiero should console Bradamante for the disappointments of the present, but Ariosto makes it impossible for the reader to trust in this consolation. As an abstract concept, the promise, echoing from the lips of Merlin beyond the grave, of a golden age to issue from the union of two people who have achieved the highest degree of faith available to human beings has powerful nostalgic appeal; however, when Melissa descends into particulars, when she exhibits the individual progeny of this union, she introduces a jarring note. The parade of descendants culminates in a description of the battle of Ravenna, where horses wade in a pool of blood up to their bellies and the survivors on all sides are insufficient in number to bury their dead. Added to this violence is the treachery of Ferrante and Giulio d'Este, which is brought into peculiar prominence by Bradamante's question and Melissa's reluctance to go into detail. "Be content with the sweet in your mouth," says Melissa, "and grieve not that I will not make it turn bitter for you at the end" (3.62). Ostensibly a compliment to the clemency of the conspirators' intended victims, Alfonso and Ippolito d'Este, this mention of the conspiracy at the conclusion of all only causes us to wonder what other bitter details may lie concealed in that lineage.

Mention of the conspiracy also brings us squarely up against that pervasive gloom hanging over Ruggiero's more immediate destiny: the treachery that is to destroy him soon after his marriage to Bradamante. Some of the descendants of this union will be no better, we learn, than the traitors who will dissolve it so swiftly after it is formed. The myth of the golden age, alluded to by Merlin, dissolves in the acid of historical inquiry, even though that inquiry is carried out by Melissa with the explicit intention of preserving the myth and encouraging Bradamante. The dynastic theme, as Ariosto represents it, offers no real promise of duration and permanence. Instead, in canto 3, it becomes a bright, dazzlingly deceptive illusion of futurity, helpful psychologically to Bradamante in a moment of despair. It serves only to keep her going in the ugly present. The future may indeed depend on endeavors like hers, but there will be no rest from those endeavors in a golden age, at least not so long as humanity goes on conspiring against itself. In the *Furioso*, the dynastic theme represents nothing more than another of those earthly paradises for which there is no room on this earth.

The dream of that golden age is useful, though, insofar as it propels Bradamante toward Ruggiero and toward the truth. Much to her credit, she is able, at the same time that the dream sustains her, to distance herself from it enough to repudiate its harsher dictates. She does not murder Brunello, as Melissa instructs her to do, nor does she use violence against Atlante, whom Merlin has characterized as a wicked thief (3.19, 74). This very slander of Atlante is enough to alert the reader to the moral and intellectual shortcomings of the dynastic imperative. It would shroud Bradamante in impercipient ruthlessness were she to abide by its requirements with perfect strictness. As it is, she learns that a love on Atlante's part every bit as selfless as her own is responsible for Ruggiero's captivity. What she fails to understand is the lesson, implicit in the text, that there is nothing she can do to release Ruggiero from the influence of this love. To anyone but Ruggiero, Atlante's love is as powerful as the mythic hippogryph that sweeps him away from Bradamante no sooner than she has burst through the enchantment of the mountaintop castle. Bitter experience alone can bring Ruggiero to a crossing of the shadow-line dividing youthful fantasy from mature reflection. Until then Ruggiero's world must remain as far from Bradamante's as any mythic landscape has ever been from the familiar world of disappointed desire, in which human striving is its own reward.

It is much to Bradamante's credit that she never quite learns this lesson of her helplessness, just as it becomes her to treat her own fantasy of a golden age with self-conscious skepticism. For it is precisely her struggle to secure the life she desires with Ruggiero, regardless of her success, that brings before the reader's eyes a human alternative to the illusions, grand and desperate, that drive Orlando and Rodomonte. When she comes to the palace of illusions in canto 13, led by Melissa— who has again been reciting the wonders of her progeny, this time the females—Bradamante cannot overcome her illusion that Ruggiero is in a kind of peril from which she can rescue him—even though she has been warned by Melissa that submission to this illusion will lose her his company forever. Neither this threat nor the promise of noble heirs is enough to make her repudiate her belief in Ruggiero's need of her and in her own ability to release him from his thralldom. To repudiate this belief, though it be illusory, though it be contradicted by every experience she has had thus far, would be for Bradamante the same as to destroy Ruggiero himself. Of course, to pursue him for the sake of begetting dynasty would even more effectively negate him.

When Astolfo dissolves the palace of illusions, Melissa turns out to have been wrong in her dire prediction. Astolfo reminds us that illusions must dissolve just as surely as they arise. States of delusion must alternate with moments of clarity. Nothing is permanent except the process itself. For Ruggiero and Bradamante, the moment of clarity leaves them face to face with each other. For them, it is a moment of recognition, while for the others, it is a moment of bewilderment. Ruggiero and Bradamante have, at least, sought each other. By this time, Ruggiero has come to recognize that Bradamante is important to him and that their illusions have been of each other. The rest of the knights trapped in Atlante's palace have been pursuing objects and people to whom they themselves were always a matter of indifference, and hence they must race to fill the vacuum created by consciousness. They must, as Orlando does, revert to their old illusions no sooner than they have been dispelled. Ruggiero and Bradamante, on the other hand, have been blessed by this time with a mutual illusion that brings them together and leaves them ready to begin, after the illusion has departed, the arduous task of becoming fully conscious of their mutual faith and its imperatives. After this encounter in the clearing left by the vanished palace, they continue to err and misunderstand each other, but there is no longer any risk that Ruggiero will be dominated by any love other than Bradamante's. She enters all of his calculations, even the most misguided ones concerning the public figure he must cut as Agramante's vassal. After the disappearance of the palace of illusions, the great tapestry of events in which the lovers find themselves becomes, as far as they are concerned, filled with light and dark threads defining the nature of their bond.

Despite her murder of Pinabello, it is appropriate that Bradamante should at this time receive from Astolfo the magic lance that once belonged to Argalia, for she has shown herself to be a moral force counterbalancing the misconception of womanhood that once made that weapon so dangerous. Nor is it any accident that the twenty-third canto of the *Furioso,* centering the entire narrative on Orlando's madness, should be framed at its beginning by Bradamante's acquisition of the lance and at its end by Orlando's abandonment of Durindana. Just as Durindana is about to fall into the hands of the enemy, who will use the sword to murder Zerbino and Brandimarte, another weapon intended for use against the faithful comes into Bradamante's hands. One weapon virtually replaces the other, and Bradamante clearly replaces Orlando in the role of champion of the faith—not faith in a public sense, though Bradamante has shown herself to be useful in the public sphere (13.45)—but faith as the word applies to relations between individuals who acknowledge each other's alterity and independence. Orlando goes mad for having treated a human being as a symbol; Bradamante grows sane in the process of vindicating her faith in another person. Argalia's lance, brought to the Occident in Boiardo's poem as an instrument by which men were to be taken into captivity in their competition over Angelica, becomes in Bradamante's hands a symbol of the invincibility of faith. Unlike Angelica, Bradamante has all along exemplified the kind of womanhood that refuses to let itself be thought of as a prize for men to fight and kill themselves over. She has conducted herself as a human being who uses her freedom of will to determine her destiny, and unlike Orlando, she has stood in a clearing and taken a disenchanted look at the object of her faith. She has recognized him as an imperfect human being, not the fulfillment of a deluded ideal.

This recognition accounts for the anguish and the uncertainty into which Bradamante is plunged when she hears the false rumor of Ruggiero's impending betrothal to Marfisa. During the course of his exploits, Ruggiero has provided her with considerable evidence of a propensity to neglect his pledges of faith to her—far more evidence, for instance, than Ginevra ever furnished Ariodante for his jealous despair. When Bradamante sets out in canto 22 to seek death at Ruggiero's hands and to revenge herself on Marfisa, she has every right to regard Marfisa as a successor to Alcina, only a successor more formidable because she is much more like Bradamante herself in the force and independence of her will. When Ruggiero later loses faith in Bradamante and goes off to revenge himself on Leone, he has scarcely any evidence in Bradamante's behavior for the despair that overtakes him. Hence, the movement of Bradamante's mind in canto 22 appears especially admirable. Her resolve to confront Ruggiero and bring him to remorse over the suffering he has caused her, or else die in the attempt, is courageous, and her belief that Marfisa has alienated his affections from her by dishonest means suggests that she has not lost faith in Ruggiero entirely. She cannot bring herself to charge him with the full responsibility for betraying her. Active confrontation, not passive, self-destructive grief, eventually restores Bradamante's peace of mind in this episode. Her decision to impress the claims of her faith upon the world rather than to yield them in adversity and suffer an obscure death brings her, just as it once did Ariodante, to a confirmation of the truth; the magic, invincible lance she carries only symbolizes the rectitude of those claims and the inevitability of her discovering the truth through asserting them.

The "Rocca di Tristano" episode, which unfolds at the center of the jealous march against Arles, heightens the seriousness of Bradamante's character. This 1532 addition to the *Furioso* broaches the question of self-determination in a variety of ways, and this is the most important question having to do with Bradamante. It is all well and good to say that as a woman Bradamante may be particularly apt to exercise that faith in the other which Ariosto extols in the *Furioso,* but in the absence of self-determination, what good is faith—faith being a voluntary gift of the self? The murals that light up the center of this episode treat the historical and political implications of this question. Whenever the French have entered Italy for the purpose of depriving the country of its self-determination, they have suffered defeat, whether in battle or by famine and disease; however, on the few occasions that they have entered as allies of Italian self-determination, they have prospered and won friends. The lesson is stark in its simplicity and impressively enough delivered for those Spanish adversaries of the French to have seen its application to themselves, even in the year 1532, when their virtual annexation of Italy was fresh. Seen in this light, the murals lend an austere dignity to Bradamante when she refuses to let her host know she is a woman if that knowledge is to mean her subjection to a vulgar beauty contest and the negation of her accomplishments in the male contest of arms. To the extent that her sex threatens to limit her power of self-determination, Bradamante repudiates it, but she begins by repudiating an outlook, represented by the castle's law, that can do nothing but leave the world drenched in antagonism.

In regarding a human being, his wife, as a possession with no will of its own, Clodione, the first lord of the castle, could do nothing but regard all other males as potential thieves. The law of the castle perpetuates the view that all women are things and all men are natural adversaries. Here the women themselves compete for the honor of being considered the prettiest thing, and their safety depends on winning the competition. In refusing to submit to the castle's law, Bradamante sets herself apart from Ullania, the representative of the queen of the Lost Islands and therefore also the representative of the kind of womanhood that makes possible the Rocca di Tristano's existence. The queen of the Lost Islands treats her sexual identity and her physical beauty as justification for abdicating every shred of self-determination and for offering herself up as a prize to whoever will fight the hardest for her. In representing this view of womanhood, Ullania deserves the uncomfortable fate that might have befallen her in the castle if Bradamante had not intervened. When Bradamante first met her on the road she lamented the harm that might come of Ullania's mission, and inside the Rocca di

Tristano, she exposes the vulgarity of all such recourse to gender for self-definition. She reminds her host that his only way of knowing that she is a woman and therefore subject to the beauty contest is to strip her naked. Many men wear their hair as long as hers, she reminds him. Definition by gender reduces humans to bare forked creatures, two-legged animals, stripping them of whatever they have been able to make of themselves with the freedom of their wills. The result is a chaotic, demented world permeated with suspicion and sexual antagonism, worthy of the dull-witted Clodione, who in a former age missed the point of Tristan's lesson in civility.

The imagery of the "Rocca di Tristano" episode, with its stormy night and the cold and the mud, matches in somberness and squalor the crude customs of the castle's inhabitants whose mural art depicts example after example of human nature brought low by unrestrained bestiality. Bradamante's refusal to submit to the mischievous stupidity of this castle's law raises her in our estimation immeasurably above Ullania and her companions. When next Bradamante meets these ladies, she finds that they have experienced an embarrassing stroke of poetic justice at the hands of Marganor. Squatting on the ground to hide their private parts, they have become symbols of what it means to seek distinction in the fulfillment of a sexual stereotype. Struggling now to hide that which they allowed to define them before, they are in ludicrous subjection to their physical being. Their sexual identity could not be more prominent.

The encounter with Ullania provides Ariosto with a means of stress-ing the difference between Bradamante and Angelica, for the character of Ullania represents nothing more than a return to the issues raised by Angelica's character—the self-abdication, the acquiescence in a sexual stereotype, the supine acceptance of oneself as an object passively to await the pleasure of others. Bradamante's open assertion of her right to be what she can make of herself, despite her sex and the pressure of inane conventions, qualifies her to be the *Furioso*'s foremost champion of the faithful. To give oneself to another, one must first be in possession of oneself, as neither Angelica nor Marfisa can be, the one in constant flight and the other driven time after time by her outrage into conflict with others. At the close of the *Furioso,* circumstance and convention force Bradamante to preserve her independence at the cost of appear-ing to be the very image of inconstant womanhood she has all along repudiated. Having been defeated in the trial by combat which she herself devised, and having been defeated (she thinks) by Leone, her only recourse is to betray her own word of honor, and she does not hesitate to do so:

Se però presa son per non avere
uccider lui né prenderlo potuto;
il che non mi par giusto; né al parere
mai son per star, ch'in questo ha Carlo avuto.
So ch'inconstante io mi farò tenere,
se da quel c'ho già detto ora mi muto;
ma né la prima son né la sezzaia,
la qual paruta sia inconstante, e paia.

Basti che nel servar fede al mio amante,
d'ogni scoglio più salda mi ritrovi,
e passi in questo di gran lunga quante
mai furo ai tempi antichi, o sieno ai nuovi.
Che nel resto mi dichino incostante,
non curo, pur che l'incostanzia giovi:
pur ch'io non sia di costui tòrre astretta,
volubil più che foglia anco sia detta.

(45.100–101)

Though I am caught for having been unable to kill or capture him, it does not seem just to me, nor will I ever stand by the decision Charles has made in this matter. I know that I shall cause myself to be considered inconstant if now I change from what I declared before, but I am not the first woman nor the last who has appeared inconstant and shall appear so. Let it be enough that in keeping faith with my lover I am found to be more solid than any rock and that in this I surpass by far as many women as ever lived in ancient times or shall live in modern ones. That they call me inconstant in all else, I care not, provided that my inconstancy serves. Provided that I am not constrained to take this man, let me be called flightier than a leaf.

Recognizing that the trial by combat was a concession on her part to conventions resembling those of the Rocca di Tristano, she recovers her integrity by breaking her own false contract, regardless of the appearance this gives her. After the obsession with public opinion we have witnessed on Ruggiero's part for almost half the narrative, Bradamante's resolution to break her word for his sake and appear in the eyes of the world the very thing of which she is the opposite—a fulfillment of the stereotype of inconstant womanhood—must strike us as heroic in the extreme. No amount of pressure applied by deceptive appearances can cause her to swerve from her constancy to the person to whom she has given her confidence and from whom she has received the same. In her moment of potentially greatest weakness, she is free and in command of herself, even freer, we suspect, than Ruggiero at the moment of his own triumph, when he grips the sword that gives him a momentary advantage over Rodomonte.

8
Conclusion

n *The Theory of the Novel,* a book that has had considerable influence in the exclusion of Ariosto from twentieth-century discussions of narrative history and theory, Georg Lukács makes a claim for Cervantes's art that might with equal justice have been made for the *Orlando Furioso.* Concerned with a modern world in which "the ways leading to the transcendental home have become impassable," Lukács declares that "*Don Quixote* is the first great battle of interiority against the prosaic vulgarity of outward life, and the only battle in which interiority succeeded, not only to emerge unblemished from the fray, but even to transmit some of the radiance of its triumphant, though admittedly self-ironising, poetry to its victorious opponent."[1] The terms Lukács uses to describe the poetry of interiority, *radiant* and *self-ironising,* apply perfectly to the *Orlando Furioso.* However, the battle described by Lukács is waged in every canto of Ariosto's poem, and also in every tercet of Ariosto's *Le satire,* which was written during the years between the first and third editions of the *Furioso.* This most important of Ariosto's minor works, filled with details of the "prosaic vulgarity" of an outward world beset with fraud and violence, makes a plea for the private virtues of loyalty, generosity, and self-awareness; however, the mild self-mockery of its poet-persona betrays a consciousness that the plea will go unheard. In the *Furioso,* the battle of interiority, with its victorious opponent, takes the shape of a magician's struggle against the kings of the earth.

In the *Furioso,* Atlante triumphs despite his failure to protect Ruggiero. Nothing is more important to Atlante than the life of his adoptive child. His errors, if they can be called errors, stem from this devotion. He may fail to distinguish between mere survival for Ruggiero and life made meaningful by heroic action, but when we look at Atlante's opponents, Agramante and Charlemagne, whose world defines Ruggiero's sphere of action, we must hesitate to pass judgment on him. Agramante's cruelty and heartless folly often make Charlemagne look good, but only because a great evil makes a lesser one seem good. The society governed by Charlemagne contains enough folly and depravity to make us wonder how anyone could perform a heroic deed in its name. It is not that there is no right or wrong in the outward world governed by the *Furioso*'s kings—that world has its standards. It is simply that there is no right in that world that can stand up to comparison with the right for which Atlante stands. Still, that outward world is victorious. Ruggiero is lured to his destruction in it because there is nowhere else for him to go. If, however, he accomplishes a heroic deed in the course of his career, it is not in the name of the causes and the purposes of that world, it is despite them. Atlante triumphs when Ruggiero's heroism takes the form of that same selfless devotion to another human being of which Atlante is the *Furioso*'s magical exponent. Ruggiero's heroism is his heritage from Atlante. The devotion of Atlante to Ruggiero, of Ruggiero to Leone, of Bradamante to Ruggiero, and of Ruggiero at last to Bradamante represents the triumph of the inner life over the squalor of the all-conquering outward world.

It follows that the *Furioso*, for all of its plot action, is not primarily about actions, but about character—about the inner, irrational life of man. Its title tells us as much.[2] Following Galileo's lead, we can focus on all of the details of a single character's career and discern a pattern that does not immediately dissolve when we turn our attention to a different character. Actions, if singled out, may yield what appears to be a cogent interpretation, but that interpretation will almost always be negated when we turn to another and yet another action. No action in the *Furioso* is final. The battle of Lipadusa is anticlimactic. At the very center of the narrative, Orlando's thunderous loss of wit leaves him no more witless than he was before and than he turns out to be afterward. If we lazily interpret the great set pieces of the *Orlando Furioso* (the rescues of Olimpia and Angelica from the sea monster) in isolation from the human context created by their actors, we will be swallowed up in the belly laugh of an author who has made us the objects of his humor. And how conclusive is the concluding scene of the *Furioso*? Rodomonte's death changes nothing, since the Maganza clan, more evil than he, still lives. In the *Furioso*, actions, and all other appearances, are misleading. It is in the inner, invisible world of character that Ariosto seeks the absolute. Rodomonte, Ruggiero, and Orlando—Angelica, Marfisa, and Bradamante—Rinaldo and Astolfo—represent complex human types and processes. They represent universals that their author could only discover through close scrutiny of the human beings of his world. To understand these characters, we as readers must apply to them the same scrutiny. Their fantastic appearance, their gaudy, anachronistic coloring, should not inhibit us from becoming involved with them, for they are only as gaudy, fantastic, and timeless as the human mind itself.

Notes

Chapter 1. Introduction: Galileo's Telescope

1. Galileo Galilei, *Opere,* ed. A. Favaro et al. (Florence: Barbèra, 1968), 18:193.
2. Dante della Terza, "Galileo, Man of Letters," in *Galileo Reappraised,* ed. Carlo L. Golino (Berkeley and Los Angeles: University of California Press, 1966), p. 13.
3. Tibor Wlassics, *Galilei critico letterario* (Ravenna: Longo, 1974), p. 184.
4. The view taken by Robert Scholes and Robert Kellogg in *The Nature of Narrative* (New York: Oxford University Press, 1966), p. 252, that the *Orlando Furioso* represents the abandonment in narrative of historicity and verisimilitude while *Lazarillo de Tormes* represents the retention of narrative's mimetic features leads to the generally accepted conclusion that Cervantes combined the mimetic with the fictitious in such a way as to provide a prototype of the novel. Implicit in this judgment is the peculiar idea that a turn toward verse, as in the *Orlando Furioso,* represents a turning away from the empirical and toward the fictitious. So it follows rather too smoothly that the beauty of the *Orlando Furioso* is a beauty of "adornment and elegant variation" (p. 208), or else, to quote Georg Lukács in *The Theory of the Novel* (Cambridge, Mass.: MIT Press, 1971), pp. 103 and 59, with whom Scholes and Kellogg are in conformity, everything in Ariosto is "ironically elegant play" and "the serene dance of [his] verse remain[s] mere lyrical play." It would be useless here to go into the ways in which nineteenth- and twentieth-century Italian criticism has contributed to this view of matters, or to speculate as to why a theorist of Northrop Frye's stature in the field of narrative criticism should be virtually silent concerning Italian romance, much less Ariosto. In part, the purpose of my entire study is to bring one of the greatest empiricists in the intellectual history of the West to Ariosto's defense. For Galileo, there was nothing contradictory at all between verse romance and the mimetic as Scholes and Kellogg use that term.
5. The *Scritti letterari* are collected in volume 9 of *Opere* cited above, cited parenthetically in the text by page number.
6. Northrop Frye, *The Secular Scripture* (Cambridge, Mass.: Harvard University Press, 1976), pp. 37–38.

7. Raffaele Colapietra, "Il pensiero estetico galileano," *Belfagor,* Sept. 1956, p. 562.

8. Camillo Pellegrino's argument is in the *Replica alla risposte de gli Accademici della Crusca* (1585), quoted by Bernard Weinberg, *A History of Literary Criticism in the Italian Renaissance* (Chicago: University of Chicago Press, 1961), 2:1020–21; Lionardo Salviati's argument is in *Lo 'Nfarinato secondo* (1588), in the same volume, p. 1041.

9. *Aristotle's Theory of Poetry and Fine Art,* a bilingual text, trans. S. H. Butcher (New York: Dover, 1951), pp. 52–55.

10. Vincenzo Viviani, *Vita di Galileo Galilei* (Florence: Società Editrice Florentina, 1856), p. 366.

11. This represents a conflation of the sixteenth-century allegories of Porcacchi and Toscanella. Both can be found in the 1730 edition of the *Orlando Furioso* published in Venice by Orlandini.

12. Toscanella, in the Orlandini edition of the *Orlando Furioso.*

13. The "Preface" to *Joseph Andrews.*

CHAPTER 2. *HOMO PRUDENS* OR "*GRAN PEDONE*"?

1. Stewart A. Baker and A. Bartlett Giamatti, eds., *Orlando Furioso* (Indianapolis: Bobbs-Merrill, 1968), p. xxxviii.

2. Both essays are available in Santoro's *Letture Ariostesche* (Naples: Liguori, 1973).

3. Northrop Frye, *The Secular Scripture,* pp. 37–38. Perhaps one measure of Frye's critical acumen is that his almost total silence concerning Ariosto does not detract from the value of his observations about romance. Instead, he proves to be of such constant aid to readers of the *Orlando Furioso* that it must be regretted that he has not turned his attention to Ariosto or to Italian romance.

4. Santoro, *Letture Ariostesche,* p. 132.

5. In the Orlandini edition of the *Orlando Furioso* (1730).

6. This judgment appears in the allegory prefacing canto 5 of the *Orlando Furioso* (Venice: Imberti, 1590).

7. Quotations from the *Orlando Furioso* are translated from the edition of Lanfranco Caretti (Milan: Ricciardi, 1963).

8. Ludovico Ariosto, *Opere minori,* ed. Cesare Segre (Milan: Ricciardi, 1964), p. 653.

9. R. W. Hanning, "Sources of Illusion: Plot Elements and Their Thematic Uses in Ariosto's Ginevra Episode," *Forum Italicum* 5 (December 1971), pp. 531–32. Hanning notes the irony of Ariosto's choice of the name *Ariodante* for the major character of a story that pays a "negative tribute to the power of art." Hanning's thesis, that Ariosto manipulates the reader's response to the story in order to upset his expectations, is undoubtedly correct. I would only add that Rinaldo's mistaken viewpoint represents a major example of this manipulation.

10. Daniela Delcorno Branca, *L'Orlando Furioso e il romanzo cavalleresco medievale* (Florence: Olschki, 1973). Branca includes a very useful chapter on the significance of Christian weapons falling into pagan hands.

11. Renzo Negri, *Interpretazione dell'Orlando Furioso* (Milan: Marzorati, 1971), p. 27.

12. Pio Rajna, *Le Fonti dell'Orlando Furioso*, 2nd ed. (1900; reprint, Florence: Sansoni, 1975), p. 57.

13. Negri, *Interpretazione*, p. 136.

CHAPTER 3. RODOMONTE

1. *Orlando Furioso di Ludovico Ariosto raccontato da Italo Calvino* (Turin: Einaudi, 1975), p. 156.

2. Negri, *Interpretazione*, p. 101; and Franco Pool, *Interpretazione dell'Orlando Furioso* (Florence: La Nuova Italia, 1968), p. 202.

3. Arnoldo Motmigliano, *Saggio su l'Orlando Furioso* (Bari: Laterza, 1928; reprint 1971), p. 263.

4. Quotations from the *Orlando Innamorato* are translated from the edition of Aldo Scaglione (Turin: UTET, 1963). To avoid confusion, I have used Ariosto's spelling of the name *Rodomonte* throughout this chapter, even though the name of Boiardo's character is spelled *Rodamonte*.

5. Eduardo Saccone's *Il soggetto del Furioso* (Naples: Liguori, 1974) and Robert Durling's chapter entitled "Ariosto" in *The Figure of the Poet in Renaissance Epic* (Cambridge, Mass.: Harvard University Press, 1965) stress these themes.

6. To the best of my knowledge, this process is first described by Giorgio De Blasi, "L'Ariosto e le Passioni," *Giornale storico della letteratura italiana,* 129 (1952), 318–62, and 129 (1953), 178–203. A passage on page 193 of the latter segment illustrates De Blasi's thought:

   For the rest, if life is a constantly shifting confine, it is also, of necessity, a conglomeration of contrasts, and Ariosto's every poetic act is informed by this inherent principle. The seizing of this innate struggle in the human spirit, this indefatigable strife between relatives, which to the inexperienced consciousness pass for absolutes and then must be demoted, in confrontation with the rhythms of life, in confrontation with the evidence born in upon the very person who had deluded himself, to relatives again and fall off consumed from the spirit because new hopes for the absolute take possession of the mind, in an incessant flow, is the given of Ariosto's poetry. It is his vision of life.

   In a note at the conclusion of his essay, De Blasi declares his intention to write a book on the *Orlando Furioso* with Ariosto's characters as its central concern. Ariosto criticism is the poorer because this book never appeared.

7. Negri, *Interpretazione*, p. 97.

8. Durling, "Ariosto" in *Figure of the Poet,* pp. 176–81.

CHAPTER 4. RUGGIERO

1. *Orlando Furioso raccontato da Italo Calvino,* p. 24.
2. In his edition of the *Orlando Innamorato,* in Canto 2, stanzas 9–10, Scaglione describes the circumstances that may have given rise to the composition of a Latin poem by Tito Vespasiano Strozzi on the origins of the House of Este.
3. A. Bartlett Giamatti, *The Earthly Paradise and the Renaissance Epic* (Princeton: Princeton University Press, 1966), p. 141.
4. In "Rescuing Ovid from the Allegorizers: The Liberation of Angelica, *Furioso* X" in *Ariosto 1974 in America* (Ravenna: Longo, 1976), pp. 85–98, Daniel Javitch gives a thorough account of Ariosto's departure from contemporary allegorical readings of Ovid.
5. Galileo, *Opere,* 9:160.
6. The narrator's insistence on justifying Ruggiero's actions in the name of honor is not, as Franco Pool would have it be, a confirmation of "the failure of the character's artificial purificatory drama" (*Interpretazione,* p. 179); on the contrary, the insistence, the preoccupation, the continual protestation of the narrator is designed by Ariosto to shed doubt on the validity of Ruggiero's code of honor. Pool confuses the author with an unreliable narrator. Here, in fact, the narrator's failure is the author's supreme artistic success.
7. Rajna, *Le Fonti,* pp. 524–25.

CHAPTER 5. ORLANDO

1. I have borrowed the image of the Moebius strip from Eduardo Saccone, who uses it in a different way in the essay that lends its title to *Il Soggetto del Furioso.* I am indebted to this fascinating essay for a number of ideas that have gone on to take a shape quite different from their source.
2. Alfredo Bonadeo, "Note sulla pazzia di Orlando," *Forum Italicum* 4 (March 1970): 42–43.
3. D. S. Carne-Ross, "The One and the Many: A Reading of *Orlando Furioso,* Cantos 1 and 8," *Arion* 5 (1966): 224.
4. Cesare Segre, *Esperienze ariostesche* (Pisa: Nistri-Lischi, 1966), pp. 31–32.
5. Coluccio Salutati, *De laboribus Herculis,* ed. B. L. Ullman (Zurich: Thesaurus mundi, 1951), pp. 256–59.
6. In "Folly in the *Orlando Furioso:* A Reading of the Gabrina Episode," *Forum Italicum* 14 (Spring 1980): 56–77, Franco Masciandaro gives a lively discussion of this phenomenon as it takes its toll on Zerbino.
7. In "Sfrenatura: Restraint and Release in the *Orlando Furioso,*" in *Ariosto 1974 in America,* pp. 33–34, A. Bartlett Giamatti takes a quite different view of this battle scene: "As in the battle with the Orc (11.35), Orlando is self-possessed when confronted by an external force or foe. Ariosto implies again, as he does so often, that we are only really fragmented in our dealings with ourselves. Now the bridle is off Mandricardo's horse as Orlando at least

symbolically unleashes the forces of ruin, the energies of self-destruction. Orlando falls; Mandricardo's horse . . . dashes off." To the extent that a sack of armor can be said to be self-possessed, perhaps Giamatti is right about Orlando. The irony of the scene lies in Orlando's having enabled Mandricardo to escape his self-destructive impulses.

8. *Opere,* 9:180.

CHAPTER 6. IL LUCIDO INTERVALLO (24.3)

1. Bononome's allegory was reprinted in the 1730 edition of the *Orlando Furioso* published in Venice by Orlandini; that edition is the source of my quotation.
2. Giamatti, *Earthly Paradise,* pp. 140–41.
3. This quotation is also from the Orlandini edition of the *Furioso.*
4. Santoro's essay entitled "L'Astolfo Ariostesco: *Homo Fortunatus*" can be found in *Letture Ariostesche* (Naples: Liguori, 1973).
5. G. G. Ferrero "Astolfo (Storia di un personaggio)," *Convivium* 29 (1961): 513–30. I am indebted to Ferrero, who gives a thorough account of the character's appearances in all works in which he figures prominently, from the *Entree d'Espagna* to the *Orlando Innamorato.*
6. David Quint, "Astolfo's Voyage to the Moon," *Yale Italian Studies* 1 (1977): 398.
7. Elissa B. Weaver, "Lettura dell'intreccio del'*Orlando Furioso:* il caso delle tre pazzie d'amore," *Strumenti critici* 11 (1977): 398.
8. D. S. Carne-Ross in "The One and the Many" has been the most influential of recent critics to reassert Burckhardt's view of characterization in the *Furioso,* and he also admits the poignancy attaching to Orlando's character.

CHAPTER 7. FABLES OF GENDER

1. Baldassare Castiglione, *Il libro del cortigiano,* in *Opere di Baldassare Castiglione, Giovanni della Casa, Benvenuto Cellini,* ed. Carlo Cordié (Milan: Ricciardi, 1960), p. 219.
2. In "Three Early Treatises on Women: *De Laudibus Mulierum* by Bartolomeo Gogio; *De Mulieribus* by Mario Equicola; *Defensio Mulierum* by Agostino Strozzi," *Italian Studies* 11 (1956): 37–38, Conor Fahy gives an account, to which I am indebted, of the contents of Equicola's treatise.
3. See Catalano's references to Mario Equicola in *Vita di Ludovico Ariosto* (Geneva: Olschki, 1930).
4. Lillian Robinson, "The Monstrous Regiment: The Woman Warrior in Renaissance Epic," Ph.D. diss., Columbia University, 1974, pp. 119, 122, 126.
5. Quoted from Fahy, "Three Early Treatises on Women," p. 46.
6. Cervantes, *Don Quixote,* part 2, chapter 1, translated by Tobias Smollett.

7. Roger Baillet, *Le monde poétique de l'Arioste: Essai d'interprétation du Roland Furieux* (Lyons: Editions l'Hermès, 1977), p. 480.
8. Carne-Ross, "The One and the Many," pp. 221 and 231.
9. Giulio Reichenbach, *L'Orlando Innamorato di M. M. Boiardo* (Florence: La Nuova Italia, 1936), p. 133.
10. In "Folly in the *Orlando Furioso*," Masciandaro argues that Zerbino, in playing Marfisa's game to the end, demonstrates himself to be the "man of single vision" who "clings to his ideas, deluding himself that they will always apply, no matter what the circumstances" (p. 63). While I do not necessarily disagree with Masciandaro, I would add that in this episode Zerbino commits an indiscretion that those who mean to keep their word should avoid. At the spectacle of Gabrina and Marfisa, he should have passed on in silence, or at least should not have let his vanity lure him into combat. It is because of his indiscretion that he winds up enlisting his constancy in the service of evil, and of course, it is Marfisa's fault in the first place, much more than Zerbino's, that this has happened at all.
11. Baillet, *Le monde poétique*, p. 485.

CHAPTER 8. CONCLUSION

1. Lukács, *Theory of the Novel*, p. 104.
2. In "Il Soggetto del *Furioso*," Eduardo Saccone points out that Boiardo's poem was far more commonly known in Ariosto's day as the *Innamoramento d'Orlando* than as the *Orlando Innamorato,* and he has much to say about what must be regarded, in consequence of this fact, as the originality of Ariosto's title—*Orlando Furioso,* proper noun and adjective, a striking grammatical combination in any case. To Saccone's speculations, I would only add the observation that Ariosto's eye-catching title focuses the reader's attention on a person, while the title by which Boiardo's poem was known stresses an event—an *innamoramento.* Perhaps Ariosto intended his title to convey the message that his poem would concern itself primarily with persons and only secondarily with events. In any case, the word *furioso*—even apart from its Senecan echo—tells us that the poem will be about irrational man.

214

Index

Aeneid, 11, 13, 42, 66–67, 112–14, 145, 151, 169, 180

Agramante, 55–56, 88, 107, 110, 113, 139, 205–6; in *Orlando innamorato,* 11, 42–44, 46, 70–71. *See also under* Astolfo; Marfisa; Rodomonte; Ruggiero

Agricane, 42, 127

Alcina, 2, 6–7, 113, 200. *See also under* Astolfo; Ruggiero

Aldigiero, 183

Alessandretta, city of, 49, 152. *See also under* Marfisa

allegory, 5–7, 11–13, 73–75, 79, 88–89, 124, 130–31

alterity, 109–10, 128

Amone (father of Rinaldo and Bradamante), 39–40

Andronica, 52

Angelica, 16, 165, 193, 206; and Bradamante, 15, 168, 172–73, 177–78, 184, 200, 202; chooses a protector, 14–16, 128, 171–72; on Ebuda, 89–90, 113–14, 176–77; and Ferraù, 128, 135, 170, 173, 178; and Marfisa, 184; and Medoro, 130, 167–68, 179–82; and Orlando, 14–15, 36, 64, 110–12, 114–16, 124, 128–36, 161, 164, 167, 169, 182; in *Orlando innamorato,* 166; and Orlando's bracelet, 178–79, 181; rescued by Ruggiero, 89–92, 105, 123–24, 150, 177–78; and Rinaldo, 20–23, 35–36, 166–67, 169–70, 173, 178, 182; and Sacripante, 15, 111–12, 169–73, 176, 178; soliloquy of, 174–76; as symbol of self-abdication, 173–74

Aquilante, 95

Arbante, 119–20

Ariodante, 37–38, 102, 105

Ariosto, Ludovico: attitude toward humanist movement, 112, 117; attitude toward women, 161–66; as Boiardo's continuator, 11, 13, 47, 71, 112, 157, 193–94; *Cinque Canti,* 25–26, 143; *le Satire,* 162–63, 205

Ariosto-Tasso controversy. *See under* Galilei, Galileo

Aristotle, 2, 8

Armida, 2

Astolfo, 68, 164, 166, 198; and Agramante, 147–49; in Alcina's paradise, 76–77, 141, 146, 149–51, 159; and Bradamante, 199; in *Cinque Canti,* 143; in Logistilla's paradise, 140, 144, 146, 150; and Orlando, 84, 98, 135–36, 143–45, 157–59; rescues Senapo, 145–46, 149; and Rinaldo, 140, 144, 159–60; and Rodomonte, 52–53, 145–49, 156–57, 159; and Ruggiero, 76–78, 92, 94, 145–46, 149–53, 156–57, 159; and Saint John the Evangelist, 154–57; in works preceding the *Furioso,* 144

Atlante, 10–11, 16, 68, 128, 152, 186, 198–99, 205–6; in *Orlando innamorato,* 11, 74. *See also under* Ruggiero

Baiardo, 32, 42

Baillet, Roger, 168, 192

Bardulasto, 70–71

Bireno, 49, 117–22, 125–26

Boiardo, Matteo Maria. See *Orlando innamorato*

Bonadeo, Alfredo, 111

Bononome, Giuseppe, 140–41

Bradamante, 2, 11, 96, 153, 163, 165, 206; and Angelica, 15, 168, 172–73, 177–78, 200–202; and Astolfo, 199; and Bradimarte, 193–94; as champion of the Faithful, 199–200; at destruction of palace of illusions, 92, 198–200; in Leone episode, 39, 104–8, 202–4; and Marfisa, 29, 184–85, 191–92, 200–202; and Orlando, 199–200; in *Orlando innamorato*, 83; and Pinabello, 194–96, 199; in Rocca di Tristano episode, 200–203; and Rodomonte, 41, 47, 53, 63–64, 147; and Ruggiero, 10, 29, 39, 78, 82, 84, 87–88, 93–100, 102, 104–8, 110, 129, 139, 193, 195–200; as symbol of self-determination, 200–201
Branca, Daniela Delcorno, 210n.10
Brandimarte, 35, 37, 41; in *Orlando innamorato*, 33. *See also under* Bradamante; Orlando; Rinaldo; Ruggiero
Brigliadoro, 135
Brunello, 191, 198; in *Orlando innamorato*, 70–72, 183
Buñuel, Luis, 75
Burckhardt, Jacob, 1–2

Caligorante, 146–47, 152
Calvino, Italo, 41–42, 44, 47, 67–68
Cantelma, Margherita, 163, 166
Caretti, Lanfranco, 152
Carne-Ross, D. S., 113–14, 168–69
Castiglione, Baldassare, 161–62, 164–65
Catullus, 171
Cervantes, 1, 8, 158, 167, 205
Charlemagne, 16, 21, 30, 36, 50, 55, 88, 97, 102, 104, 126, 144, 153, 186, 195, 205–6. *See also under* Galilei, Galileo; Orlando
Charles V, emperor, 52
Chaucer, 53
Cimosco, 117–22
Cinque Canti. See under Ariosto, Ludovico
Clarice (wife of Rinaldo), 35–36
Clodione, 201–2
Cloridano, 179–81
Colapietra, Raffaelle, 7–8
courtois, 112, 115–16, 128, 159

Dalinda, 19, 26–30, 50
Dante, 30, 42, 76, 78, 114–15, 120, 151, 169
Dardinello, 31, 37, 167, 179–81
DeBlasi, Giorgio, 210n.6
della Terza, Dante, 2–3
d'Este, Alfonso, 10, 13, 68
d'Este, Ferrante, 197
d'Este, Giulio, 197
d'Este, Ippolito, 10, 13, 68
d'Este, Isabella, 163
dolce stil novo, 111
Don Quixote. See Cervantes
Doralice, 41, 96–97. *See also under* Rodomonte
Dudone, 102
Durindana, 31–32, 42, 64, 125–26, 132, 135, 139, 199
Durling, Robert, 60, 210n.5
dynasty theme, 68, 196–98

earthly paradise theme, 73, 81, 87, 111, 114–15, 145–46, 154–57, 160
Ebuda, 122–25. *See also under* Angelica
Equicola, Mario, 163–64
Erifilla, 70, 74, 80, 86, 90
Erminia, 6

Fahy, Conor, 212n.2
fede theme, 22, 26–27, 29, 34–35, 48–50, 68–69, 91–92, 104–5, 194–95
Ferraù, 51, 92; in *Orlando innamorato*, 47. *See also under* Angelica; Rinaldo
Ferrero, G. G., 212n.5
Fielding, Henry, 2, 8–10, 13
Fiordiligi, 35, 41, 64, 115, 138, 193
Frye, Northrop, 5, 18, 209n.3

Gabrina, 51, 196. *See also under* Marfisa
Galafrone (father of Angelica), 176
Galilei, Galileo, 19, 40, 75, 206; on allegory, 5–7, 11–13; on Angelica, 14–16; in Ariosto-Tasso controversy, 8–9; on Charlemagne, 13–14; comparing Ariosto and Tasso, 2, 4; comparing poetry and the visual arts, 4; on consistency of character, 7–13, 90; on decorum, 7–9, 13–14; on Melissa, 10–13; on Orlando, 4–5, 7, 115, 121, 133;

on Tasso, 3, 6–7, 10, 14–15; on veri-
similitude, 6–9, 14–16
Giamatti, A. Bartlett, 18, 73, 140–41,
211n.7
Ginevra and Ariodante episode, 50, 113,
117, 119, 126, 200. *See also under*
Rinaldo
Gradasso, 51, 92, 139; in *Orlando in-
namorato*, 31, 42. *See also under*
Rinaldo
Grifone, 52, 95, 166
Guidon Selvaggio, 95

Hanning, Robert W., 209n.9
hippogryph, 12, 15, 87, 91, 144
honor theme, 100–101
Horace, 18–19, 170

innkeeper's tale, 57–59, 162
invasions of Italy, 52–53, 62–63, 201
Isabella, 4, 41, 127, 193. *See also under*
Orlando; Rodomonte

Javitch, Daniel, 89
John the Evangelist, Saint, 154–57

Leone, 68. *See also under* Bradamante;
Rinaldo; Ruggiero
le Satire, 162–63, 205
Lidia, 166
Lipadusa. *See under* Orlando; Rinaldo
Logistilla. *See under* Astolfo; Ruggiero
Lukács, Georg, 205
Lurcanio, 21–23, 28, 29

Machiavelli, Niccolò, 21
Maganza, House of, 11, 68, 92
magic book, 140–41, 153
magic goblet, 17–18, 33–36
magic lance, 184, 199–200
magic ring, 14–16, 84–87, 91, 178
magic shield, 79, 87, 90–91, 95, 152
Malagigi, 36, 94, 96, 183
Mandricardo, 190. *See also under* Orlando; Rodomonte; Ruggiero
Marfisa, 163, 165, 193, 206; and Agramante, 71, 185, 191–92; in Alessandretta, 187, 189, 190–91; and
Angelica, 184; and Bradamante, 29,

184–85, 200–202; as child, 185–86;
defeats Pinabello, 187–89; defeats Zer-
bino, 188–90; denial of gender, 190–
91; in female attire, 182–83; and
Gabrina, 186–90; in *Orlando in-
namorato*, 71, 183, 185; relations with
Ruggiero and Bradamante, 191–92; re-
proaches Ruggiero, 98–99; and Rodo-
monte, 57, 182, 184–85; and Ruggiero,
29, 92, 98–99, 184; as symbol of mili-
tant self-sufficiency, 184–85
Marganor, 50, 202
Masciandaro, Franco, 211n.6, 213n.10
Medea, 25–26
Medoro. *See under* Angelica
Melissa, 10–13, 16, 82–83, 197–98
Merlin, 196–97
Michael, Archangel, and Discord, 50
Milton, John, 51
Momigliano, Arnoldo, 41–42, 44
Montaigne, Michel Eyquem de, 40

narrative theory, 4, 205, 208n.4
Negri, Renzo, 38, 41, 58

Oberto, 124–25
O'Keeffe, Georgia, 172
Olimpia, 193, 206. *See also under*
Orlando
Oliviero, 33, 137, 139
orca, 89–91, 124–25, 173
Orlando, 4–5, 7, 16, 35, 41, 47–48, 206;
and Angelica, 14–15, 36, 64, 110–12,
114–16, 124, 128–36, 161, 167, 169,
178–79, 181–82; and arms, 135–37;
and Astolfo, 84, 98, 135–36, 143–45,
157–59, 164; and Bradamante, 199–
200; and Charlemagne, 114–16, 131,
137; as Hercules, 110, 117, 123–24;
and Isabella, 125–26; on Lipadusa,
31–33, 38, 134, 136–37, 139; madness
of, 67, 129–35; and Mandricardo, 32,
125–28, 132; in *Orlando innamorato*,
42, 44, 46, 110–11, 113, 127; rescues
Olimpia, 49, 116–26, 128, 130, 132;
responsible for Brandimarte's death,
31–32, 64, 104–5, 115, 134, 137–39,
199; responsible for Zerbino's death,
32, 64, 125–27, 132, 199; and Rinaldo,

Orlando (*continued*)
23, 117, 131; and Rodomonte, 51, 53, 61–64, 113, 127, 131–32, 137; and Ruggiero, 92, 98, 102, 110, 117, 137, 139; speech against firearms, 122

Orlando innamorato, 11, 62, 66, 68, 112, 144, 200, 213n.2. *See also under* Agramante; Angelica; Atlante; Brandimarte; Brunello; Ferraù; Marfisa; Orlando; Rinaldo; Rodomonte; Ruggiero

Orrigille, 166

Orrilo, 146–47, 152

Ovid, 89, 117, 123

palace of illusions. *See under* Bradamante; Ruggiero

Pellegrino, Camillo, 8

Petrarca, 111, 116

Pinabello, 94–96, 187–89. *See also under* Bradamante

Polinesso, 21–23, 28–31, 40, 51, 127

Pontano, Giovanni, 18–19, 141–43

Pool, Franco, 41, 211n.6

Porcacchi, Tommaso, 22

preux, 112, 115–16, 128, 159

Proteus, 90

Proust, Marcel, 169

Pulci, Luigi, 40

querelle des femmes, 58, 162

Quint, David, 146

Rajna, Pio, 36, 103

Ravenna, battle of, 197

Reichenbach, Giulio, 182

Ricciardetto, 94, 183

Rinaldo, 88, 104, 109, 144, 179; and Angelica, 20–23, 35–36, 166–67, 169–70, 173, 178, 182; and Astolfo, 140, 144, 159–60; exhortation of British reinforcements, 30–31; and Ferraù, 20–22, 37, 65; in *Gerusalemme liberata,* 2; in Ginevra and Ariodante episode, 17–19, 21–30, 33–35, 39, 162; and Gradasso, 31–33, 37–38; in Leone episode, 38–40; on Lipadusa, 22, 31–33, 38; and Orlando, 23, 117, 131; in

Orlando innamorato, 45–47, 166; refuses magic goblet, 33–36; responsible for Brandimarte's death, 32–34, 139; and Ruggiero, 38–39, 102; and his wife, 35–36

Robinson, Lillian, 163–64

Rocca di Tristano episode. *See under* Bradamante

Rodomonte, 31, 47, 69, 110, 206; and Agramante, 51, 57, 65, 131; and Astolfo, 52–53, 145–49, 156–57, 159; and Bradamante, 41, 47, 53, 63–64, 147; and Doralice, 47, 53–58, 60, 62, 147, 182–83; and innkeeper's tale, 57–59; and Isabella, 47, 53, 59–62, 127, 131–32, 147; and Mandricardo, 51, 54–57, 182–83, 185; and Marfisa, 57, 182, 184–85; and Orlando, 51, 53, 61–64, 127, 131–32, 137; in *Orlando innamorato,* 42–48, 157; in Paris, 47–48, 51–52, 61, 146; and Ruggiero, 53, 55, 57, 64–66, 68, 92, 96, 103, 107–8, 134, 153, 204

Ruggiero, 2, 11, 47–48, 51, 109, 139, 166, 205–6; and Agramante, 10, 39, 65, 93–101, 107, 110; in Alcina's paradise, 10–12, 69–70, 72–92, 105, 146, 149–52, 156, 173, 195; and Astolfo, 76–78, 92, 94, 145, 149–53, 156–57, 159; and Atlante, 12, 69, 73–74, 83–84, 92, 199; and Bradamante, 10, 29, 39, 78, 82, 84, 87–88, 93–100, 102, 104–8, 110, 129, 139, 193, 195–200; as Brandimarte reborn, 102–3, 139; and British reinforcements, 88, 93; confronts law of Pinabello's lady, 94–96; at destruction of palace of illusions, 92, 198–99; and Doralice, 55; in Leone episode, 94, 103–8, 123, 129, 192, 200; in Logistilla's paradise, 12, 86–92, 105, 146, 195; and Mandricardo, 92, 96–97, 99, 103; and Marfisa, 29, 92, 98–99, 184, 191–92; and Orlando, 92, 98, 102, 110, 117, 137, 139; in *Orlando innamorato,* 11, 42–43, 47, 69–72, 74–75, 80, 83, 157; rescues Angelica, 89–92, 105, 123–24, 150, 177–78; and Rinaldo, 38–39, 88, 101–

The Johns Hopkins University Press

Figures in Ariosto's Tapestry

This book was composed in Simoncini Garamond text and Jenson display type by The Composing Room of Michigan Inc., from a design by Chris L. Smith. It was printed on 50-lb. Glatfelter paper and bound in Holliston Roxite A by Thomson-Shore.